The Future of Anomie Theory

THE FUTURE OF ANOMIE THEORY

edited by NIKOS PASSAS & ROBERT AGNEW

Northeastern University Press
BOSTON

Northeastern University Press

Copyright 1997 by Nikos Passas and Robert Agnew

Library of Congress Cataloging-in-Publication Data
The future of anomie theory / edited by Nikos Passas & Robert
Agnew.
    p. cm.
    Includes bibliographical references and index.
    ISBN 1-55553-321-3 (cl. : alk. paper)
    1. Anomy. 2. Criminology. 3. Deviant behavior. I. Passas,
Nikos. II. Agnew, Robert, 1953– .
  HM291.F867   1997
  301.5'42'01—dc21   97-15769

Designed by Ann Twombly

Composed in Bodoni by Coghill Composition, Richmond, Virginia
Printed and bound by Maple Press, York, Pennsylvania. The paper is
Maple Antique, an acid-free stock.

MANUFACTURED IN THE UNITED STATES OF AMERICA
01 00 99 98 97   5 4 3 2 1

To my wonderful partner Hilli —NP

To Mary and Willie —RA

Contents

Foreword

In a felicitous stroke of conceptual and terminological recoinage, the historian of science Derek de Solla Price extended Robert Boyle's seventeenth-century term, "invisible college," to refer to those informal collectives of closely interacting scientists that generally limit themselves to a size "that can be handled by interpersonal relationships." This welcome volume indicates that the long tradition of what has come to be known as "anomie theory" probably has its own array of invisible colleges. For one thing, we find Nikos Passas and Robert Agnew, the editors of the volume with its telling title, *The Future of Anomie Theory*, contributing major essays to another, quite recent volume, with its correlative title, *The Legacy of Anomie Theory*. For another, the overlapping rosters of references and citations in these nicely complementary volumes further suggest, if they do not demonstrate, that invisible colleges are at work in the domain of anomie theory. And, as we know from Derek Price, Diana Crane, and Daryl Chubin, it is principally such invisible colleges that reconfigure the research fronts of scientific knowledge.

That is clearly the case in this far-reaching and, as its title implies, far-seeing volume, which deals penetratingly with both the systematics and the history of anomie theory. With regard to its systematic aspect, even those of us who, like myself, are not committed Popperians can say in a Karl Popper vein that theories that cannot be falsified have little worth. However plausible or otherwise gratifying, such theories are doomed to remain inconclusive speculation. It follows then that finding ways of putting a theory to new and exacting empirical tests provides an authentic contribution, both theoretical and methodological. As even more notably, of course, does extending a theory in new directions. The fortunate reader of this volume will find ample theoretical and empirical contributions of both these types, along with keen observations on the historical continuities and discontinuities in the evolution of anomie theory.

The editors orient the reader to the explicit and, on occasion, the implicit contents of the volume in their fine opening chapter, and, after summarizing current extensions of anomie theory, they go on to examine an array of what they see as impending extensions. To this I shall add only a few quite personal observations by way of providing further contexts.

The first of these has to do with what the editors Passas and Agnew, as well as other contributors to the volume, instructively note for themselves. As the editors put it, ". . . researchers often misinterpreted or oversimplified the original statements of anomie theory." They go on to observe: "Most notably, anomie theory was often reduced to the simple assertion that crime results when people cannot achieve monetary success through legitimate channels." In long retrospect, it has become plain to me that I virtually colluded in that misunderstanding. For one thing, the initial, 1938, version of "Social Structure and Anomie" (SS&A) had failed to make it clear enough that its paradigmatic analysis was not confined to the sphere of "monetary success." To be sure, SS&A had noted that to apply its analytical scheme to "various spheres of conduct would introduce a complexity unmanageable within the confines of this paper" and that "for this reason, we shall be concerned primarily with economic activity." Published misunderstandings soon made it clear that this limiting caveat should have been expanded. So it was that the 1957 "Continuities in the Theory of Social Structure and Anomie" plaintively observed that "we have considered the emphasis on monetary success as [only] *one* dominant theme in American culture, and have traced the strains which it differentially imposes upon those variously located in the social structure. . . . It is the conflict between cultural goals and the availability of using institutional means—*whatever the character of the goals*—which produces a strain toward anomie" (the latter italics added).

Another frequent and understandable misunderstanding variously noted in this volume argues that the anomie-and-opportunity-structure paradigm had been confined to deviant behavior in the lower social class. (The term "underclass," with its various connotations, had not yet come into being.) As though to anticipate that misleading imputation, again in 1957, I applied the paradigm in the domain of science to demonstrate that this probabilistic theory of deviant behavior was not at all limited to the lower reaches of the social structure. There is much in this volume that makes distinct contributions by similarly applying the paradigm to other kinds of white-collar and organizational deviance and by variously demonstrating that it does not, as still often misconceived, apply only to the lower social strata.

Another important subject that turns up in the Introduction by Agnew and Passas and elsewhere in the volume holds further personal as well as generically theoretical resonance. This is the question of the applicability of the SS&A paradigm to the pattern of much lower rates of criminal behavior among women who, after all, have long had less access to the legitimate means, or resources, for fulfilling many of their aspirations. That basic question inevitably brings to mind an undergraduate honors thesis at Radcliffe College entitled "Delinquent Girls: An Exploratory Study of Sociological Factors in Female Delinquency" that appeared (but not in print) back in 1961. In its essentials, this small-scale study found that girls who identified themselves with the sex (now, of course, "gender") roles traditionally assigned to men (rather than women) were more likely to engage in delinquent behavior, thus providing an early suggestion that as women increasingly entered the labor market and were subjected to much the same pattern of culturally mandated success aspirations coupled with differential access to legitimate means, they would probably exhibit increasing rates of deviant behavior. Because that limited study appeared at a time when there was next to nothing in sociological print about patterns of delinquency among girls and women, I have long been inclined to consider it as something of a landmark study, all the more, be it confessed, because it was written by one Stephanie Merton. A pity that, activated by the firm sense of personal autonomy presumably quite common among Radcliffe undergraduates in the 1960s, the author rejected her father's mild suggestion that she at least condense the modest thesis into a journal article. Happily, as Agnew and Passas make clear, recent years are seeing systematic studies of gender-related patterns of deviant behavior.

One more personal association with the contents of this much appreciated volume, and I am done. It has to do with the self-exemplifying problem in the sociology of science of the part played in problem-choice in science by sociocultural contexts. As a specific case-in-point, one might ask: What has led to varying degrees of interest among sociologists in the problem of anomie? Rather than essaying an even speculative answer to that question, I convey an apposite observation by the Russian sociologist, Nikita E. Pokrovsky of the Moscow State University, of a new focus on the theory of anomie in deeply and widely anomic post-Soviet Russia. Throughout the period of Soviet hegemony, he observes,

> the theory of anomie did not enjoy any success in Russia and was known only to a narrow circle of experts on Western social theory and criminology. . . . Anomie, as a social phenomenon, was seen as existing in Russia either in the depths of society or as not present at all. However, the deterioration and further collapse of the social structure of the Soviet society has changed the whole picture. From a state of total "filling-up" of social space, Russian society has made a dramatically fast transition to a condition where there is

a complete vacuum in cultural goals and institutionalized means. This transitional period in Russian society has brought the theory of anomie to the fore as an efficient method of analysis. (personal communication)

Congruently enough, Professor Pokrovsky's own second "doctoral dissertation" (required for a full professorship at the Moscow State University) is entitled *Loneliness and Anomie.*

Personal associations aside, I bear witness that to judge from the consequential essays in this volume, the future of anomie theory has already begun.

ROBERT K. MERTON

ROBERT AGNEW & NIKOS PASSAS

Introduction

Anomie theory dominated the criminology literature during the 1950s and 1960s but then entered a period of decline (Bernard, 1984; Burton and Cullen, 1992; Cole, 1975; Passas, 1988; Rosenfeld, 1989). By the 1980s, most criminologists probably would have questioned whether anomie theory had a future. The empirical evidence seemed to provide little support for the theory (Kornhauser, 1978; Agnew, 1995a). Empirical researchers were starting to ignore the theory in their models, and certain prominent criminologists were arguing that the theory should be abandoned (Hirschi, 1969; Kornhauser, 1978).

During the last few years, however, several criminologists have rallied to the defense of anomie theory. They felt that we were on the verge of rejecting a theory that had much to offer criminology. These criminologists criticized the empirical evidence against anomie theory, began to conduct more sophisticated tests of the theory, and suggested revisions and extensions in anomie theory.

There has been a resurgence of interest in anomie theory as a result of their work. Articles on the theory are becoming more common, the theory is receiving substantially more attention at professional meetings such as those of the American Society of Criminology, and several students are now completing dissertations on strain/anomie theory. Most recently the Advances in Criminological Theory series devoted a special issue to "The Legacy of Anomie Theory" (Adler and Laufer, 1995).

This volume presents eight chapters that we believe reflect the future of anomie theory. These chapters are written by most of the figures who played a central role in the revival of anomie theory, as well as by a major figure in the original development of the theory. The chapters reflect what we see as the three central themes in the recent work on anomie theory: a reexamination of the empirical research on classic anomie theory, more sophisticated tests of classic anomie theory, and efforts to revise and extend classic anomie theory. Some of this work is proceeding at the microlevel, with such work often being classified under the rubric of "strain theory." Other parts are proceeding at the macrolevel, with such work retaining the designation "anomie theory."

This introductory chapter briefly reviews the three central themes listed above, discusses the relationship between strain and anomie theory, and then provides a preview of the eight articles that follow. We conclude by pointing to the major issues or research topics likely to dominate the future research on anomie (and strain) theory. We begin, however, with a brief discussion of the core ideas of anomie theory.

What Is Anomie Theory?

Anomie theorists in criminology trace their roots to Durkheim ([1897] 1951) and Merton (1938). Merton, in particular, has directly inspired hundreds of studies on anomie theory and crime (Burton and Cullen, 1992; Clinard, 1964; Cole and Zuckerman, 1964; Cole, 1975). There remains some confusion, however, over the core ideas of anomie theory (see the discussion in Passas, 1995a). Some theorists, in fact, have argued that Durkheim and/or Merton are actually social control rather than anomie theorists—or that anomie theory is a type of control theory (Bernard, 1987, 1989; 1995; Burton and Cullen, 1992; Cullen, 1984; Hirschi, 1969, p. 3, n. 1; Messner, 1988; Messner and Rosenfeld, 1994). There are certainly links between anomie and control theory, but we believe that there are key differences as well. Anomie theory is best understood by recognizing that it has both a macroside, where the links to control theory are most clear, and a microside.

The macroside of anomie theory focuses on the inability of society to regulate individual conduct effectively (see the discussions in Messner, 1988; Passas, 1995a). Durkheim focuses on the regulation of individual goals, arguing that society may fail to set reasonable limits on the goals that individuals pursue (or, in the case of the economic sphere, society may encourage individuals to pursue unattainable goals). Individuals unable to set limits on their desires come to pursue unattainable or ever-escalating goals. Merton argues that society may encourage individuals to pursue lofty goals, although the precise nature of these goals is not clearly described. At times it sounds as if Merton is talking about unattainable or ever-escalating goals ("in the American Dream there is no final stopping point"); at other times it sounds as if he is talking about lofty but attainable goals. Merton, however, explicitly argues that society may fail to place sufficient emphasis on the norms regulating goal attainment. In the extreme case, "any and all procedures which promise attainment of the all-important goal [are] permitted" (1968, p. 187). Merton and Durkheim, then, both focus on a breakdown in societal regulation, although Durkheim focuses primarily on the failure to regulate individual goals, and Merton focuses on the encouragement of lofty goals coupled with the failure to regulate norms for goal attainment (for fuller discussions of the differences between Durkheim and Merton, see Agnew, in this volume; Cullen, 1984; Passas, 1995a).

This focus on the regulation of individual conduct is why Hirschi states that "Durkheim's theory is one of the purest examples of control theory" (1969, p. 3, n. 1) and why others have made similar arguments regarding Merton (Bernard, 1987; Burton and Cullen, 1992; Cullen, 1984; Messner, 1988). The macro arguments of Durkheim and Merton, however, constitute only one part of their theory. Durkheim and Merton also go on to describe *why* the breakdown in societal regulation increases the likelihood of individual deviance; that is, they present a theory of individual motivation (see Cohen on "levels of analysis" in this volume; Messner, 1988). This brings us to the microside of their theory, and it is here where they clearly depart from control theory. The breakdown in societal regulation does not *free* the individual to engage in deviance. Rather, it creates *pressure* to engage in deviance (see the Agnew article in this volume for a fuller discussion). In Durkheim this pressure arises from the inevitable failure that results from the pursuit of unattainable or ever-escalating goals. In Merton this pressure arises from the failure to achieve culturally prescribed goals. Merton argues that this pressure is greatest in the lower classes, because lower-class individuals are said to face the greatest barriers to goal achievement.

This idea of being *pressured* into deviance is at the core of anomie theory. As Merton states at the beginning of his classic article "Social Structure and Anomie," "our primary aim is to discover how some *social structures exert a definite pressure upon certain persons in the society to engage in nonconforming rather than conforming conduct*" (1968, p. 186, emphasis in the original). Most definitions of anomie theory likewise stress the idea that individuals are pressured into deviance. Vold and Bernard (1986, p. 185), for example, state that "strain theories propose that there are certain socially generated pressures or forces that drive people to commit crimes."

Anomie theory, in sum, focuses on a breakdown in the social regulation of individual conduct and argues that this breakdown creates *pressure* for individual deviance. This pressure stems from the inability of individuals to satisfy their desires through legitimate channels. (Although Passas [1990, this volume] argues that once a regulatory breakdown has occurred, the influence of normative reference groups may bring about *deviance without pressure or strain.*)

Most work on anomie theory has been at the microlevel, focusing on the relationship between the individual experience of goal blockage and crime/delinquency. As several authors have noted, the macroside of anomie theory has been largely ignored (Bernard, 1987; Burton et al., 1992; Messner, 1988; Messner and Rosenfeld, 1994; Rosenfeld, 1989). Textbook treatments of Merton, for example, typically focus on the effect of goal blockage on crime and ignore his related argument about the cultural imbalance between goals and norms (Hilbert and Wright, 1979; Passas, 1988). Fortunately, the past few years have seen a resurgence of interest in the macroside of anomie theory. This interest is represented in several articles in this volume, including the article by Messner and Rosenfeld on their institutional-anomie theory.

Several macroanomie theorists have recently argued that the macroside of anomie theory can be "decoupled" from the microside (Bernard, 1987; Messner and Rosenfeld, 1994; Messner, 1988). They claim, for example, that the macrolevel arguments of Durkheim and Merton are compatible with control theory at the microlevel. In particular, they argue that the breakdown in the social regulation of individual conduct may *free* individuals to engage in deviance, rather than *pressuring* them to do so (also see Kornhauser [1978], who makes a similar point in her critique of Merton). These arguments raise new questions regarding the underlying assumptions of anomie theory. Agnew (1987) acknowledges that the macroside of anomie theory is compatible with control theory but claims that efforts to link the two rob anomie theory of that which makes it unique. Macrolevel anomie theory becomes another version of control theory, albeit a somewhat distinctive and important version. Microlevel anomie theory, however, remains truly distinct from control theory (see Agnew, 1995b, 1995c). The relationship between the macro- and microsides of anomie theory (i.e., between "anomie" and "strain" theory) is a persistent theme in the chapters in this volume and the topic of a subsequent section in this chapter.

The Three Central Themes in Current Anomie Research

I. A REEXAMINATION OF THE EMPIRICAL RESEARCH ON CLASSIC ANOMIE THEORY

There were several reasons for the decline of classic anomie theory beginning in the late 1960s (see Cole, 1975; Burton and Cullen, 1992; Hagan and

McCarthy, this volume; Passas, 1988, 1995a; Rosenfeld, 1989). Researchers seemed to have exhausted the research puzzles provided by the classic theories. Several alternative theories, providing new research puzzles, emerged. The conservative shift in political climate was at odds with anomie theory, particularly given the association of the theory with the "liberal" policies of the 1960s—such as the War on Poverty. The fact that the economic growth of the 1960s was accompanied by rising crime rates caused many to question the underlying logic of anomie theory (see Hagan and McCarthy, this volume). And, quite importantly, empirical studies provided little support for the theory (see Agnew, 1995a; Hirschi, 1969; Liska, 1971; Kornhauser, 1978; Jensen, 1995).

Contemporary anomie theorists, however, argue that the empirical data do not provide a sufficient basis for rejecting anomie theory. They point to several fundamental problems in much of the previous research on the classic anomie theories of Merton (1938, 1968), Cohen (1955), and Cloward and Ohlin (1960).

First, researchers often misinterpreted or oversimplified the original statements of anomie theory (see Agnew, 1995a, 1995b; Bernard, 1984, 1987; Burton and Cullen, 1992; Cullen, 1984, 1988; Hoffman and Ireland, 1995; Menard, 1995; Messner, 1988). Most notably, anomie theory was often reduced to the simple assertion that crime results when people cannot achieve monetary success through legitimate channels (see Hilbert and Wright, 1979). The complex models advanced by Merton, Cohen, and Cloward and Ohlin were ignored. Several researchers have tried to correct these simplistic interpretations of anomie theory. Most notably, several criminologists have pointed to the neglect of the macroside of anomie theory, which attempts to explain the higher rate of crime in certain groups or in total societies (Messner, 1988; Messner and Rosenfeld, 1994; Rosenfeld, 1989). The Rosenfeld and Messner article in this volume falls into this category. Researchers have also argued that the microside of anomie theory, often referred to as "strain" theory, has been misinterpreted (Bernard, 1984; Burton and Cullen, 1992; Cullen, 1984, 1988; Hoffman and Ireland, 1995). The Agnew, Menard, and Cullen and Wright articles in this volume fall into this category. These articles suggest more complex theoretical models than those typically tested in the literature.

Second, not only did researchers oversimplify or misinterpret the *original* statements of anomie theory, they also ignored the revisions made in these theories by their authors and others (e.g., Cloward, 1964; Cohen, 1965; Cohen and Short, 1958; Merton, 1959, 1964, 1968; Mizruchi, 1964;

Vaughan, 1983). Such revisions addressed many of the central criticisms of anomie theory. These revisions, in particular, better defined the nature and determinants of strain and anomie, more precisely specified the conditions under which strain or anomie might lead to crime, and extended the scope of the theory to new types of crime or deviance and new populations. The neglect of these revisions is therefore a serious shortcoming. Several researchers have attempted to remind criminologists of such revisions and thereby improve the quality of research on anomie theory (e.g., Agnew, 1992, 1995a; Bernard, 1984; Burton and Cullen, 1992; Burton and Dunaway, 1994; Burton et al., 1994; Farnworth and Leiber, 1989; Hoffman and Ireland, 1995; Menard, 1995; Messner, 1988; Passas, 1987; Rosenfeld, 1989). Several of the chapters in this volume attempt to do the same. Agnew, Passas, and Cohen, for example, remind readers of the central role that reference groups play in the interpretation of and reaction to strain. Passas and Vaughan remind readers that anomie theory is applicable not just to lower-class individuals.

Third, the empirical research on anomie theory was plagued by methodological as well as theoretical problems (see especially Agnew, 1992; Bernard, 1984; Burton and Cullen, 1992; Burton and Dunaway, 1994; Burton et al., 1994; Farnworth and Leiber, 1989; Hoffman and Ireland, 1995). The standard paradigm for testing anomie theory involved the creation of a single measure focusing on the disjunction between aspirations and expectations (typically, education or occupational aspirations/expectations). The impact of this measure on minor delinquency was then examined with survey data from a school population. Serious questions have been raised about the appropriateness of this paradigm (see especially Agnew, 1992; Bernard, 1984; Burton and Cullen, 1992; Hagan and McCarthy, this volume). Further, such tests ignore the macrolevel arguments of anomie theory. Several of the chapters in this volume discuss methodological problems in previous tests and point to more appropriate ways to test anomie theory.

Finally, contemporary anomie theorists have argued that many empirical data are in fact supportive of the theory. Certain of these data involve quantitative studies at the individual level and macrolevel (Bernard, 1984; Burton and Cullen, 1992; Burton and Dunaway, 1994). Other data involve qualitative studies of offenders and groups, including studies of female offenders, gangs, and organizations (see Box, 1983; Broidy and Agnew, forthcoming; Hagan, 1994; Passas, 1994a; Vaughan, 1983).

Based on the above arguments and data, it would seem safe to conclude that any effort to reject anomie theory based on the current empirical research is premature. Most of the studies critical of anomie theory are flawed, and many empirical studies provide tentative support for the theory or elaborated versions of it. At the very least, it would seem that further research is warranted.

II. CONDUCTING BETTER TESTS OF CLASSIC ANOMIE THEORY

Researchers have not been content simply to criticize previous tests of classic strain theory. They have also attempted to provide more appropriate tests of classic anomie/strain theory. Certain of these tests have been at the individual level. Such tests employ more sophisticated measures of strain/anomie and often attempt to examine the intervening mechanisms between anomie and crime, explore the factors that condition the effect of anomie on crime, and test the theory with more appropriate populations (Agnew et al., 1996; Burton and Dunaway, 1994; Burton et al., 1994; Hagan and McCarthy, 1996; Menard, 1995). The Menard article in this volume provides an excellent example of the new research being done in this area. The Hagan and McCarthy article discusses their groundbreaking work in this area, particularly their development of a "street criminology" that is more suitable for testing strain/anomie theory.

Other tests have been at the macrolevel, with certain of these tests being more qualitative in nature. Several researchers, for example, have conducted case studies of organizational deviance using anomie theory (D. Cohen, 1995; Passas, 1990, 1994a, 1994b; Vaughan, 1983, 1992a, 1992b). The Vaughan chapter in this volume provides a good example of the research in this area. Although these studies have not been conducted in the positivist tradition aiming to "test the theory," all of them provide support for elaborated versions of anomie theory.

Although contemporary anomie theorists have rejected the previous paradigm for testing anomie theory, a new paradigm has yet to emerge. This is perhaps a good thing, because it would be unfortunate to close off experimentation prematurely. Anomie theory is quite complex. As will be evident from reading the articles in this volume, there are a variety of ways to conceptualize and measure strain and anomie, there are several routes by which anomie and strain might lead to crime, and there is a host of factors that might condition the effect of anomie and strain on crime. Further, there is still some uncertainty over the types of deviance and the types of populations for which anomie theory is most relevant. What is most needed now is diversity in research. This diversity, we hope, will lead to theoretical refinement.

III. EXTENDING STRAIN/ANOMIE THEORY

Although contemporary anomie theorists have devoted much effort to the defense of their theory, they also recognize that the theory suffers from certain problems and is in need of revision and extension. Indeed, the founders of anomie theory viewed their theoretical statements not as finished products but as preliminary efforts—and they specifically encouraged others to build on their work. Fortunately, contemporary anomie theorists have been able to overcome the tendency toward "theoretical reification" that Cullen and Wright (this volume) describe.

Some contemporary anomie theorists have attempted to revise the classic anomie theories. Examples include the work of Agnew et al. (1996), Bernard (1987), Burton and Cullen (1992), Burton and Dunaway (1994), Burton et al. (1994), Elliott and Voss (1974), Elliott et al. (1979), Greenberg (1977); Hagan and McCarthy (this volume), Passas (1988, 1990, this volume), and Vaughan (1983, 1992a, this volume). It is argued, for example, that individuals may pursue goals other than economic success, that goal achievement is a function of more than economic position, that comparative and normative reference groups play a large role in the creation of and reaction to strain, and that anomie theory can be applied to individuals in all social strata as well as to organizational actors.

Others have suggested more fundamental alterations in anomie and strain theory (e.g., Agnew, 1985, 1992, 1995b; Bernard, 1990; Messner and Rosenfeld, 1994; Simon and Gagnon, 1976). Certain of these alterations are at the microlevel, involving efforts to apply anomie theory to the explanation of individual-level deviance. Agnew's (1992) general strain theory is the most prominent example. It points to new sources of strain beyond the inability to achieve economic success/middle-class status, and it more fully specifies the factors that condition the impact of strain on crime. Other alterations are at the macrolevel, involving efforts to explain the higher rates of deviance in certain groups, communities, or entire societies. Messner and Rosenfeld's (1994) institutional-anomie theory is the most prominent example. They considerably extend the work of Merton by discussing how the dominance of the economic system leads to a breakdown in social control in other institutional spheres.

Finally, other elaborations specifically aim at bridging the gap between micro- and macrolevels (Passas, this volume, forthcoming; Vaughan, 1983, 1992b, this volume).

In most of the above cases, researchers have attempted to remedy certain weaknesses in anomie theory by drawing on research and theory in related areas. Agnew, for example, draws heavily on the stress, emotions, and equity/ justice literatures in his revisions of strain theory. Messner and Rosenfeld draw on the broad literature dealing with the "markets and morality" debate, as well as several literatures dealing with institutions such as the family, school, and polity. Passas draws on the reference group, symbolic interaction, relative deprivation, conflict theory, religion, political science, and organizational theory literatures. Vaughan draws on organizational theory, family, and general sociology literatures. Several of the chapters in this volume employ the same strategy to advance anomie theory. Cohen draws on several different literatures, including the literatures on reference groups and identity theory. Hagan and McCarthy draw on the stratification, life-course development, and social-capital literatures. Cullen and Wright draw on the large literature dealing with social support.

As a result of the above revisions and extensions, anomie theory is now quite broad in its scope. The theory is applicable to both micro- and macro-level issues and to virtually all types of crime and all groups—including different class, gender, age, and racial groups (see Box, 1983; Broidy and Agnew, 1996; D. Cohen, 1993, 1995; Cole and Zuckerman, 1964; Hoffman and Su, forthcoming; Merton, 1957; Ogle et al., 1995; Passas, 1990, 1994a, 1994b, 1995a; Savelsberg, 1995; Vaughan, 1983). Many of the revisions and extensions in anomie theory are now in the process of being explored and tested, with such tests being both quantitative and qualitative in nature. The preliminary results of such tests provide some basis for optimism regarding anomie theory (Agnew et al., 1996; Agnew and White, 1992; Chamlin and Cochran, 1996; Hoffman and Su, forthcoming; Passas, forthcoming; Paternoster and Mazerolle, 1994; Vaughan, this volume). So it now once again appears to be the case that the theory has a future.

Does Strain/Anomie Theory Constitute a Unified Theoretical Tradition?

One might, however, ask about the nature of that future. Although the theoretical revision and extension described above is quite exciting, many of the theoretical elaborations appear to be moving in different directions. As a result, many criminologists may wonder whether it is still possible to speak of anomie/strain theory as constituting a single theoretical tradition. In particular, what do the microlevel strain theories of criminologists such as Agnew have in common with the macrolevel anomie theories of researchers such as Messner and Rosenfeld?

This issue is evident in many of the articles in this volume. Agnew, for example, notes that several prominent theorists have questioned the association between anomie and strain theory—claiming that anomie theory may be more compatible with control than strain theory at the microlevel. Rosenfeld and Messner emphasize the strong links between their institutional-anomie theory and control theory but do not discuss links with strain theory—except to note that their theory is not incompatible with strain theory. Cohen also raises questions about the links between anomie theory and strain theory, particularly Agnew's general strain theory. Passas argues that there is an important nonstrain component in anomie theory.

As suggested above, we believe that strain and anomie theories are both direct descendants of Durkheim and Merton. There are at least two major theoretical traditions represented in their work. At one level, these theorists discuss the disjunction between goals and means and the pressure that this disjunction creates for deviance. It is from this discussion that all strain theories flow. Agnew (1992) simply broadens the scope of strain theory, focusing on *all* situations where individuals are not treated as they want to be treated. This includes situations where others prevent one from achieving one's goals, as well as situations where others remove positively valued stimuli that one possesses or present one with negatively valued stimuli. In the tradition of strain theory, all these situations are said to create pressure for deviance.

At a second level, both Durkheim and Merton focus on the inability of society to regulate conduct effectively. Macrolevel anomie theories such as Messner and Rosenfeld's institutional-anomie theory derive from this aspect of anomie theory. Following Merton, they argue that the high rate of crime in the United States is due partly to a cultural system that places great stress on monetary success but little emphasis on the legitimate means to achieve such success. Further, they argue that the cultural emphasis on money is paralleled by an institutional structure that is dominated by the economy. Noneconomic functions and roles are devalued. Noneconomic institutions must accommodate themselves to the demands of the economy. And economic norms have come to penetrate these other institutions (see Passas, 1994b; Passas and Escamilla, 1992, for a discussion involving religious institutions). As a result, institutions such as the family, school, and polity are less able to socialize individuals and apply external sanctions effectively. This latter part of their theory represents a fundamental extension of Durkheim and Merton but is still in keeping with their emphasis on the regulation of individual conduct.

Durkheim and Merton, then, present versions of both strain and anomie theory. The strain and anomie theories advanced by these theorists, however, are closely linked. Durkheim argues that little restraint at the macrolevel (i.e., anomie) leads to strain at the individual level (i.e., the pursuit of unlimited goals). Merton argues that the cultural imbalance between goals and norms at the macrolevel (i.e., anomie) contributes to strain at the individual level. Strain at the individual level, in turn, contributes to the low emphasis on institutional norms at the cultural level. (The reciprocal relationship between micro- and macrolevel variables is a central theme in Vaughan's analysis of the Challenger disaster.) Recent theories, however, tend to devote less attention to these links between anomie and strain theory.

Agnew (1995b, this volume) does state that strain may contribute to low social control and vice versa, but his arguments are phrased primarily at the microlevel. Only limited attention is devoted to macro-micro links. Likewise, Messner and Rosenfeld (1994, this volume) do not discuss the links between their institutional-anomie theory and strain theory. It is easy to think of ways in which the cultural and social conditions described by Messner and Rosenfeld might promote strain at the individual level. The strong emphasis on monetary success directly contributes to goal blockage, and the weakening of noneconomic institutions almost certainly contributes to a wide range of strainful conditions, from child abuse to role overload. Likewise, one can argue that strain at the individual level may reduce concern for institutional norms and undermine the ability of the major social institutions to exercise social control. The theories of Cohen (1955) and Cloward and Ohlin (1960), in fact, devote considerable attention to the ways in which strain ultimately leads to the attenuation or rejection of institutional norms. Nevertheless, the links between strain and anomie theory have not received much attention in recent theory and research.

There are, then, signs of divergence in the recent work on anomie and strain theory. The theories of Durkheim and Merton are multilayered and complex, so perhaps it should come as no surprise that the progeny of Durkheim and Merton differ in significant ways. Also, anomie theorists have been especially eager to stress the macroside of their theory, because this side has often been overlooked in theory and research. Strain theorists, meanwhile, have often felt compelled to focus on the microlevel in responding to numerous empirical and theoretical assaults on their theory.

The divergence of strain and anomie theory may have certain useful consequences. In particular, it may foster the integration of both strain and anomie theory with other theories, such as control, labeling, and conflict theories (e.g., Passas, forthcoming). Anomie at the societal level certainly produces low control at the individual level, and the work of theorists such as Bernard (1987) and Messner and Rosenfeld (1994, this volume) has helped clarify this link. Likewise, strain at the individual level is certainly a function of more than anomie at the societal level. The macrolevel determinants of the types of strain described in Agnew can be explained using a variety of theories, including conflict, feminist, and social-disorganization theories.

At the same time, we hope that theorists do not overlook the close connection between anomie and strain theory, and we suspect that these links will receive further attention as the new versions of strain and anomie theory become more firmly established.

A Preview of the Eight Essays

We begin with a chapter on Durkheim and Merton by Agnew. Although Agnew is best known for his work on general strain theory, the chapter in this volume focuses on the individual-level strain theories advocated by Durkheim and Merton. Agnew begins by challenging the recent argument that Durkheim and Merton are actually control rather than strain theorists. He then describes the individual-level strain theories advocated by Durkheim and Merton. He contends that empirical researchers have neglected most of the core arguments of Durkheim and Merton. Researchers, in particular, have never explored Durkheim's conception of strain as the pursuit of unlimited goals or his suggestion that a breakdown in societal regulation (or low social control) leads to strain. Likewise, researchers have never fully explored Merton's arguments regarding the components of individual-level strain, the macrolevel determinants of strain, or the factors that condition the effect of strain on deviance. The empirical tests of Merton's theory that have been done have little relevance to the theory that Merton actually advocates. According to Agnew, the theories of Durkheim and Merton have never received an adequate test, and they contain many useful suggestions regarding the nature and sources of individual-level strain.

The next two chapters, by Cohen and Passas, suggest major extensions in the classic anomie theories. Cohen's paper builds on his classic 1965 article, "The Sociology of the Deviant Act: Anomie Theory and Beyond." This article pointed to several weaknesses in anomie theory and suggested ways in which such weaknesses might be remedied. Unfortunately, Cohen's suggestions had little impact on research efforts. We hope that will not be the case with the chapter in this volume. Cohen describes several strategies for strengthening classic anomie theory, including the development of more explicit linkages between anomie and reference-group theory, so as to better understand the origins of and reaction to strain. He then points to a source of strain largely neglected in anomie research: the inability to establish, maintain, or demonstrate a desired identity through legitimate channels. Such strain may sometimes result in deviance, an argument that bears much in common with recent work in social psychology (e.g., Thoits, 1991) and recent accounts of deviance in certain groups (e.g., Anderson, 1994). Cohen also suggests a major extension of strain theory. He argues that we should treat collectivities as actors—with anomie theory being used to understand the deviance of such collectivities. Cohen's essay not only offers suggestions for strengthening anomie theory but also makes us more aware of the intimate links between anomie and other theories—including differential-association and control theories.

The third chapter, by Passas, is an elaboration of an earlier, unpublished paper on relative deprivation (Passas, 1987). Passas elaborates Merton's theory by following up on Cohen's remark that it is important to consider "what other people say, do and feel." He discusses the links between anomie theory, (comparative) reference-group theory, and relative deprivation theory. In particular, he argues that anomie theory certainly talks about strains that are socially produced and make for higher rates of deviance in some social groups than in others. Yet for structural strain to translate into individual deviant behavior, it is indispensable that at some point people *experience* the ends-means discrepancy. This experience varies in different social locations, depending on one's comparative reference point. A macro-micro link is attempted here by the realization that the U.S. culture, the ideology of the American Dream, and high rates of social mobility encourage *nonmembership* referents. However, not everyone will succeed in attaining the goals of his or her socially distant referents (because of lack of available means). This increases the likelihood of unfavorable comparisons, of *feelings* of relative deprivation, and of deviant responses. Passas goes on to suggest that as such experiences, interactions, and responses may accumulate and crystallize in subcultures, *deviance without strain* is a possible consequence. Passas's chapter also demonstrates the relevance of anomie theory to the conduct of people in relatively high social positions (see also Passas, 1990).

In the fourth chapter, Vaughan elaborates on a second theme emphasized by Cohen—the treatment of collectivities as actors (see also Box, 1983; D. Cohen, 1992, 1993, 1995; Passas, 1990, 1994a, 1995b; Vaughan, 1983). Vaughan's chapter involves a qualitative case study of NASA and the space shuttle Challenger disaster, and her analysis illustrates how Merton's anomie theory can be used to explain the organizational deviance of white-collar workers. Drawing on and extending Merton, she argues that individuals and organizations are in competition over scarce resources (which may include money and other resources). The resources representing success are said to be scarce across the stratification system, so that all organizations and individuals in all social positions face the prospect of defeat in this competitive struggle. Vaughan argues that organizations threatened with defeat may turn to deviance, a prospect enhanced by the fact that "societal standards guiding the conduct of organizations are ambiguous." Organizational deviance, then, is most likely when there is pressure to deviate in a context of limited social regulation. These arguments are illustrated in her case study of NASA. NASA lacked the resources to meet its flight schedule, and NASA decision makers knowingly risked the safety of its flight crews. In the process, NASA developed a subculture that came to justify their behavior—to "normalize" the deviance in which they engaged. Vaughan provides a fascinating and important account of the development, persistence, and operation of this subculture—an account that illustrates and extends Cohen's work on the origin of deviant subcultures (also see Braithwaite, 1989a; Passas, 1995b). This account also strongly underscores one of the central arguments of Cohen and Passas: one cannot treat the individual in isolation—the experience of and reaction to strain is heavily dependent on others in the environment.

In the fifth chapter, Hagan and McCarthy describe their pioneering work on "street" criminology. As they note, the dominant paradigm in crime research since the 1960s has been the study of self-reported delinquency among school populations. Although such studies have produced valuable results, they have neglected the serious criminal behavior committed by "street youth"—that is, youth without any permanent place to live who spend much of their time on the street. In studying crime among street youth, Hagan and McCarthy combine elements from Merton's anomie theory, Coleman's (1988, 1990) work on social capital, and the life-course perspective. They focus on the social capital available to youth over the life course, with such capital having a fundamental impact on the individual's life chances and the attainment of goals. In particular social capital—such as the assistance provided by family—is instrumental in building human and cultural capital. Youth from families with diminished social capital are more likely to end up on the street, which reduces their level of control and increases their exposure to the types of strain outlined in Agnew's general strain theory. Further, they may become embedded in networks that increase their commitment to crime. As a result, crime is quite likely. The impact of life on the street, however, is also influenced by social capital available in the community. The focus on social capital broadens Merton's theory, because goal achievement is seen as more than a simple function of economic resources. Several others in this volume make a similar argument (see Cullen and Wright, Passas).

In the sixth chapter, Menard provides an excellent illustration of the more sophisticated tests of classic strain and anomie theory that are beginning to appear (also see Agnew et al., 1996; Burton et al., 1994; Burton and Dunaway, 1994; Menard, 1995). In particular, he focuses on the version of strain theory proposed by Cloward (1959). This theory is similar to Cloward and Ohlin's (1960) theory of delinquent subcultures, except that the focus is on the explanation of *individual* deviance in all groups—regardless of class, gender, age, and area of residence. Like Cloward and Ohlin, Cloward extends Merton's theory by considering access to legitimate and illegitimate opportunity structures. Menard describes this theory, in all its complexity. He then builds on his previous test of Merton's theory (Menard, 1995) and tests Cloward's theory with data from the National Youth Survey. He constructs a complex model that includes measures of access to legitimate opportunity, anomia, modes of adaptation, and access to illegitimate opportunity structures (both "learning and performance structures"). Unlike previous tests of anomie theory, which simply focused on the disjunction between aspirations and expectations, Menard's data are generally supportive of anomie (and differential-opportunity) theory.

The final two chapters discuss significant extensions in anomie theory. In the seventh chapter, Cullen and Wright discuss the links between Cullen's social-support theory of crime and Agnew's (1992) general strain theory on the one hand, and Messner and Rosenfeld's (1994) institutional-anomie theory on the other. Cullen and Wright argue that differences in social support can help explain why only *some* strained individuals turn to crime. This is a crucial issue in strain theory, and one that has been largely neglected in empirical research—despite Cullen's (1984) excellent treatise on the importance of taking account of "structuring" variables. Most researchers simply assume that strain has a direct effect on crime. This assumption, as Cullen and Wright point out, is seriously flawed. A consideration of social support may help us understand the different responses to strain—including crime. Further, Cullen and Wright build on Messner and Rosenfeld's institutional-anomie theory by arguing that the American Dream promotes crime not only by reducing social control but also by weakening social support. The American Dream, in particular, is said to erode communal ties and undermine the ability of noneconomic institutions to provide social support. The Cullen and

Wright paper, in sum, points to a major factor that may both condition and mediate the effect of strain and anomie on crime.

In the eighth and final chapter, Messner and Rosenfeld discuss the relationship of their institutional-anomie theory of crime to a central debate in sociology: the "markets and morality" debate; that is, "do markets enhance or erode the moral order of a capitalist society?" Messner and Rosenfeld argue that markets both enhance and erode the moral order and that their "net" moral consequences vary over time and between societies. They then argue that their institutional-anomie theory helps specify the conditions under which markets erode rather than enhance morality. Merton has been criticized for not relating his theory to the nature of the capitalist system, that is, for not taking full account of those social conditions and historical factors that lead to anomic societies (Gouldner, 1973; Pfohl, 1985; Taylor et al., 1973). Messner and Rosenfeld, however, show that there is a strong connection between certain types of capitalist markets and anomie (also see Passas, 1990). The final part of their chapter discusses the similarities and differences between their theory and Merton's anomie theory—as well as other theories of crime. Institutional-anomie theory is starting to stimulate additional research (Chamlin and Cochran, 1995) and promises to direct much attention to the long-neglected area of macroanomie theory.

Conclusion

Although the chapters differ from one another in many ways, they give the reader an idea of the future directions in which strain/anomie theory may proceed. Drawing on these chapters and other recent research, we want to conclude by speculating about the directions in which we feel strain/anomie research will and should proceed.

1. Anomie and strain theorists will focus on a much broader range of strainful events and conditions. Previous research on strain theory focused largely on the disjunction between aspirations and expectations, particularly occupation/educational aspirations and expectations. Researchers will continue to study the blockage of conventional success goals (e.g., Agnew et al., 1996; Burton et al., 1994; Burton and Dunaway, 1994; Menard 1995, this volume): this type of strain clearly occupies a central place in the history of anomie theory. However, examinations of this type of strain will become more sophisticated. They will move away from the focus on the disjunction between aspirations and expectations: it is fairly well established that this disjunction bears little relationship to crime. Alternative measures of strain will be em-

ployed, such as perceptions of blocked opportunities, measures of relative deprivation, and the disjunction between expectations and actual achievements (Agnew, 1992; Agnew et al., 1996; Burton et al., 1994; Burton and Dunaway, 1994; Menard, 1995, this volume).

Researchers, however, will likely direct the bulk of their attention to additional types of strain, such as those identified in Agnew's general strain theory (e.g., Agnew and White, 1992; Hoffman and Su, forthcoming; Paternoster and Mazerolle, 1994). That is, they will explore a wide range of goals, as well as examining types of strain other than goal blockage, such as the loss of positive stimuli and the presentation of negative stimuli. Several of the articles in this volume point to types of strain other than the blockage of success goals (e.g., Cohen; Hagan and McCarthy). Efforts to examine these new types of strain have been somewhat limited by existing data sets, but this is beginning to change as researchers start to conduct surveys that focus specifically on the types of strain identified by Agnew and others.

Researchers will likely find that certain types of strain have a stronger relationship to crime than other types, because they are likely to be more upsetting than others. For example, a severe physical assault is likely to be more upsetting than a minor verbal disagreement. Also, it is likely that certain types of strain are more conducive to crime than other types. For example, female adults are often overburdened with family and other demands. Although these demands may be quite upsetting, they may not lead to crime because family demands reduce opportunities for crime and are often associated with a high level of social control (family violence, however, may be a response to such demands). Interpersonal disputes between adolescent males, however, may be very conducive to violence.

A major challenge for strain researchers is to determine which types of strain are most likely to lead to crime and *why* they are most likely to lead to crime. Those types of strain that are most upsetting may be those that are thought to be intentionally inflicted and those that threaten core identities, challenge core values, interfere with the achievement of dominant goals, violate strongly held justice norms, or represent unconditioned or conditioned negative stimuli. The types of strain most conducive to crime may be those that provide opportunities for crime, are associated with low social control, and involve members of deviant peer groups (as the source of strain, the fellow victims of strain, or part of the audience to strain).

Further, researchers need to determine if some types of strain are more consequential in certain subgroups—including age, gender, race, and class groups—and for certain types of crime. In this volume, Menard examines the utility of his strain model across three age groups and for several different types of crime. Cullen and Wright, Hagan and McCarthy, and others discuss the relevance of their strain models across the life cycle (also see Agnew, 1997). Several authors in this volume also discuss the relevance of structurally induced strain across different class groups, and this, of course, has been a popular topic in the larger literature on strain theory. There has also been some discussion of the relevance of strain theory among males versus females (see Broidy and Agnew, forthcoming; Hoffman and Su, forthcoming). In this connection, it should be noted that many feminist models of crime employ what is essentially a strain model, arguing that the oppression of females is responsible for much female crime. Likewise, Messerschmidt (1993) employs what is essentially a strain model in explaining male crime. Unfortunately, there has been little discussion of the extent to which strain theory can explain crime in different racial groups. Strain theory, however, would seem to have much potential in this area and, in particular, would call attention to the impact of discrimination and other negative life experiences associated with race—factors that are neglected in most other microtheories of crime. We hope that research in these areas will lead to theoretical refinement, so that we might reach a point where we can state that certain types of strain are more likely to lead to certain types of crime in certain groups (and we can explain why this is the case).

2. Strain and anomie theorists will devote more attention to the micro- and macrosources of strain. Not everyone is equally likely to experience strainful events and conditions. Previous research has focused primarily on position in the stratification system as a source of strain. Current researchers continue to assign an important place to this variable, but they also emphasize the importance of additional factors. Cohen and Passas, for example, emphasize the importance of one's comparative and normative reference groups. So, for example, objectively advantaged individuals may feel strain if they compare their situation with even more advantaged others. Likewise, objectively deprived individuals may feel little strain if they compare themselves with other deprived individuals. Hagan and McCarthy emphasize the importance of social capital in the generation of strain, with social capital being only partly a function of economic position. Cullen and Wright emphasize the importance of the closely related concept of social support. Although their chapter focuses on how social support may condition the effect of strain on crime, social support can also play a central role in preventing or causing strain. Still other research has explored the effect of variables such as gender,

age, and race on strain—although much more research is obviously needed in these areas. Strain, then, is clearly more than a function of social class.

Future research will also more fully examine the macrodeterminants of individual strain. Passas, for example, discusses how certain features of our cultural system and social structure may lead some individuals to select nonmembership reference groups, which, in turn, may increase their level of strain. Hagan and his associates have described how certain macrolevel changes in the stratification system may affect individual-level strain (see Hagan, 1994). Hagan and McCarthy also note that community-level variations in social capital can have a dramatic impact on the strain experienced by individuals. Bernard (1990) describes how conditions in the urban underclass may foster individual strain. Messerschmidt (1993) describes how larger cultural and social forces create strain for males in various social locations in our society. Additional examples can be given, and we expect that eventually we will have an integrated statement describing the major ways in which cultural and structural forces lead to individual-level strain and ways of coping with it.

It should be emphasized that research on the micro- and macrosources of strain will be challenging, because the different types of strain may be differentially related to social and cultural variables.

3. Strain theorists will devote more attention to the factors that *intervene* between strainful events or conditions and crime (see Menard, this volume). In particular, more attention will be devoted to the role of negative affect as an intervening variable (see Agnew, 1995b, 1995c; Brezina, 1996). According to Agnew, strain promotes crime by increasing the individual's level of negative affect, especially anger and frustration. This negative affect creates pressure for corrective action, with crime being one possible response. The focus of strain theory on negative affect sets it apart from other theoretical traditions (see Agnew, 1995b, 1995c), and we expect researchers to devote more attention to the role of such affect in explaining the link between strain and crime.

4. Anomie and strain researchers will pay more attention to the factors that *condition* the link between strain and crime. As Agnew points out in his chapter, Merton did discuss such factors. Such factors were a central focus of Cohen (1955) and especially of Cloward and Ohlin (1960). And conditioning or "structuring" effects were the central theme in Cullen (1984). Nevertheless, empirical researchers have largely ignored the factors that might condition the effect of strain on crime. Such effects, however, should receive increased attention by researchers and theorists. Several of the chapters in

this volume devote extended discussions to such effects. Cohen and Passas, for example, argue that one's reference groups can exert a large effect on how one reacts to strain. More research, however, is needed on the impact of such groups and on the factors that influence the selection of reference groups. Hagan and McCarthy note that only some street youth turn to crime, and they discuss certain possible reasons for this—such as the social capital provided by the communities in which these youth reside. Drawing on Cloward (1959), Menard discusses the role played by access to illegitimate opportunities and finds some empirical support for conditioning effects involving illegitimate opportunities. Cullen and Wright provide an excellent discussion of the importance of conditioning variables, with a focus on social support. Others have listed additional variables that may condition the effect of strain on crime (see Agnew, 1992; Cullen, 1984, for extended discussions).

5. Researchers will continue extending anomie and strain theory to new populations, ranging from street youth to corporate executives. Strain theory was originally developed with lower-class individuals in mind, but most empirical research has focused on school populations. Researchers such as Bernard (1984, 1990) and Hagan and McCarthy (this volume) emphasize the special relevance of strain theory to those in low social positions. At the same time, researchers such as Passas and Vaughan remind us that anomie theory is quite relevant to individuals in high social positions as well.

6. There will be a surge of work on macrolevel anomie theory. Certain of this work will focus on corporate or organizational deviance, with the research of D. Cohen (1995), Passas (1990, 1994a), and Vaughan (1983, this volume) serving as excellent prototypes. Such research will investigate the types of strain experienced by organizations and individuals within organizations and will examine the ways in which organizations adapt to this strain— with such adaptations often involving deviance (see Braithwaite, 1984; Clinard and Yeager, 1980; Passas, 1995b). Organizations, in particular, may develop subcultures that facilitate, approve of, or justify deviance. Whether such subcultures develop, however, is conditioned by a number of factors internal and external to the organization (see the Vaughan chapter in this volume). Such factors and contexts need to be explored in a systematic fashion. An international or comparative perspective will be most helpful, as it will introduce elements of cultural differences and conflict, power struggles and inequalities, and it will assist in linking the developing literature on anomie and strain to that on globalization.

Messner and Rosenfeld's institutional-anomie theory of crime is already starting to revive research and theorizing at the societal level. Their theory, in particular, not only represents a fundamental extension of Merton but also significantly extends other macrolevel theories, such as social-disorganization theory. Unlike most disorganization theories, they assign a fundamental role to the cultural sphere. Further, they focus on how culture and social structure may lead to a breakdown in social control in the various institutions. Here, too, they extend disorganization theories—most of which focus on the community and fail to consider the larger sources of weak social control (although see Bursik and Grasmick, 1993). Messner and Rosenfeld are in the process of testing key ideas in their theory, and their tests should serve as prototypes for others.

7. Finally, anomie and strain theorists will continue to explore the links between their theories, as well as the links between anomie/strain theory and other theories (Passas, 1988). Strain and anomie theorists will devote more attention to the influence of anomie on the experience of and reaction to strain. And we hope researchers will explore the ways individual-level strain affects anomie. As several theorists have noted, cultural and structural variables structure but do not fully determine the behavior of individuals. Individual behavior, in turn, reacts to and helps shape culture and social structure.

Further, the close links between strain/anomie and other theories will receive more attention (Passas, forthcoming). These links have been emphasized in virtually every chapter in this volume, as well as in other recent work on strain and anomie theory (Agnew, 1995a, 1995b). It is clear that anomie/strain contribute to low control and increase the likelihood that individuals will form or join deviant subcultures. It is also reasonably clear that low social control and association with deviant others may increase strain/anomie (Agnew, this volume). We expect to see a fuller recognition of these links in the integrated theories emerging in the near future. Strain and anomie theorists have focused much of their recent effort on the refinement and revision of their theory but should become more interested in exploring the links between different theories now that their revisions in strain/anomie theory are assuming a more definitive form.

We predict, then, that strain and anomie theorists will focus on several related issues in their future research. And in focusing on these issues, we expect that they will employ a range of methodological techniques, ranging from sophisticated quantitative techniques—such as structural equation models using longitudinal survey data—to more qualitative techniques— such as intensive interviews with offenders and case studies of organizations. Further, we expect that a variety of strategies for theory development will be employed, ranging from the traditional deductive approaches to more inductive approaches, such as the strategy of "theory elaboration" described by Vaughan in this volume. The ultimate future of anomie and strain theories, of course, will depend on the interpretation of empirical data. We hope, however, that the articles in this volume demonstrate that anomie theory is alive and kicking, that it has a distinctive contribution to make to the explanation of deviance and crime, and that it is worthy of serious consideration.

References

Adler, Freda, and William S. Laufer. 1995. *Advances in criminological theory*, Vol. 6: *The legacy of anomie*. New Brunswick, N.J.: Transaction.

Agnew, Robert. 1985. A revised strain theory of delinquency. *Social Forces* 64:151–67.

———. 1992. Foundation for a general strain theory of crime and delinquency. *Criminology* 30(1):47–87.

———. 1995a. Strain and subcultural theories of criminality. In *Criminology: A contemporary handbook*, edited by Joseph F. Sheley, 305–27. Belmont, Calif.: Wadsworth.

———. 1995b. The contribution of social-psychological strain to the explanation of crime and delinquency. In *Advances in criminological theory*, Vol. 6: *The legacy of anomie*, edited by Freda Adler and William S. Laufer, 113–37. New Brunswick, N.J.: Transaction.

———. 1995c. Testing the leading crime theories: An alternative strategy focusing on motivational processes. *Journal of Research in Crime and Delinquency* 32:363–98.

———. 1997. Stability and crime over the life course: A strain theory explanation. In *Advances in criminological theory*, Vol. 7: *Developmental theories of crime and delinquency*, edited by Terrence P. Thornberry, 101–32. New Brunswick, N.J.: Transaction.

Agnew, Robert, Francis T. Cullen, Velmer S. Burton Jr., T. David Evans, and R. Gregory Dunaway. 1996. A new test of classic strain theory. *Justice Quarterly* 13:681–704.

Agnew, Robert, and Helene Raskin White. 1992. An empirical test of general strain theory. *Criminology* 30:475–99.

Anderson, Elijah. 1994. The code of the streets. *Atlantic Monthly* 273 (May):81–94.

Bernard, Thomas J. 1984. Control criticisms of strain theories: An assessment of theoretical and empirical adequacy. *Journal of Research in Crime and Delinquency* 21:353–72.

———. 1987. Testing structural strain theories. *Journal of Research in Crime and Delinquency* 24(4):262–80.

———. 1989. A theoretical approach to integration. In *Theoretical integration in the study of deviance and crime: Problems and prospects*, edited by Steven F. Messner, Marvin D. Krohn, and Allen E. Liska, 137–59. Albany: State University of New York Press.

———. 1990. Angry aggression among the "truly disadvantaged." *Criminology* 28:73–109.

———. 1995. Merton versus Hirschi: Who is faithful to Durkheim's heritage? In *Advances in criminological theory*, Vol. 6: *The legacy of anomie*, edited by Freda Adler and William S. Laufer, 81–90. New Brunswick, N.J.: Transaction.

Box, Steven. 1983. *Ideology, crime and mystification*. London: Tavistock.

Braithwaite, John. 1984. *Corporate crime in the pharmaceutical industry*. London: Routledge and Kegan Paul.

———. 1989a. Criminological theory and organizational crime. *Justice Quarterly* 6(3):333–58.

———. 1989b. *Crime, shame and reintegration*. Cambridge: Cambridge University Press.

———. 1993. Beyond positivism: Learning from contextual integrated strategies. *Journal of Research in Crime and Delinquency* 30(4):383–99.

Brezina, Timothy. 1996. Adapting to strain: An examination of delinquent coping responses. *Criminology* 34:39–60.

Broidy, Lisa, and Robert Agnew. Forthcoming. Gender and crime: A general strain theory perspective. *Journal of Research in Crime and Delinquency*.

Bursik, Robert J., and Harold G. Grasmick. 1993. *Neighborhoods and crime: The dimensions of effective community control*. New York: Lexington.

Burton, Velmer S., Jr., and Francis T. Cullen. 1992. The empirical status of strain theory. *Journal of Crime and Justice* 15:1–30.

Burton, Velmer S., Jr., Francis T. Cullen, T. David Evans, and R. Gregory Dunaway. 1994. Reconsidering strain theory: Operationalization, rival theories, and adult criminality. *Journal of Quantitative Criminology* 10:213–39.

Burton, Velmer S., Jr., and R. Gregory Dunaway. 1994. Strain, relative deprivation, and middle-class delinquency. In *Varieties of criminology: Readings from a dynamic discipline*, edited by Greg Barak, 79–95. Westport, Conn.: Praeger.

Chamlin, Mitchell B., and John K. Cochran. 1995. Assessing Messner and Rosenfeld's institutional anomie theory: A partial test. *Criminology* 33:411–29.

Clinard, Marshall B., ed. 1964. *Anomie and deviant behavior: A discussion and critique*. New York: Free Press.

Clinard, Marshall B., and Peter Yeager. 1980. *Corporate crime*. New York: Free Press.

Cloward, Richard A. 1959. Illegitimate means, anomie, and deviant behavior. *American Sociological Review* 24:164–76.

Cloward, Richard A., and Lloyd Ohlin. 1960. *Delinquency and opportunity*. New York: Free Press.

Cohen, Albert K. 1955. *Delinquent boys: The culture of the gang*. New York: Free Press.

———. 1965. The sociology of the deviant act: Anomie theory and beyond. *American Sociological Review* 30:5–14.

Cohen, Albert K., and James F. Short. 1958. Research in delinquent subcultures. *Journal of Social Issues* 14:20–37.

Cohen, Deborah V. 1992. Ethical choice in the workplace: Situational and psychological determinants. Ph.D. diss., Columbia University.

———. 1993. Creating and maintaining ethical work climates: Anomie in the workplace and implications for managing change. *Business Ethics Quarterly* 3:343–58.

———. 1995. Ethics and crime in business firms: Organizational culture and the impact of anomie. In *Advances in criminological theory*, Vol. 6: *The legacy of anomie*, edited by Freda Adler and William S. Laufer, 183–206. New Brunswick, N.J.: Transaction.

Cole, J. R., and H. Zuckerman. 1964. Inventory of empirical and theoretical studies of anomie. In *Anomie and deviant behavior: A discussion and critique*, edited by Marshall B. Clinard, 243–313. New York: Free Press.

Cole, S. 1975. The growth of scientific knowledge: Theories of deviance as a case study. In *The idea of social structure*, edited by Lewis A. Coser, 175–220. New York: Harcourt Brace Jovanovich.

Coleman, James. 1988. Social capital in the creation of human capital. *American Journal of Sociology* 94:95–120.

———. 1990. *Foundations of social theory*. Cambridge, Mass.: Harvard University Press.

Cullen, Francis T. 1984. *Rethinking crime and deviance: The emergence of a structuring tradition*. Totowa, N.J.: Rowman & Allanheld.

———. 1988. Were Cloward and Ohlin strain theorists?: Delinquency and opportunity revisited. *Journal of Research in Crime and Delinquency* 25:214–41.

———. 1994. Social support as an organizing concept for criminology. *Justice Quarterly* 11:527–59.

Durkheim, Emile. 1951 [1897]. *Suicide*. New York: Free Press.

Elliott, Delbert S., Suzanne S. Ageton, and Rachelle J. Canter. 1979. An integrated theoretical perspective on delinquent behavior. *Journal of Research in Crime and Delinquency* 16:3–27.

Elliott, Delbert S., and Harwin Voss. 1974. *Delinquency and dropout*. Lexington, Mass.: D.C. Heath.

Farnworth, Margaret, and Michael J. Leiber. 1989. Strain theory revisited: Economic goals, educational means, and delinquency. *American Sociological Review* 54:263–74.

Giddens, Anthony. 1979. *Central problems in social theory: Action, structure, and contradiction in social analysis*. Berkeley: University of California Press.

———. 1990. R. K. Merton on structural analysis. In *Robert K. Merton: Consensus and controversy*, edited by Jon Clark, Celia Modgil, and Sohan Modgil, 97–110. London, New York, and Philadelphia: Falmer Press.

Gottfredson, Michael R., and Travis Hirschi. 1990. *A general theory of crime*. Stanford, Calif.: Stanford University Press.

Gouldner, Alvin. 1973. Foreword. In *The New Criminology*, Ian Taylor, Paul Walton, and Jock Young, ix–xiv. London: Routledge & Kegan Paul.

Greenberg, David F. 1977. Delinquency and the age structure of society. *Contemporary Crises* 1:189–223.

Hagan, John. 1994. *Crime and disrepute*. Thousand Oaks, Calif.: Pine Forge Press.

Hagan, John, and Bill McCarthy. 1996. *Mean streets*. New York: Cambridge University Press.

Hilbert, R. E., and Charles W. Wright. 1979. Representations of Merton's theory of anomie. *American Sociologist* 14:150–56.

Hirschi, Travis. 1969. *Causes of delinquency*. Berkeley: University of California Press.

———. 1979. Separate and unequal is better. *Journal of Research in Crime and Delinquency* 16:34–38.

Hoffman, John P., and Timothy Ireland. 1995. Cloward and Ohlin's strain theory reexamined: An elaborated theoretical model. In *Advances in criminological theory*, Vol. 6: *The legacy of anomie*, edited by Freda Adler and William S. Laufer, 247–70. New Brunswick, N.J.: Transaction.

Hoffman, John P., and S. Susan Su. Forthcoming. The conditional effects of negative life events on delinquency and drug use: A strain theory assessment of gender differences. *Journal of Research in Crime and Delinquency.*

Jensen, Gary F. 1995. Salvaging structure through strain: A theoretical and empirical critique. In *Advances in criminological theory*, Vol. 6: *The legacy of anomie*, edited by Freda Adler and William S. Laufer, 139–58. New Brunswick, N.J.: Transaction.

Kornhauser, Ruth. 1978. *Social sources of delinquency*. Chicago: University of Chicago Press.

Liska, Allen E. 1971. Aspirations, expectations, and delinquency: Stress and additive models. *Sociological Quarterly* 12:99–107.

Menard, Scott. 1995. A developmental test of Mertonian anomie theory. *Journal of Research in Crime and Delinquency* 32:136–74.

Merton, Robert K. 1938. Social structure and anomie. *American Sociological Review* 3:672–82.

———. 1956. The socio-cultural environment and anomie. In *New perspectives for research on juvenile delinquency*, edited by L. H. Witmer and R. Kotinsky, 24–50. Washington, D.C.: U.S. Department of Health, Education and Welfare.

———. 1957. Priorities in scientific discovery: A chapter in the sociology of science. *American Sociological Review* 22:635–59.

———. 1964. Anomie, anomia, and social interaction: Contexts of deviant behavior. In *Anomie and deviant behavior: A discussion and critique*, edited by M. B. Clinard, 213–42. New York: Free Press.

———. 1968. *Social theory and social structure*. New York: Free Press.

———. 1995. Opportunity structure: The emergence, diffusion, and differentiation of a sociological concept, 1930s–1950s. In *Advances in criminological theory*, Vol. 6: *The legacy of anomie*, edited by Freda Adler and William S. Laufer, 3–78. New Brunswick, N.J.: Transaction.

Messerschmidt, James W. 1993. *Masculinities and crime*. Lanham, Md.: Rowman and Littlefield.

Messner, Steven F. 1988. Merton's "Social structure and anomie": The road not taken. *Deviant Behavior* 9:33–53.

Messner, Steven F., Marvin D. Krohn, and Allen E. Liska, eds. 1989. *Theoretical integration in the study of deviance and crime: Problems and prospects*. Albany: State University of New York Press.

Messner, Steven F., and Richard Rosenfeld. 1994. *Crime and the American dream*. Belmont, Calif.: Wadsworth.

Mizruchi, Ephraim. 1964. *Success and opportunity*. New York: Free Press.

Ogle, Robbin S., Daniel Maier-Katkin, and Thomas J. Bernard. 1995. A theory of homicidal behavior among women. *Criminology* 33:173–93.

Orrù, Marco. 1987. *Anomie: History and meanings*. Boston: Allen & Unwin.

Passas, Nikos. 1987. Anomie and relative deprivation. Paper presented at the plenary session of the annual meeting of the Eastern Sociological Society, Boston.

———. 1988. Merton's theory of anomie and deviance: An elaboration. Unpublished Ph.D. diss., University of Edinburgh.

———. 1990. Anomie and corporate deviance. *Contemporary Crises* 14:157–78.

———. 1994a. I cheat, therefore I exist? The BCCI scandal in context. In *Emerging global business ethics*, edited by W. M. Hoffman, J. Kamm, R. E. Frederick, and E. Petry, 69–78. Newport, Colo.: Quorum Books.

———. 1994b. The market for gods and services: Religion, commerce and deviance. *Religion and Social Order* 4:217–41.

———. 1995a. Continuities in the anomie tradition. In *Advances in criminological theory*, Vol. 6: *The legacy of anomie*, edited by Freda Adler and William S. Laufer, 91–112. New Brunswick, N.J.: Transaction.

———. 1995b. The mirror of global evils: A review essay on the BCCI affair. *Justice Quarterly* 12:801–29.

———. Forthcoming. *Consolidating criminology*. Albany: State University of New York Press.

Passas, Nikos, and Manuel Escamilla. 1992. Scientology and its "Clear" business. *Behavioral Sciences and the Law* 10:103–16.

Paternoster, Raymond, and Paul Mazerolle. 1994. General strain theory and delinquency: A replication and extension. *Journal of Research in Crime and Delinquency* 31:235–63.

Pfohl, Steven J. 1985. *Images of deviance and social control: A sociological history*. New York: McGraw-Hill.

Rosenfeld, Richard. 1989. Robert Merton's contribution to the sociology of deviance. *Sociological Inquiry* 59:453–66.

Savelsberg, Joachim J. 1995. Crime, inequality, and justice in Eastern Europe: Anomie, domination, and revolutionary change. In *Crime and inequality*, edited by John Hagan and Ruth D. Peterson, 206–24. Stanford, Calif.: Stanford University Press.

Simon, William, and John H. Gagnon. 1976. The anomie of affluence: A post-Mertonian conception. *American Journal of Sociology* 82:356–78.

Simpson, Sally S., and Christopher S. Koper. 1992. Deterring corporate crime. *Criminology* 30:347–75.

Taylor, Ian, Paul Walton, and Jock Young. 1973. *The new criminology*. London: Routledge & Kegan Paul.

Thoits, Peggy A. 1991. On merging identity theory and stress research. *Social Psychology Quarterly* 54:7–22.

Vaughan, Diane. 1983. *Controlling unlawful organizational behavior*. Chicago: Chicago University Press.

———. 1992a. Theory elaboration: The heuristics of case analysis. In *What is a case? Exploring the foundations of social inquiry*, edited by Charles C. Ragin and Howard S. Becker, 173–202. Cambridge: Cambridge University Press.

———. 1992b. The macro-micro connection in white-collar crime theory. In *White-collar crime reconsidered*, edited by Kip Schlegel and David Weisburd, 124–45. Boston: Northeastern University Press.

Vold, George, and Thomas J. Bernard. 1986. *Theoretical criminology*. New York: Oxford University Press.

ROBERT AGNEW

The Nature and Determinants of Strain: Another Look at Durkheim and Merton

Strain theorists in criminology trace their roots to Durkheim (1951) and Merton (1938). These theorists were among the first to argue that crime stems from the frustration/anger that results from goal blockage. And although new versions of strain theory have been developed (e.g., Agnew, 1992), Durkheim and especially Merton still exert a strong influence on the field. They are the inspiration behind the new versions of strain theory, and they still continue to guide contemporary empirical research (e.g., Agnew, 1995a; Burton and Cullen, 1992; Farnworth and Leiber, 1991; Jensen, 1995; Menard, 1995). Their strain theories, however, have been the subject of heavy attack since the late 1960s.

Researchers argue that the empirical evidence does not support Merton's theory and that it should therefore be abandoned. Most notably, they point to studies suggesting that the discrepancy between aspirations and expectations for goal achievement is unrelated to delinquency (Agnew, 1995a; Burton and Cullen, 1992; Hirschi, 1969; Jensen, 1995; Kornhauser, 1978). There has been little empirical research on Durkheim's version of strain theory, although that has not prevented some individuals from claiming that it too is wrong (e.g., Cloward and Ohlin, 1960).

Further, control theorists argue that a close reading of Durkheim actually reveals him to be a control theorist. Hirschi (1969, p. 3, n. 1) states that "Durkheim's theory is one of the purest examples of control theory," with deviance being the automatic result of a breakdown in societal regulation (also see Kornhauser, 1978, p. 165). Others have come to accept this view. Cullen, for example, states that "Durkheim contended that suicide is the ultimate by-product of the inability of society—to be more exact, the normative structure of society—to regulate social needs" (1984, p. 58). So, like other control theorists, Durkheim explains deviance in terms of "society's failure or inability to control or regulate people's deviant impulses" (1984, p. 77).

More recently, a number of "anomie" theorists have even argued that Merton is a control theorist or that his arguments are compatible with control theory (see the review in Bernard, 1995).[1] Bernard (1987) argues that Merton did not propose a microlevel strain theory. Rather, Bernard states that Merton's focus is on *structural strain* and anomie, and his theory in this area is said to be quite compatible with control theory. He believes that Merton's theory "does not require that people in situations of social structural strain experience stress or frustration. When legitimate means to monetary success are unavailable, people will tend to chose illegitimate means regardless of whether they feel frustrated or not. . . . It would not contradict Merton's theory if it were found that people experience social structural strain as freedom rather than stress, or as some combination of freedom and stress. In that case, Merton's theory could be construed as consistent with Hirschi's (1969)" control theory (1987, p. 266; also see Bernard, 1989, p. 147; and the somewhat modified view in Bernard, 1995).

Burton and Cullen (1992) make a similar argument (also see Cullen, 1984). They claim that Merton did not propose a theory of "individually felt strain," but rather he focused on the social condition of anomie and used anomie to explain variations in the crime rate across social units. Anomie refers to a "breakdown in normative control," and Merton is said to be "more a 'control' theorist than a 'strain' theorist" (1992, p. 5). Other theorists are less extreme, although they argue that Merton presents an anomie theory that is distinct from his strain theory, with his anomie theory being compatible with control theory (e.g., Messner, 1988).[2]

The strain theories of Durkheim and Merton, then, have been attacked on two fronts. One line of attack contends that they are wrong; another questions whether Durkheim and Merton even advocate individual-level strain theories.

This essay challenges both sets of arguments. First, the theories of Durkheim and Merton are briefly reviewed. I argue that Durkheim is best viewed as a strain theorist rather than a control theorist. The argument that Merton advocates a version of strain theory is presented in Agnew (1987) and so is not reviewed here. Next, I discuss the views of Durkheim and Merton on the nature of individual-level strain and the macrolevel determinants of such strain. I argue that researchers have neglected most of the core arguments of Durkheim and Merton and that the empirical studies of Merton's strain theory have little relevance to the theory that Merton actually advocates (also see Bernard, 1984; Burton and Cullen, 1992; Menard, 1995). Further, I argue that the neglect of Durkheim by empirical researchers is undeserved. In making these arguments, I point to several new directions for further research.

Durkheim

Durkheim has much to say regarding the nature of strain and the macrolevel determinants of strain, but most of his arguments have been neglected in contemporary research and theory (although see Adler, 1983; Krohn, 1978; Vold and Bernard, 1986).[3] I begin with a brief description of Durkheim's theory, as well as a comment on the issue of whether he is best viewed as a control or a strain theorist.

According to Durkheim ([1897] 1951), all healthy societies set limits on the goals that individuals pursue. These limits are set so that individuals have a reasonable chance of achieving their goals: those individuals with greater social resources have higher limits. Such limits make people "contented with their lot while stimulating them moderately to improve it" (1951, p. 250). Under certain conditions, however, societies may lose their ability to regulate individual goals. When this occurs, goals become unlimited or at least unattainable. This occurs because individuals are inherently unable to set limits on their desires. The needs of nonhuman animals are naturally limited: they simply need enough to satisfy their physical requirements. Once satisfied, they aspire to no more. Most human needs, however, are not strongly tied to the body. In humans, "a more awakened reflection suggests better conditions, seemingly desirable ends craving fulfillment" (1951, p. 247). But according to Durkheim (1951, p. 247), "nothing appears in man's organic nor in his psychological constitution which sets a limit to" these desires. People will restrain their desires only in response "to a limit they recognize as just," which means that this limit must come from "an authority which they respect" (p. 249). That authority is society or "one of its organs." When society fails to play this role, goals become unlimited or unattainable. And as Durkheim states, "to pursue a goal which is by definition unattainable is to condemn oneself to a state of perpetual unhappiness" (1951, p. 248).

Durkheim describes several situations in which societies are unable to regulate individual goals adequately. The first situation occurs during periods of economic crisis. Many individuals are suddenly "cast into a lower state than their previous one." As such, they must lower their desires. "But society cannot adjust them instantaneously to this new life and teach them to practice the increased self-repression to which they are unaccustomed" (Durkheim, 1951, p. 252). Consequently, they are unable to achieve their *limited* goals.

The second situation occurs during periods of economic boom. During such booms, the standard by which goals are regulated becomes obsolete. A new standard, taking account of the "abrupt growth in power and wealth," must be imposed. But such a standard cannot be imposed immediately, and so there is no restraint on aspirations for a period of time. "The limits are unknown between the possible and the impossible, what is just and unjust, legitimate claims and hopes and those which are immoderate" (Durkheim, 1951, p. 253). Aspirations increase in the absence of societal regulation. The prosperous are "no longer resigned to [their] former lot," and the jealousy aroused by their good fortune prompts others to increase their aspirations— particularly in the context of normative deregulation (Durkheim, 1951, p. 253).

In the third situation, Durkheim argues that anomie has recently become a chronic state in one sphere of life—industry and trade. He argues that economic activity is now largely free of all regulation, including regulation by religion, government, and occupational groups. Economic prosperity has become the ultimate end, and "appetites thus excited have become freed of any limiting authority . . . restraint seems like a sort of sacrilege" (Durkheim, 1951, p. 255). "From top to bottom of the ladder, greed is aroused without knowing where to find ultimate foothold. Nothing can calm it, since its goal is far beyond all it can attain" (1951, p. 256). In his discussion of the economic sphere, Durkheim suggests that heightened aspirations not only are a result of the absence of societal restraint but are also positively encouraged. "These dispositions are so inbred that society has grown to accept them and is accustomed to think them normal. It is everlastingly repeated that it is man's nature to be externally dissatisfied, constantly to advance, without relief or rest, toward an infinite goal. The longing for infinity is daily represented as a mark of moral distinction. . . . The doctrine of the most ruthless and swift progress has become an article of faith" (1951, p. 257). Finally, Durkheim speaks of conjugal anomie, noting that marriage functions as a regulator of sexual relations—both physical and emotional.

Durkheim argues that the pursuit of unlimited or unattainable goals is a source of "constantly renewed torture" (1951, p. 247). It is for this reason that anomie may lead to suicide and sometimes violence. In particular, Durkheim argues that anomie may result in violence if individuals blame others for their problems (1951, p. 285) or if they are of "low morality" (1951, p. 357).

Is Durkheim a Strain Theorist?   Given this brief description of Durkheim, we are now in a better position to ask whether he is a control or a strain theorist. Control theory is distinguished from strain theory in terms of its independent variables and, most especially, its specification of intervening processes (Agnew, 1993, 1995b, 1995c). Control theory argues that deviance results from the *absence of society* (independent variable), and this absence creates deviance because it provides individuals with the *freedom to satisfy universal needs and desires* through the most expedient means—which is often deviance (intervening process). Strain theory argues that deviance results from negative treatment by others, with most strain theories focusing on goal blockage; *and* this negative treatment increases the likelihood of deviance because it frustrates/angers the individual, with deviance being one method of dealing with this frustration/anger. In control theory, then, individuals are *freed* to engage in deviance, whereas in strain theory, individuals are *pressured* into deviance (Hirschi, 1969; Kornhauser, 1978; Vold and Bernard, 1986).

Durkheim's theory clearly focuses on the absence of society. Deviance ultimately is caused by the failure of society (or its organs) to regulate individual goals adequately. The absence of such regulation is what Durkheim means by anomie. To this extent, Durkheim appears to be a pure control theorist. The position of Durkheim becomes muddied, however, if we focus on intervening processes and ask *why* the absence of societal regulation leads to deviance. Here we find ourselves phrasing the answer in terms of strain theory. The absence of society does *not* free individuals to satisfy their universal desires in the most expedient manner. Rather, the absence of society leads individuals to develop unlimited or unattainable goals, and the failure to achieve these goals leads to "anger and all the emotions customarily associated with disappointment" (Durkheim, 1951, p. 284). It is these emotions that *drive* individuals to suicide and violence. These emotions are *not* universally shared, and the absence of society does *not* free individuals to act on them. The intense anger/frustration described by Durkheim is not *released* by the absence of society, it is *created* by the absence of society. The absence of society is important, then, not because it increases freedom but because it increases the frustration/anger that drives individuals to deviance. So the absence of society leads to strain at the individual level in Durkheim, and it is this strain that causes deviance. For this reason, Durkheim is best viewed as a strain rather than a control theorist.

THE NATURE AND DETERMINANTS OF STRAIN

Durkheim's arguments regarding the nature of strain and the macrolevel determinants of strain have been largely neglected in contemporary research.

As argued below, this neglect is undeserved, and contemporary researchers should attempt to build on and test Durkheim's insights.

Strain as the Pursuit of Unlimited Goals.   Most contemporary work on strain theory focuses on the inability to achieve limited or fixed goals, such as middle-class status or a certain level of monetary success. Limited goals were also important in Durkheim: economic crises might result in a situation where the downwardly mobile are unable to achieve their limited goals (set in the period before the economic crisis). Durkheim, however, argues that a lack of normative regulation most often results in the pursuit of unlimited goals. And he appears to mean two things by unlimited goals. First, he refers to a situation where the individual pursues some limited goal, experiences little or no satisfaction from the achievement of that goal, and immediately turns to the pursuit of some other goal. In describing anomie in the economic sphere, for example, Durkheim states,

> a thirst arises for novelties, unfamiliar pleasures, nameless sensations, all of which lose their savor once known. The wise man, knowing how to enjoy achieved results without having to constantly replace them with others, finds in them an attachment to life in the hour of difficulty. But the man who has always pinned all his hopes on the future and lived with his eyes fixed upon it, has nothing in the past as a comfort against the present's afflictions, for the past was nothing to him but a series of hastily experienced stages. (1951, p. 256)

We have, then, the image of an individual with an insatiable appetite, moving from one limited goal to the next and not obtaining any gratification from his or her accomplishments. Second, Durkheim refers to a situation where the individual desires the impossible: that which could never be achieved under any circumstances. In describing conjugal anomie, for example, Durkheim states that "if one happens to exhaust the range of what is possible, one dreams of the impossible: one thirsts for the nonexistent" (1951, p. 271).

Durkheim's arguments in this area have been largely ignored. Cloward and Ohlin, for example, quickly dismiss the idea of unlimited goals by stating that "probably relatively few people are afflicted with insatiable aspirations" (1960, p. 83). And I know of no study that has attempted to operationalize strain in terms of the pursuit of unlimited goals, either ever-escalating goals or impossible goals. This neglect is surprising, because certain accounts suggest that unlimited goals may be common among delinquents. Summarizing previous research on delinquent values, Matza and Sykes state that the delinquent is "deeply immersed in a restless search for excitement, 'thrills,' or 'kicks' "; that he or she has "grandiose dreams of quick success"; and that "the sudden acquisition of large sums of money is his goal" (1961, pp. 713–14). Other researchers have similarly suggested that delinquents often have unrealistic or unlimited goals (Crenkovich, 1978; England, 1960; Lerman, 1968; Agnew, 1994). Still other researchers have argued that such goals characterize many adults (e.g., Agnew, 1980; Mizruchi, 1964).

Merton himself has suggested that goals may be unlimited, for example, when he states that "in the American Dream there is no final stopping point. The measure of 'monetary success' is conveniently indefinite and relative. At each income level . . . Americans want just about twenty-five percent more (but of course this 'just a bit more' continues to operate once it is obtained). In this flux of shifting standards, there is no stable resting point, or rather, it is the point which manages always to be 'just ahead' " (1968, p. 190; also see the discussion of the "anomie of success" in Merton, 1964, and Passas 1987, 1995). There is a sharp difference in Merton's and Durkheim's discussions of unlimited goals: Merton believes that such goals are fostered by society, and Durkheim believes that such goals are largely rooted in the absence of society. Merton's arguments regarding unlimited goals, however, have received no more attention than Durkheim's. Merton's theory is usually interpreted to mean that there is a disjunction between means and *limited goals*.

This neglect of unlimited goals is unfortunate. Not only is there good reason to believe that such goals exist, but their existence—if confirmed—would have important policy implications. If goals are unlimited, means to achieve goals are unimportant, and efforts to prevent crime by fostering goal achievement are doomed to failure. Future research should attempt to explore the extent of unlimited goals, their determinants (more below), and their relation to delinquency. It would not be difficult to measure the second type of unlimited goals (impossible goals), and—with some probing—it would also seem possible to measure the first type (ever-escalating goals). Certain preliminary efforts have already been made in this area (Agnew, 1980, 1994).

The Absence of Society as a Source of Strain. Merton's anomie theory has heavily influenced contemporary views regarding the link between macrosocial conditions and individual-level strain. As depicted in numerous accounts (see Hilbert and Wright, 1979), society actively fosters strain by encouraging individuals in all social classes to pursue the goal of monetary success and by preventing large numbers of individuals from achieving this goal through legitimate channels. Durkheim presents an alternative view that I believe has been prematurely rejected by researchers.

According to Durkheim, society promotes strain by its absence rather than its presence. As noted above, Durkheim argues that the absence of societal regulation leads to unlimited or unattainable goals, because individuals are inherently unable to limit their own desires. These unlimited or unattainable desires then lead to strain. Many researchers, I believe, are uncomfortable with this argument. It is not clear why individuals are inherently unable to limit their desires. If individuals are able to use their reflective abilities to aspire beyond their physical needs, why can't they draw on these same abilities to limit their desires in response to limited opportunities? Numerous theorists, in fact, have argued that individuals often adjust their aspirations downward in response to limited opportunities (Agnew, 1995a; Kornhauser, 1978). Also, Durkheim's argument has certain biological overtones that leave researchers uneasy: unlimited goals seem to be at least partly a product of human nature. In this area, it has been argued that Durkheim's theory has much in common with the Freudian perspective on biological impulses that Merton attacked (Cullen, 1984; Mestrovic, 1988). And Merton's revision of Durkheim is said to "reject the notion of anomie as a result of society's failure to prevent the leakage of biological impulse" (Taylor et al., 1973, p. 96; also see Clinard, 1964; Horton, 1964; Lukes, 1967; Orru, 1987, p. 121).

Although I am sympathetic to these arguments, I still believe that there is some merit to Durkheim's basic argument. Durkheim states that at least two conditions must obtain if individuals are to avoid strain and find contentment: they must have a reasonable chance of achieving their goals, and they must view their goals as just. For this to occur, their goals must be proportionate to their resources, and they must come from an authority they respect, that is, society or one of its organs. Although individuals may sometimes be capable of limiting their own goals, it seems reasonable to argue that they will have an easier time in this effort *if they are assisted by society*. This seems especially true in those circumstances described by Durkheim. Durkheim speaks of individuals who suddenly experience dramatic increases or decreases in wealth, who are surrounded by others who have experienced increases in wealth, or who are encouraged by certain elements of society to pursue unlimited goals. Without the assistance of others, it may be difficult for such individuals to realistically appraise their situation and set reasonable goals for themselves.

But, as Durkheim points out, society and its organs are often unable to regulate individual goals effectively. There seem to be two reasons for this. First, society may simply fail to provide individuals with limits for their goals. This may be due to rapid social change (limits are in a state of flux) or to the dominance of noneconomic institutions by the economy (noneconomic institutions are prevented from imposing limits; also see Messner and Rosenfeld, 1994). In certain cases, individuals may even be deliberately encouraged to pursue unattainable goals—although here we are no longer talking about the absence of society. Second, individuals may reject the limits that society does try to impose. Most notably, individuals may reject such limits because they are not attached to or do not respect society or its organs. As indicated, Durkheim argues that regulations must come from an authority that is respected if they are to be accepted as just. Durkheim makes a similar point when he discusses the close relation between anomic and egoistic suicide, noting that it is "almost inevitable that the egoist should have some tendency to nonregulation; for, since he is detached from society, it has not sufficient hold upon him to regulate him" (1951, p. 288). This explanation, of course, relates to Hirschi's (1969) bond of attachment and to notions of internal social control. Durkheim also goes on to suggest that individuals may reject societal limits if they no longer feel dependent on society for the satisfaction of their desires. Durkheim states, for example, that wealth fosters unlimited desires, because it "deceives us into believing that we depend on ourselves only" (1951, p. 254). This explanation relates to his concept of organic solidarity and to the concepts of external control and commitment in control theories.

Unlimited or unattainable goals are most likely, then, when society or its organs fail to set reasonable limits on individual goals or society specifically encourages the pursuit of unlimited goals, and when individuals are not attached or committed to society or its organs, such as family, peers, school, mass media, and work. Durkheim discusses certain of the factors that foster these conditions, such as rapid social change. It would not be difficult to expand on Durkheim. The social-control and social-disorganization literatures, in particular, discuss those macro- and microfactors that lead to low attachment and commitment.

These arguments imply that control variables, such as attachment and commitment, may be important not only because they increase the internal and external sanctions for deviance but because they are implicated in the process of regulating goals. Durkheim's arguments regarding the absence of society, then, suggest a new perspective on the relationship between social control and deviance; low control may increase strain by contributing to the pursuit of unlimited or unattainable goals.

We might also broaden Durkheim's argument and point to another way in which the absence of society may encourage strain. Society not only plays an important role in regulating individual goals but also in satisfying individual goals. Individuals have certain needs that must be met through society. Some have suggested that these needs are biologically based, and others have suggested that they may be existentially based or a product of the cultural system (e.g., Kornhauser, 1978, p. 169; Nye, 1958; Thrasher, 1927). Whatever the case, the satisfaction of these needs might be jeopardized by the absence of society (low social control). And individuals, in their frustration and discontent, might turn to delinquency for the satisfaction of their needs. Thrasher, for example, focuses on Thomas's four wishes: new experience, security, affection, recognition (also see Nye, 1958, p. 8). He argues that the disorganized areas in which gang boys live make the satisfaction of many of these needs problematic. Gang boys, in particular, are confronted by the "disintegration of family life, inefficiency of schools, formalism and externality of religion, corruption and indifference in local politics, low wages and monotony in occupational activities, unemployment, and lack of opportunity for wholesome recreation" (1927, p. 37). The failure of society to satisfy their needs not only creates low social control but also strain or frustration. Individuals then seek to satisfy their needs through other, often deviant channels. As Thrasher notes, the gang "offers a substitute for what society fails to give; and it provides a relief from suppression and distasteful behavior. It fills a gap and affords an escape" (1927, p. 38). The gang is not necessarily delinquent, although certain factors increase the likelihood of delinquency, including a "general soreness against the world" (1927, p. 95). Nye (1958) and Shaw and McKay (1942) make similar arguments, suggesting that the failure of major social institutions to satisfy basic needs creates pressure for deviance (as well as reducing social control). And although Messner and Rosenfeld (1994) do not make this argument, it is certainly compatible with their theory. They describe how the dominance of economic goals undermines the effectiveness of noneconomic institutions. In particular, institutions such as the family and school become less able to fulfill their distinctive functions. Messner and Rosenfeld claim these effects are important because they weaken social control and thereby contribute to deviance. These effects, however, may also contribute to strain by undermining the ability of these institutions to satisfy human needs/goals.

According to these arguments, then, the absence of society (i.e., social disorganization/low social control) may contribute to strain in two ways—by fostering the pursuit of unattainable goals and by interfering with the achievement of goals. Such arguments are seldom made in contemporary research: the effects of social disorganization and low control on deviance are interpreted not in terms of strain but in terms of the freedom to deviate. Researchers do sometimes argue that strain may reduce social control (e.g., Elliott et al., 1985; Kornhauser, 1978, p. 140; Reis, 1951), but they seldom argue that low "control" may increase strain.

Merton

Although Durkheim's arguments regarding strain and anomie have been largely neglected, those of Merton dominate the literature. Merton presents a rather different view of strain and its macrolevel determinants. Despite certain statements to the contrary, he tends to present strain as the inability to achieve *limited* goals. And he argues that strain stems primarily from the *presence* rather than the absence of society (for discussions of the differences between Merton and Durkheim on anomie, see Cullen, 1984; Hilbert, 1989; Horton, 1964; Mestrovic, 1988; Mestrovic and Brown, 1985; Orru, 1987; Passas, 1995; Taylor et al., 1973). Further, Merton devotes significant attention to those factors that condition the effect of strain on deviance. The dominance of Merton's paradigm, however, has not prevented researchers from neglecting key aspects of it in their tests of strain/anomie theory.

Merton begins his theory by arguing that societies differ in the relative emphasis they place on goals and the legitimate norms governing goal achievement. In some societies, equal emphasis is placed on goals and norms, so that individuals achieve satisfaction from both goal achievement and following the institutional norms for goal achievement (1968, p. 188).[4] Other societies, however, place great emphasis on goals and little emphasis on the legitimate means to achieve goals. In extreme cases, "the behavior of many individuals [is] limited only by considerations of technical expediency . . . the technically most effective procedure, whether culturally legitimate or not, becomes typically preferred to institutionally prescribed conduct" (1968, p. 189). Such societies are characterized by a state of anomie or normlessness (1968, p. 289). For Merton, normlessness refers to those norms regulating goal achievement, whereas for Durkheim, it refers to those norms regulating goals.

Merton argues that in the United States there is a cultural imbalance between goals and norms. The cultural system encourages all individuals, rich and poor, to place a relatively high emphasis on the goal of monetary success and to strive for large sums of money. At the same time, there is relatively little emphasis on the legitimate norms to achieve this goal. Messner and Rosenfeld (1994) provide a discussion of how the particular historical circumstances of the United States have led to this cultural imbalance. And this cultural imbalance is said to explain the high rate of deviance in the United States.[5]

Merton goes on to argue that although the cultural system encourages deviance in all classes, the "greatest pressures toward deviation are exerted upon the lower strata" (1968, p. 198). Although members of the lower class are encouraged to strive for monetary success, the stratification system limits their ability to achieve such success through legitimate means. Such individuals may withdraw their support from legitimate norms and turn to deviance. The goal blockage experienced by these individuals, in fact, is perhaps the major reason for the low emphasis on legitimate norms in the cultural system (Messner, 1988). "When the cultural and social structure are malintegrated, the first calling for behavior and attitudes which the second precludes, there is a strain toward the breakdown of norms, toward normlessness" (1968, p. 217). Merton's assertion that lower-class individuals are less able to achieve their goals than higher-class individuals is the reason his theory is assumed to focus on limited rather than unlimited goals.

Merton states that individuals who are unable to achieve monetary success do not necessarily turn to deviance. In fact, he says that conformity is the most common adaptation to strain (1968, pp. 207, 237). He discusses certain of the factors that condition the effect of strain on deviance, although he never presents a systematic overview of such factors (more below).

THE NATURE AND DETERMINANTS OF STRAIN

Merton's theory is more complex than is typically portrayed in empirical research. Those studies that attempt to test the theory by simply examining the disjunction between aspirations and expectations for some goal fail to appreciate this complexity, and they have little relevance to Merton's theory. As with Durkheim, let us begin by discussing Merton's image of strain.

Strain as the Failure to Achieve Limited Goals.   Although Merton clearly advocates a version of strain theory (Agnew, 1987), it is true that the bulk of Merton's work focuses on the macrolevel. Nevertheless, a careful reading of Merton allows us to develop a description of strained individuals. Such individuals, products of the larger cultural and social system, (1) place a high relative value on the goal of monetary success (or some other goal, such as scientific productivity); (2) have high aspirations for monetary success; (3) do not view adherence to legitimate norms as a source of status or prestige (see n. 5); and (4) feel that they will not be able to achieve monetary success through legitimate channels. One very important feature to be noticed from this description is that strained individuals have placed "all their eggs in one basket." Their satisfaction is a function of their ability to achieve high levels of monetary success; there is no satisfaction to be gained from the achievement of other goals or from the adherence to legitimate norms.

All the above factors must be present before we can state that strain is present. No test of strain theory that I am aware of has taken all these factors into account. The typical test simply measures strain in terms of the disjunction between aspirations and expectations (items 2 and 4 above) for some goal, usually educational or occupational success (although see Menard, 1995). Such tests do not consider the relative importance attached to this goal or the importance attached to the legitimate means for goal achievement. This may be *one reason* why such tests usually fail to support strain theory. Individuals who are unable to achieve the goal of monetary success (or occupational/educational success) may *not* place a high relative emphasis on this goal. They may, in particular, achieve satisfaction from the achievement of other goals that were not considered or, perhaps, from simple adherence to the legitimate norms for goal achievement. As will be discussed below, Merton acknowledges that this is a possibility. Further, evidence suggests that most people pursue a variety of goals, that they are able to achieve at least some of their important goals, and that this partial goal achievement is sufficient to prevent strain or frustration (Agnew 1984, 1986).

The Macro Sources of Individual Strain. What structural and cultural factors promote individual strain, as described above? Merton lists or implies several such factors, and his arguments have been supplemented by other strain/anomie theorists.

First, Merton argues that the cultural system places a high relative emphasis on monetary success. He states that "the goal of monetary success is entrenched in American Culture" and that "Americans are bombarded on every side by precepts which affirm the right or, often, the duty of retaining the goal even in the face of repeated frustration" (1968, pp. 190–91). This goal, in particular, is emphasized by the "prestigeful representatives of society," including parents, school officials, and those in the workplace. It is stressed in textbooks and in the mass media, and it is exemplified by the cultural heros of our society. In addition, individuals are encouraged to identify not with their co-peers, but with those at the top (1986, p. 193; also see Passas, 1987). Cohen (1955) and Cloward and Ohlin (1960) make similar arguments, although there is some disagreement about the nature of the goals stressed in American society and whether there are class differences in the goals that are stressed. Nevertheless, the cultural system is said to encourage everyone to place much emphasis on success and to discourage everyone from drawing in their ambitions. Merton supports these assertions through a brief content analysis of mass media materials (also see Messner and Rosenfeld, 1994).

Merton goes on to note that not everyone adopts the cultural emphasis on success; there are, in fact, class and race differences in the extent to which the emphasis on success is assimilated (1968, pp. 234–40). It is not clear why only *some* individuals adopt the cultural emphasis on success, but the larger literature suggests that there is a tendency for deprived individuals to adapt to their deprivation by lowering their aspirations or focusing on alternative goals (Agnew, 1986). Further exploration of this issue is important, because it will shed light on the factors that condition the effect of macrolevel variables on the individual (see Agnew and Jones, 1988). Nevertheless, Merton argues that his theory only assumes that a *"sizable minority* of the lower strata" adopt the cultural emphasis on monetary success (1968, p. 225).

Second, the social structure blocks access to this goal for large numbers of people. In particular, Merton notes that every social system provides certain opportunities for success and that access to these opportunities is strongly influenced by one's position in the social structure. On the one hand, then, there is the "opportunity structure" of the society—the "scale and distribution of conditions that provide various probabilities for acting individuals and groups to achieve specifiable outcomes" (Merton, 1995, p. 25; also see Merton, 1964, p. 216; Bernard, 1989). On the other hand, access to the opportunity structure is largely a function of one's "status set," which defines the individual's location in the social structure. One's status set is made up of such social attributes as occupation, neighborhood, age, sex, gender, race, education, and religion; each of these attributes or statuses has certain "resources, rights, privileges, and constraints" associated with it (Merton 1995, pp. 58, 76–77). In this area, Cohen (1955) provides an excellent discussion of how the class system prevents working-class boys from achieving middle-class status. Both Cohen and Merton note that the connection between status and goal achievement is not perfect, but it is strong (again, raising the issue of why macrolevel variables like status have a differential impact on individuals).

Third, there is a final way in which the larger social environment contributes to strain, although it is only hinted at in Merton. Merton implies that strain is simply a function of the discrepancy between "the accepted goal and its accessibility": the greater the discrepancy the greater the strain toward deviance (Merton, 1968, p. 229). The implication is that individuals evaluate their actual and/or expected levels of goal achievement and experience strain/frustration if they feel that they have failed in the quest for monetary success. As several theorists have pointed out, this represents a very atomistic view of the individual (see especially Agnew, 1992, pp. 53–55; Burton and Cullen, 1992, p. 21; Burton and Dunaway, 1994; Cohen, 1965, pp. 6–7, this volume; Passas, 1987, this volume). Strain is not only a function of the discrepancy between goals and achievements, but also a function of the inputs and outcomes (or attainments) of those in one's comparative reference group(s). Individuals do not determine whether they are strained or frustrated in isolation from one another; rather, they compare themselves with one another, and such comparisons have a major impact on determining their level of strain. The larger social environment is important in this process not only because it provides a range of reference groups for selection, but because it also affects the actual reference group(s) that is selected for comparison. Cohen (1955, p. 122), for example, argues that the democratic tendency in America leads us to compare ourselves against "all comers," at least of one's age and sex—whatever their family background or material circumstances. Passas (1987, this volume) provides an excellent discussion of this point in a paper designed to link Merton's theory of anomie with his work on reference groups and relative deprivation. He notes that there is much pressure for individuals in the United States to select nonmembership reference groups. In particular, the "American Dream," our egalitarian ideology, and high rates of social mobility often lead us to compare ourselves against those higher in the stratification system.

In sum, the macrosocial environment contributes to individual strain in at least three ways: (1) by leading individuals to place an exaggerated emphasis on the goal of monetary success; (2) by preventing large groups of individuals from achieving such success through legitimate channels; and (3) by fostering the selection of comparative reference groups from the upper strata or from broad strata.

None of these arguments has received serious examination. Although anomie theorists frequently assert that the cultural system places an exaggerated emphasis on monetary success, the only data they present involve the content analysis of nonrandom samples of mass media stories. Data from other sources, such as the socialization literature, suggest that there is much emphasis on nonmonetary goals and on the legitimate norms for goal achievement (Agnew, 1986). Individuals, in particular, appear to pursue a wide range of goals—ranking many of these goals above monetary success in their goal hierarchies. More research is clearly needed in this area. If such research reveals that monetary success does not occupy the central place claimed by anomie theorists, that does not mean that anomie theory is wrong. It may still be the case that certain *subgroups* in the United States place great emphasis on one or a small number of goals. Qualitative accounts suggest this may be the case in certain highly deprived environments, such as the urban underclass (MacLeod, 1987; Sullivan, 1989). Data, then, are needed on the relative and absolute emphasis placed on various goals by people in general as well as people in different status sets.

We also need better information on the nature of opportunity structures and the factors that influence the individual's access to such structures. Burton and Cullen (1992, p. 18) make this same point and provide several suggestions for research in this area. Finally, we know little about the comparative reference groups that individuals select, the types of comparisons made with these groups, and how such comparisons impact strain. Agnew (1992) argues that the justice/equity and social comparison literatures can be of much use in this area. The justice/equity literature suggests that the comparison process often takes account of others' inputs *and* outcomes, although the specific principles used to make comparisons vary by social situation. And the social comparison literature focuses on those factors that influence the choice of comparison others or groups. The consideration of comparison processes is quite important because, as the recent research of Burton and Dunaway (1994) illustrates, measures of strain that take account of social comparison may be important predictors of deviance. The macro-level research on social inequality and crime reinforce this point (Burton and Dunaway, 1994, p. 83).

Finally, researchers should focus on those factors that affect the link between the macrosocial environment and the individual. As indicated above, strain theorists recognize that individuals do not respond in a passive manner to social and cultural forces. For example, the cultural emphasis on monetary success is not internalized by all individuals. Likewise, one's location in the social structure does not fully determine opportunities for goal achievement or the individual's *perceptions* of opportunities. Individual traits and features of the microsocial environment can affect the individual's response to the larger social environment, and such traits and features should be explored. They will constitute a central part of any theory that seeks to integrate macro-level and microlevel variables.

Factors Affecting the Impact of Strain on Deviance.   Unlike Durkheim, Merton had much interest in the factors that affect one's reaction to strain. Merton recognized that individuals seldom react to strain with deviance. He listed a variety of nondeviant and deviant adaptations to strain, and he discussed certain of the factors that affect the choice of these adaptations. Cohen (1955), Cloward and Ohlin (1960), Cullen (1984), Agnew (1992), and others have elaborated on his arguments. All theorists suggest that, at best, strain should have only a weak main effect on deviance. If we are going to salvage strain theory, then, we must pay close attention to those factors that condition the effect of strain on deviance: to what Cullen (1984) calls "structuring variables."

First, Merton suggests that some strained individuals do not turn to deviance because they are able to cope in ways that reduce their strain. They may turn to the pursuit of "alternative goals in the repository of common values" (1968, pp. 211, 237), with Merton providing the examples of artistic and intellectual goals. They may also employ that adaptation known as ritualism, which involves lowering the amount of money that is desired. The cultural system does not encourage these two adaptations (1968, pp. 192–93), but Merton suggests that the adaptation of ritualism is "fairly frequent" (1968, p. 204)—he does not comment on the frequency of the first adaptation. Merton states that the choice of ritualism is a function of social class and residence. Lower middle-class individuals are said to be more likely to choose ritualism, because they place great stress upon conformity to institutional means. And he notes that residents of the city are less likely to lower their aspirations, because it is more difficult to lower aspirations when "one is confronted with evidence that others have been able to realize [their aspirations], and in the city, the mass media trumpet this evidence on every side" (1964, pp. 223–24). Finally, strained individuals may adapt by developing the belief that they will *eventually* achieve monetary success. Merton notes that the cultural system fosters this belief, with a central cultural axiom being that "present seeming failure is but a way station to ultimate success" (1968, p. 193). So we have the image of the failed individual, who nevertheless believes that success is "just around the corner." These adaptations, then, alleviate the individual components of strain listed above.

Second, Merton suggests that deviance is unlikely to occur even when individuals are not able to alleviate their strain or frustration. One reason is that many individuals have a strong commitment to institutional norms. This commitment is partly a function of class, with commitment being greatest in the lower middle class and lowest in the lower class. And it is partly a function of one's exposure to deviant others. Merton states that a high frequency of "deviant but 'successful' behavior" tends to reduce the legitimacy of the institutional norms for others and thereby increases the likelihood of a deviant response by others (1968, p. 234; 1964, pp. 228–39). Merton also suggests that the likelihood of deviance is affected by external social control, noting that such control is lower in the city (1964, p. 224).

Finally, Merton argues that many strained individuals do not turn to deviance because they blame their failure on themselves. The cultural system encourages individuals to make such attributions, and these attributions have the function of deflecting blame away from the system (1968, pp. 191, 201–3, 222). Merton states that a central message conveyed by the cultural system is that "success or failure are wholly results of personal qualities; that he who fails has only himself to blame" (1968, p. 222). As a result, "aggression provoked by failure should therefore be directed inward and not outward, against oneself and not against a social structure which provides free and equal access to opportunity" (1968, p. 191). The attributions one makes regarding the source of goal blockage, then, play an important role in determining how one reacts to strain. Durkheim (1951) makes the same point when he notes that anomie may result in violence (as well as suicide) if individuals attribute their misfortune to others, and Cloward and Ohlin (1960) argue that one's attributions regarding the source of goal blockage are a central variable determining whether strain leads to deviance. They then list certain of the factors that determine whether failure is attributed to oneself or to the social order, factors such as the visibility of external barriers.

There are still other factors that condition the impact of strain on deviance. Cohen (1955) and Cloward and Ohlin (1960) stress the importance of contact with other strained or delinquent individuals. Interaction with such individuals increases the opportunities and social support for delinquency. Such social support includes instruction in delinquent techniques and exposure to "definitions favorable to crime." Whether individuals join or form delinquent subcultures is dependent on a number of factors, including one's attachment to and supervision by parents and the availability of delinquent groups in one's neighborhood. Additional theorists have listed still other factors that may condition the impact of strain on delinquency (see Agnew, 1992, the other chapters in this volume). With limited exceptions, however, these factors have been ignored in research. This may be another major reason why empirical studies generally fail to support Merton's theory.

Conclusion

Despite recent statements to the contrary, Durkheim and Merton do advocate individual-level strain theories. In fact, they have much to say about the nature of individual-level strain and the macrolevel determinants of such strain. Merton also has much to say about the factors that condition the effect of strain on deviance. Further, most of their arguments have been ignored in contemporary research. Researchers have never explored Durkheim's conception of strain as the pursuit of unlimited goals, and they have never considered all the components of individual-level strain identified by Merton. Further, the macrolevel determinants of strain have seldom been examined. Few researchers have pursued Durkheim's suggestion that the absence of society (or low social control) leads to strain. Likewise, few researchers have explored the macrolevel determinants of strain identified by Merton and his followers. The theories of Durkheim and Merton, then, have yet to receive an adequate test, and they contain many useful suggestions regarding the nature and sources of strain.

This review also challenges those researchers who argue that strain theory is distinct from anomie theory. There is, in fact, a close connection between strain and anomie in the work of Durkheim and Merton. In Durkheim, we find that anomie at the societal level (i.e., the failure to regulate individual goals) leads to strain at the individual level. This strain, involving the pursuit of unlimited or unattainable goals, leads to anger/frustration and may drive the individual to suicide and violence. In Merton, strain at the individual level, involving the failure to achieve monetary success, is perhaps the major cause of anomie at the societal level (i.e., the low emphasis on legitimate norms by the cultural system). Individual-level strain in Merton is a function of the larger cultural and social environment; specifically the strong emphasis on monetary success by the cultural system, the systematic denial of opportunities for such success by the stratification system, and the pressure by the social and cultural system to adopt comparative reference groups from higher strata. It is individual-level strain, however, that leads individuals to withdraw their support from legitimate norms. This occurs as individuals realize that such norms are not effective in securing access to monetary success. As Merton states, "appreciable numbers of people become estranged from a society that promises them in principle what they are denied in reality. And this withdrawal of allegiance from one or another part of prevailing social standards is what we mean, in the end, by anomie" (1964, p. 218; also see 1964, p. 227; 1968, pp. 220, 199). Although such strain is not the only cause of anomie,[6] it nevertheless plays a key role in its generation.[7]

Finally, it should be noted that although the theories of Durkheim and Merton differ in their fundamental emphases, these theories are best viewed as complementary rather than contradictory. Strain may involve the pursuit of unlimited and limited goals. In fact, Durkheim and Merton talk about both types of strain. Likewise, strain may stem from the absence of society and the presence of society. In particular, unlimited or unattainable goals may stem from the failure of society to regulate effectively individual goals and from the deliberate encouragement of unlimited goals. Durkheim, in fact, mentioned both sources of unattainable goals.[8] In addition, the failure to achieve goals may be the result of the absence of society (e.g., the failure of parents to teach skills and attitudes necessary for goal achievement) or barriers imposed by society (e.g., discrimination based on race). In many cases, it is difficult to state whether we are dealing with the absence or the presence of society. The failure of the school system to offer effective instruction may be viewed as the absence of society from one perspective, and it may be viewed as a deliberate barrier to goal achievement from another.

So, contrary to recent accounts, Durkheim and Merton have much to say about the nature of individual-level strain and the macrolevel determinants of such strain. Further, researchers have only begun to explore properly their varied arguments in these areas.

Notes

1. Anomie theorists draw on the macrolevel arguments of Durkheim and Merton and attempt to explain differences in crime *rates* among social units in terms of anomie or normlessness. Strain and anomie theory have traditionally been viewed as the microlevel and macrolevel counterparts of the same theory (see Messner and Rosenfeld 1994, p. 49). Many contemporary anomie theorists, however, have distanced themselves from strain theory and allied themselves with control theory.

2. Messner (1988) acknowledges that Merton does attempt to explain the deviant behavior of individuals in terms of the frustration generated by goal blockage. At the same time, he argues that Merton presents a distinct theory of social organization that attempts to explain crime rates across social units in terms of anomie or normlessness. Messner argues that these two theories are "logically independent" and that "evidence inconsistent with one is not necessarily inconsistent with the other" (1988, pp. 33, 43; also see Messner and Rosenfeld, 1994, p. 61). Further, he contends that there is no conflict between "control approaches and Merton's theory of social organization" and that "it is possible to link the two" (1988, p. 42). Messner and Rosenfeld have extended Merton's theory of social organization, advancing what is essentially a control theory of crime. Still other theorists, such as Hilbert and Wright (1979) and Adler (1995), have pointed to the sharp distinction between anomie and strain theory or have stressed the close connection between anomie and control theory.

3. There are at least three possible reasons for this neglect. First, Merton's (1938) classic article "Social Structure and Anomie" is widely regarded as a reinterpretation and extension of Durkheim. Durkheim's theory was reinterpreted to fit American Society and

extended to explain a wider range of deviant behavior (see Clinard, 1964; Cloward and Ohlin, 1960; Hilbert, 1986; Orru, 1987). The resultant popularity of Merton's theory (Cole 1975) may have diverted attention from the Durkheimian theory on which it was allegedly based. Second, Durkheim's theory has certain biological overtones that may leave researchers uneasy. Durkheim's theory, in fact, has much in common with the Freudian perspective on biological impulses that Merton was attacking (see Clinard, 1964; Cullen, 1984; Horton, 1964; Lukes, 1967; Mestrovic, 1988). Third, the neglect of Durkheim's work on anomie and strain may stem from the recent argument that Durkheim is actually a control theorist (Hirschi, 1969, p. 3, n. 1; Kornhauser, 1978; Lilly et al., 1989).

4. Several researchers have questioned the distinction between goals and legitimate norms in Merton. If one may obtain satisfaction from achieving goals and from following legitimate norms, then how do we distinguish goals from norms (see Turner, 1954; Lemert, 1964)? In the words of Kornhauser (1978, p. 162), "to say that culture equally values goals and means can only mean that there is more than one goal." Kornhauser (1978, p. 162) argues that it makes more sense to speak of the *number* of goals in a society. Balanced or stable systems are those that provide a variety of goals that can be achieved by all or most members of society. Our culture is imbalanced, because "it does not provide a sufficient variety of values whose achievement carries *public* recognition of moral worth" (1978, p. 163). This seems a useful clarification of Merton's theory.

5. Kornhauser (1978, pp. 144–46) argued that Merton's concept of cultural imbalance is sufficient account for deviance and that additional concepts such as goal blockage are unnecessary. If the cultural system places little emphasis on institutional norms, that alone should result in high rates of deviance, because deviance is usually a more efficient mechanism for goal achievement than conformity. Messner (1988, p. 38, n. 5) responded by arguing that the cultural imbalance described by Merton is the result of goal blockage, although he acknowledged that Merton is somewhat unclear on this point (1988, pp. 37–38). Several researchers, however, have argued that Merton's statements regarding cultural imbalance do in fact constitute a distinct theory of crime, claiming that this theory can explain societal differences in crime rates (Bernard, 1987; Vold and Bernard, 1986; Hilbert and Wright, 1979). Societies that place great emphasis on goals and little emphasis on legitimate norms should have higher rates of crime. Kornhauser (1978, pp. 162–65) took a different approach and went on to challenge Merton's notion of cultural imbalance. She argued that there is much evidence suggesting that our cultural system places great stress on institutional norms such as truth and honesty. Support for such norms is heavily institutionalized, and violations of such norms are heavily sanctioned. At the same time, however, she acknowledged that adherence to such norms is not a source of status or prestige in our society. Such adherence, then, does not provide the individual with satisfaction, so our culture is imbalanced not because it emphasizes goals and deemphasizes legitimate norms. Our culture is imbalanced because adherence to institutional norms does not carry "public recognition of moral worth." If we accept Kornhauser's arguments, cultural imbalance does not lead directly to deviance. Deviance results only when the emphasis on monetary success is combined with the inability to achieve such success. It should be noted that Kornhauser's arguments are compatible with other aspects of Merton's theory. Merton notes, for example, that lower- and middle-class parents "exert continuous pressure upon children to abide by the moral mandates

of society" (1968, p. 205). Lower-class Americans, however, are said to be less likely to adhere to institutional norms because they have been "imperfectly socialized" (1968, pp. 203, 205). Such statements imply that the cultural system does stress institutional norms, even though such norms are not a source of status.

6. Merton states that the "cultural . . . exaggeration of the success-goal leads men to withdraw emotional support from the rules" (1968, p. 190). Also, the presence of widespread deviance in society causes others to reduce their attachment to legitimate norms.

7. Although these arguments point to the close connection between strain and anomie theory, that is not to deny that anomie theory is compatible with control theory. The lack of normative regulation described by Durkheim and Merton may well increase the freedom to deviate. A society that is unable to regulate the goals that individuals pursue may be unable to regulate other aspects of the individual's behavior. And a society that places little emphasis on legitimate norms certainly increases the freedom of individuals to satisfy their needs and desires through deviance (although such freedom is partially a result of prior strain). As I have argued here and elsewhere (Agnew 1987), Durkheim and Merton do not make these control arguments. The central variable leading to deviance in their theories is the pressure generated by goal blockage. It is this pressure that drives individuals to suicide and violence in Durkheim and that leads individuals to reject legitimate norms and turn to deviance in Merton. Merton, in fact, explicitly rejects control interpretations (1968, pp. 175, 185).

8. Merton focused on the deliberate encouragement of unattainable goals, but he later acknowledged that some individuals may limit their goals, despite the cultural emphasis on lofty aspirations. He did not indicate why this is so, but it may be that our society is more pluralistic than suggested by Merton. Cultural transmission agents like the media and family may differ in the extent to which they encourage individuals to pursue lofty goals—some attempting to limit goals, some providing no guidance on goals, and some encouraging the pursuit of lofty goals.

References

Adler, Freda. 1995. Synnomie to anomie: A macrosociological formulation. In *Advances in Criminological Theory*, Vol. 6: *The Legacy of Anomie*, edited by Freda Adler and William S. Laufer, 271–83. New Brunswick, N.J.: Transaction.

Agnew, Robert. 1980. Success and anomie: A study of the effect of goals on anomie. *Sociological Quartery* 21:53–64.

———. 1984. Goal achievement and delinquency. *Sociology and Social Research* 68:435–51.

———. 1986. Challenging strain theory: An examination of goals and goal blockage. Paper presented at the annual meeting of the American Society of Criminology, Atlanta.

———. 1987. On "Testing Structural Strain Theories." *Journal of Research in Crime and Delinquency* 24:281–86.

———. 1992. Foundation for a general strain theory of crime and delinquency. *Crimonology* 30:47–87.

———. 1993. Why do they do it?: An examination of the intervening mechanisms between "Social Control" variables and delinquency. *Journal of Research in Crime and Delinquency* 30:245–66.

———. 1994. Delinquency and the desire for money. *Justice Quarterly* 11:411–27.

———. 1995a. Strain and subcultural theories of criminality. In *Criminology: A Contemporary Handbook*, edited by Joseph F. Sheley, 305–27. Belmont, Calif.: Wadsworth.

———. 1995b. The contribution of social-psychological strain theory to the explanation of crime and delinquency. In *Advances in Criminological Theory*. Vol. 6: *The Legacy of Anomie*, edited by Freda Adler and William S. Laufer, 113–37. New Brunswick, N.J.: Transaction.

———. 1995c. Testing the leading crime theories: An alternative strategy focusing on motivational processes. *Journal of Research in Crime and Delinquency* 32:363–98.

Agnew, Robert, and Diane Jones. 1988. Adapting to deprivation: An examination of inflated educational expectations. *Sociological Quarterly* 29:315–37.

Bernard, Thomas J. 1984. Control criticisms of strain theories: An assessment of theoretical and empirical adequacy. *Journal of Research in Crime and Delinquency* 21:353–72.

———. 1987. Testing structural strain theories. *Journal of Research in Crime and Delinquency* 24:262–80.

———. 1989. A theoretical approach to integration. In *Theoretical Integration in the Study of Deviance and Crime: Problems and Prospects*, edited by Steven F. Messner, Marvin D. Krohn, and Allen E. Liska, 137–59. Albany: State University of New York Press.

———. 1995. Merton versus Hirschi: Who is faithful to Durkheim's heritage? In *Advances in Criminological Theory*, Vol. 6: *The Legacy of Anomie*, edited by Freda Adler and William S. Laufer, 81–90. New Brunswick, N.J.: Transaction.

Burton, Velmer S., and Francis T. Cullen. 1992. The empirical status of strain theory. *Journal of Crime and Justice* 15:1–30.

Burton, Velmer S., and R. Gregory Dunaway. 1994. Strain, relative deprivation, and middle-class delinquency. In *Varieties of Criminology*, edited by Greg Barak, 79–95. Westport, Conn.: Praeger.

Clinard, Marshall B. 1964. The theoretical implications of anomie and deviant behavior. In *Anomie and Deviant Behavior*, edited by Marshall B. Clinard, 1–56. New York: Free Press.

Cloward, Richard A., and Lloyd E. Ohlin. 1960. *Delinquency and opportunity*. New York: Free Press.

Cohen, Albert. 1955. *Delinquent boys*. New York: Free Press.

———. 1965. The sociology of the deviant act: Anomie theory and beyond. *American Sociological Review* 30:5–14.

Cullen, Francis T. 1984. *Rethinking crime and deviance theory*. Totowa, N.J.: Rowman and Allanheld.

Durkheim, Emile. 1951. *Suicide*. New York: Free Press.

Elliott, Delbert S., David Huizinga, and Suzanne Ageton. 1985. *Explaining delinquency and drug use*. Beverly Hills: Sage.

England, Ralph. 1960. A theory of middle-class juvenile delinquency. *Journal of Criminal Law, Criminology and Police Science* 50:535–40.

Farnworth, Margaret, and Michael J. Leiber. 1989. Strain theory revisted: Economic goals, educational means, and delinquency. *American Sociological Review* 54:263–74.

Hilbert, Richard E. 1986. Anomie and the moral regulation of reality: The Durkheimian tradition in moral relief. *Sociological Theory* 4:1–19.

Hilbert, R. E., and Charles W. Wright. 1979. Representations of Merton's theory of anomie. *American Sociologist* 14:150–56.

Hirschi, Travis. 1969. *Causes of delinquency.* Berkeley: University of California Press.

Horton, John. 1964. The dehumanization of anomie and alienation: A problem in the ideology of sociology. *British Journal of Sociology* 15:283–300.

Jensen, Gary F. 1995. Salvaging structure through strain: A theoretical and empirical critique. In *Advances in Criminological Theory,* Vol. 6: *The Legacy of Anomie,* edited by Freda Adler and William S. Laufer, 139–58. New Brunswick, N.J.: Transaction.

Kornhauser, Ruth. 1978. *Social sources of delinquency.* Chicago: University of Chicago Press.

Krohn, Marvin. 1978. A Durkheimian analysis of international crime rates. *Social Forces* 57:654–70.

Lemert, Edwin M. 1964. Social structure, social control, and deviation. In *Anomie and Deviant Behavior,* edited by Marshall B. Clinard, 57–97. New York: Free Press.

Lerman, Paul. 1968. Individual values, peer values, and subcultural delinquency. *American Sociological Review* 33:219–35.

Lilly, Robert J., Francis T. Cullen, and Richard A. Ball. 1989. *Criminological theory: Context and consequences.* Newbury Park, Calif.: Sage.

Lukes, Steven. 1967. Alienation and anomie. In *Philosophy, Politics, and Society,* edited by Peter Laslett and W. G. Runciman, 134–56. New York: Barnes and Noble.

MacLeod, Jay. 1987. *Ain't no makin' it.* Boulder, Colo.: Westview Press.

Matza, David, and Gresham Sykes. 1961. Juvenile delinquency and subterranean values. *American Sociological Review* 26:713–19.

Menard, Scott. 1995. A developmental test of Mertonian anomie theory. *Journal of Research in Crime and Delinquency* 32:136–74.

Merton. Robert K. 1938. Social structure and anomie. *American Sociological Review* 3:672–82.

———. 1964. Anomie, anomia, and social interaction: Contexts of deviant behavior. In *Anomie and Deviant Behavior,* edited by Marshall B. Clinard, 213–42. New York: Free Press.

———. 1968. *Social theory and social structure.* New York: Free Press.

———. 1995. Opportunity structure: The emergence, diffusion, and differentiation of a sociological concept, 1930s–1950s. In *Advances in Criminological Theory,* Vol. 6: *The Legacy of Anomie,* edited by Freda Adler and William S. Laufer, 3–78. New Brunswick, N.J.: Transaction.

Messner, Steven F. 1988. Merton's "Social Structure and Anomie": The road not taken. *Deviant Behavior* 9:33–53.

Messner, Steven F., and Richard Rosenfeld. 1994. *Crime and the American dream.* Belmont, Calif.: Wadsworth.

Mestrovic, Stjepan G. 1988. Durkheim, Schopenhauer, and the relationship between goals and means: Reversing the assumptions in the Parsionian theory of rational action. *Sociological Inquiry* 58:163–81.

Mestrovic, Stjepan G., and Helene M. Brown. 1985. Durkheim's concept of anomie and dereglement. *Social Problems* 33:81–99.

Mizruchi, Ephraim. 1964. *Success and opportunity*. New York: Free Press.

Nye, Ivan. 1958. *Family relationships and delinquent behavior*. New York: Wiley.

Orrù, Marco. 1987. *Anomie: History and meanings*. Boston: Allyn and Unwin.

Passas, Nikos. 1987. Anomie and relative deprivation. Paper presented at the annual meeting of the Eastern Sociological Society, Boston.

———. 1995. Continuities in the anomie tradition. In *Advances in Criminological Theory*, Vol. 6: *The Legacy of Anomie*, edited by Freda Adler and William S. Laufer, 91–112. New Brunswick, N.J.: Transaction.

Reiss, Albert J. 1951. Delinquency as the failure of personal and social controls. *American Sociological Review* 16:196–207.

Shaw, Clifford R., and Henry D. McKay. 1942. *Juvenile delinquency and urban areas*. Chicago: University of Chicago Press.

Sullivan, Mercer L. 1989. *Getting paid*. Ithaca, N.Y.: Cornell University Press.

Taylor, Ian, Paul Walton, and Jock Young. 1973. *The new criminology*. New York: Harper.

Thrasher, Frederick M. 1927. *The gang*. Chicago: University of Chicago Press.

Turner, Ralph H. 1954. Value conflict in social disorganization. *Sociology and Social Research* 38:301–8.

Vold, George B., and Thomas J. Bernard. 1986. *Theoretical criminology*. New York: Oxford University Press.

ALBERT K. COHEN

An Elaboration of Anomie Theory

The construction of so-called "integrated" theories of crime commonly begins by confronting some set of theories, none of which appears to provide a satisfactory explanation of crime in general but all of which appear to identify some variables and relationships that a satisfactory general theory should take into account. An empirical study is undertaken that is designed to yield correlations of all the independent variables with the dependent variable and with one another. An attempt is made to formulate a single comprehensive theory or model in which all the independent variables, either directly or through their influence on one another, determine the value of the dependent variable. The challenge is to find a formulation that does not look stitched or patched together, that is not just a more abstract description of the network of correlations that it is supposed to explain, and whose propositions constitute a logically coherent system.

I do not question this manner of proceeding, but in this essay I am doing something else. My object is not to find another way to an integrated theory. It is, rather, to realize more fully the potentialities inherent in anomie theory. I will show how anomie theory can be strengthened by taking more fully into account some very elementary and general principles of sociology that are, or should be, part of the foundation of *any* theory of crime. I will show that some of Merton's terms, if thoughtfully considered, include significantly more than Merton seems to have had in mind at the time of writing and that these expanded meanings include some of the territory claimed by other theories of crime and deviance. More generally, I will show that anomie theory, fleshed out and elaborated in these and other ways, will—although still unified by its original underlying logic—incorporate or otherwise take into account many of the ideas that are thought to be distinctive of the theories with which it is sometimes contrasted.

Reference Groups, Differential Association, Subcultures: Three Theories or One?

Some years ago I pointed out (Cohen, 1965[1]) that Merton's actors appeared to experience strain and to work their way through it as though each were contained within a box, uninfluenced by other human beings. I suggested that comparison processes and the opinions of authoritative others help to determine the importance of goals, the interpretation of attainments, the perceived magnitude of disjunction, and, above all, the choice of mode of adaptation ("above all," because Merton's failure to deal with determinants of choice among his adaptations was the most obvious and most noted lacuna in his theory). For our present purposes, let us call this bundle of ideas reference-group theory. Note our manner of proceeding: We did not go looking for a way to harness reference-group theory to anomie theory; rather, we found something amiss in anomie theory, and reference-group theory appeared to fill the niche.

Consider now that the relatively sophisticated concepts and propositions of advanced versions of reference-group theory are themselves elaborations and refinements of very elementary and very general sociological principles: human beings, whatever they are doing, are always concerned with what other human beings are thinking and doing, which requires that they see the world and themselves as the others do and that they "take the role of the other." Starting from that premise, Edwin H. Sutherland developed the theory of differential association. Differential-association theory is what we get when we apply to the learning process the presuppositions and logic that lead to reference-group theory. The two bodies of theory could hardly be more intimately related. Indeed, one of the "modalities" of associations in differential-association theory is "intensity," which "has to do with such things as the prestige of the source of a criminal or anticriminal pattern and with emotional reactions related to the associations" (Sutherland and Cressey, 1970, p. 76). The other modalities—frequency, duration, and priority—have to do with location and duration in time; only intensity identifies the *character* or *quality* of those associations that count in learning, and that character or quality is the most prominent feature of reference groups—at least those that are called "normative" reference groups.

Let us return now to the question, "Why do we choose this or that mode of adaptation?" Although actors always take into account, in arriving at a judgment or a decision, the views of their reference groups, clearly they do not, like well-oiled weather vanes, simply point in the direction of their current reference groups. They have some autonomy, in the sense that they bring to the situation some norms or standards—"their own"—that they have built up over a period of time. How they define a particular situation and, therefore, what they will do, will depend on those "internalized" norms and on the immediate reference-group context. Furthermore, every such event or experience will leave the actor's "own" norms strengthened, weakened, or otherwise modified, depending on the immediate reference-group context. And this, it turns out, is another way of describing the theory of differential association!

Note that if, via these reference-group processes, patterns of value and belief diffuse to and are shared by others, we are talking about the transmission of subcultures, which is still another way of describing differential-association theory. Finally, let us assume that a number of individuals who are capable of serving as reference objects for one another experience strain arising from the same source. Assume, furthermore, that there do not exist among them patterns of value and belief that can provide a resolution to the strain. The same elementary social processes that lead to the phenomena described by reference-group theory and differential-association theory should, under these conditions, lead to the genesis and elaboration of new and shared adaptations—that is to say, subcultural solutions to strain (Cohen, 1955).

In sum, to answer the question about choice of adaptation, we have developed some implications of an elementary "principle of sociology." These implications include what are called "reference-group theory," "theory of differential association," and "theory of subcultures," and these theories fit naturally and comfortably within the larger body of anomie theory. (Whether they are best thought of as three discrete theories or as facets of a single theory—or theoretical system—is an interesting question, but it need not be debated here.)

Social-Control Theory

The disjunction and consequent strain that weaken devotion to the established norms, produce anomie, and, ultimately, motivate deviance result from the "unavailability," according to Merton, of legitimate means. The words available and unavailable suggest two values of a discontinuous variable: either my arm is long enough to reach the apple or it is not. Or, less figuratively, either I have the money I need to pay for the education I want or I don't. Sometimes things are like that: there is literally no honest way I can lay my hands on all that money. However, it is probable that as often as not, when we speak of unavailability, we are speaking of other valued objects, pleasures, projects, relationships, and investments that might be lost, damaged, or forgone if we decide to pursue the goal. I *could* scrape together, by working, saving, begging, borrowing, and selling off possessions, enough money to reach my educational goal; in that sense the goal is available. But the damage to my standard of living and that of others dependent on me, the loss of participation with family and friends in customary and gratifying activities, the unpleasantness of asking for help and being beholden to others, and the moral discomfort for the sacrifices that others, no matter how willingly, are making on my behalf—these and other costs seem so overwhelming that I hardly give any serious thought to going to college. "Impossible," I say. "I can't afford it." The goal may not be categorically unavailable, but it is certainly *less* available.

Consider now Travis Hirschi's control theory (Hirschi, 1969). People refrain from crime, according to Hirschi, because (among other reasons) they are not prepared to pay the price for the damage that the deviance will do to their social relationships and other projects and enterprises. He calls these attachments and commitments. They are two of his four controls, the others being beliefs and involvement. Both Merton and Hirschi are saying that actors have investments in certain relationships and projects and that they will stay away from those activities that threaten to undermine them. But there is, of course, a large difference as well. Hirschi is talking about the costs that attach to deviance; these costs explain conformity. (Conformity is what you get when you can't afford deviance.) Merton is talking about the costs that attach to conformity; these costs explain deviant behavior.

However, Cloward's amendment to Merton's theory—his recognition that illegitimate means may also be unavailable and that they, too, may be out of reach or may entail unacceptable costs—has the interesting consequence that now one of Hirschi's fundamental ideas is part and parcel of anomie theory. Actually, to the best of my knowledge, Cloward's first publication of this idea (Cloward, 1951) preceded Hirschi's publication of this version of control theory (Hirschi, 1969) by almost twenty years. He could not, therefore, have been responding to control theory. I take it that he just saw that there was something amiss in anomie theory, and he fixed it.

There is still an important difference between the two theories at a very fundamental level. Hirschi's failure to recognize that conformity may damage one's attachments and commitments and encourage consideration of deviant alternatives was not an oversight on his part. He starts from the premise that deviance is not really problematical. What needs explaining is why people don't follow the deviant path to their goals. The failure to accept the fully symmetrical stance taken by anomie theory—that both deviance and nondeviance may be categorically unavailable or too costly—is reasoned, deliberate, and conscious. It is not possible for anomie theory to adopt this premise of control theory and still be anomie theory.

Identity Theory

Consider the following and where it might fit in the framework of anomie theory. I have an exchange of words with another patron in a bar. He informs me that my mother is a whore, I am a bastard, and my claim to be a man is a joke, and he describes to a large and amused audience the various kinds of deviant sexual acts in which I engage. I go out, I come back with a gun, I kill the son of a bitch. What has anomie theory to say about this?

It can be argued that most human action is oriented to the achievement, preservation, or demonstration of an identity. Whatever I am about, part of my agenda is to conduct my business in a way that will promote, or at least not jeopardize, the claims I make about myself. In the example above—we must, of course, assume a certain cultural setting—there may be available to me no other course of action that would be compatible with my claims to manhood.

What I do may relate to identity in two ways. I may do things because they signify, embody, somehow communicate to others that I am a certain kind of person. Or I may do things to acquire the skills, the tools, the money, the props I may need to perform the behavior that directly expresses or communicates my claimed identity. Both serve the same purpose, the one directly, the other indirectly. Both are clearly a means to an end. And once it is clear that we are talking about ends and means, we have a candidate for inclusion in the domain of anomie theory.

First, identities are culturally patterned. They are drawn from a repertoire provided by the culture in the same way as other goals. Their meanings, and therefore the behavior that will express them, are defined by the culture. Of course, individuals, in constructing their identities, modify and adapt the materials provided by their culture, but this is true of cultural goals generally.

Second, building identity is work. We have to make use of time, money, skills, physical equipment, connections, social positions, ascribed and achieved, and other more or less scarce resources. The means for accomplishing this identity work in lawful and legitimate ways may or may not be at hand. If they are not, then we are faced with a disjunction, strain, and the other ramifying consequences that are spelled out in anomie theory. In short, identity-oriented behavior is a species of means-ends behavior that lends itself readily to analysis in terms of anomie theory.

Collectivities as Actors

Collectivities commit vast numbers of crimes and aberrations short of crime. It is proper, therefore, to ask of any theory how it proposes to deal with all that crime and deviance. This comes down to asking how it proposes to deal with the idea of collectivity. A collectivity is not a person—not a real person, anyway. But is it a real actor? Does it really do things? Or is it really short-hand for a lot of people doing their respective things, some of which we then call acts of the collectivity?

Ordinary people—and this includes criminologists when they are not doing criminology—take it for granted that these entities are truly actors. It does not occur to them to brood upon the question: The United States of America, the Baltimore Orioles, Dow Chemical, the university I work for, and the church I belong to—are they just fictions, conventions of speech? Are they really—and only—collections of biological individuals, so-called "natural persons," who alone are truly capable of doing things? But when criminologists take off their baseball cap and put on their thinker's cap, they are of not so clear a mind. The tension between the philosophical realism of common sense and the nominalistic and individualistic propensities of American scholarly and intellectual culture tends to immobilize them and to discourage systematic theorizing about the conduct of collectivities.

I have written on this subject at length elsewhere (Cohen, 1990). I will not repeat the argument here. My conclusion, however, is that the instincts of everyday life are, in this respect, valid. The collectivities we treat as actors *are* actors. There are problems of how we go about establishing that a collectivity did this or that, but that is also true of natural persons. We are not saying that any theory meant to explain the behavior of human beings will make sense if applied to collectivities. There is no reason, however, that we should not get on with the business of explaining the deviance of collectivities and stop worrying that we are explaining something that does not exist.

If collectivities are truly actors, then is it reasonable to ask whether their conduct can be dealt with literally and not just figuratively in the language of anomie theory? To begin with, do they have goals? They do. Indeed, it is hard to talk about collectivities without reference to their goals, intentions, plans, targets, and so on. Economists have produced a significant literature on the goals of business corporations. They could, for example, include, with varying emphasis, to make money, to be the biggest, to provide their workers with lifetime employment, and otherwise to ensure their economic security, to preserve a reputation for probity and integrity, to capture market share, to be famous for the quality of their products, and so on. These goals, like those of natural persons, include building and validation of identities. And these goals, whether we are speaking of business firms, universities, or families, are largely shaped by their cultural contexts. It is, perhaps, better to say that each collectivity builds its commitments and identity from the repertoires provided by its culture and modifies and adapts them to the concrete circumstances and exigencies of its existence, but again, this would be no less true of natural persons.

We need not belabor the point; it is obvious where we are going. The activities of collectivities can be seen as the employment of means to realize their culturally patterned goals. These means (or opportunities) may be legitimate or illegitimate, and the prospective costs (and, therefore, deterrents) of any course of action consist of other opportunities forgone, diminished, or sacrificed. These costs are a measure of the unavailability of the opportunities. The unavailability constitutes a disjunction that produces, in turn, strain, anomie, and adaptation, deviant or conforming. In sum, the deviant behavior of collectivities falls within the domain of anomie theory.

Levels of Analysis

Merton deals with anomie on two levels. First, he offers a model of motivation to account for the behavior of individuals and differences among individuals. The motivation consists of a concatenation of circumstances—goals, on the actor side, and available means or opportunities, on the situation side—that together create the disjunction that eventually leads to deviance. This essay has consisted mostly of elaboration of the Mertonian model of deviant motivation.

On another level, he deals with the properties of systems—of their culture and social organization—that account for the rates and distribution of deviance (also system properties) and for differences in these respects among systems. For example, he claims that American society is distinguished by levels of aspiration that are extraordinarily high in all strata of the society, coupled with a very unequal distribution of legitimate opportunities. I have not had much to say on this level. However, the two levels are intimately related. In effect, Merton is saying that the culture and social organization of American society are such that they engender a distribution of motivational fields—the "concatenations of circumstances" that I allude to in the paragraph above—that corresponds to the actual distribution of deviance. If the theory of motivation were different—if the "concatenations of circumstances" that are supposed to produce deviance were different—the analysis of American culture and social organization would have to account for the distribution of *that* motivational field and *that* would have to correspond to the actual distribution of deviance. Our elaboration of the model of motivation implies a more complex and differentiated motivational field than Merton proposes. If the elaboration is valid, if the circumstances to which it calls attention really make a difference in outcomes, then a theory, on either the individual or social system level, that ignores them will encounter departures from expectations that it cannot explain.

For example, proof of Merton's theory as it stands would require data on the distribution of the availability of legitimate means and a demonstration that the unavailability of legitimate means is associated with higher rates of deviance. But our analysis has highlighted obscurities in the term "availability" and has noted that availability is often—perhaps more often than not—a function of cost in terms of opportunities forgone, which would include the sorts of things that figure in Hirschi's controls: attachments and commitments. Research employing measures of availability that leave these out might produce predictions on the dependent variable that do not conform to reality only because the measure of the independent variable is blind to important information.

Anomie Theory and Strain Theory

It is of some interest that Agnew, in words reminiscent of the opening paragraphs of this essay, says that "much of the recent theoretical work in criminology has focused on the integration of different delinquency theories," whereas he "has taken an alternative track and . . . has focused on the refinement of a single theory" (Agnew, 1992, p. 74). That theory is strain theory, whose "traditional" or "classic" versions are exemplified by the early work of Merton, Cohen, Cloward, and Ohlin.

In point of fact, none of these authors described what they were doing as strain theory (or some equivalent expression). Of course, in our (if I may use that pronoun) theory, strain played a key role in the transformation of ends-means disjunction into deviance, but it was not the defining attribute; it was not what distinguished anomie theory from other theories. What distinguished it was that it was couched in terms of the means-ends scheme and was concerned with the social origins and consequences of the disjunction between ends and means. If it did not deal with those things, it was not anomie theory. Other theories as well as ours—theories featuring mental conflict, psychoanalytical mechanisms, and frustration and aggression—provided a role for strain or some such thing, but that did not make of them—and us—a family of theories. We did not see in them kin, much less bedfellows, of anomie theory.

The perspective of general strain theory is different. It looks at a variety of seemingly unrelated theories and research findings, drawn from a number of disciplines, and draws out what appears to be a commonality: the experience of noxious stimuli and consequent delinquent or otherwise deviant conduct. It sets itself a task of constructing a general theory of crime and delinquency in which the independent variable is some kind of dysphoric state, that is, strain. From this perspective, the tension produced by the disjunction between ends and means is only one of many possible kinds of strain. General strain theory entails an effort to develop an exhaustive classification of kinds of strain, of possible mechanisms of coping with strain (compare Merton's "modes of adaptation"), and determinants of choice among such mechanisms. It is less, I think, an effort at "refinement of a single theory" than it is an attempt to replace a class of theories with a single theory whose domain comprehends the domains of all the theories it replaced or, perhaps better, synthesized. This is an ambitious and daring attempt to move toward a comprehensive and general theory of deviance, but its strategy is different from that of this essay, which perhaps comes closer to the description "refinement of a single theory." But, as Agnew correctly points out, general strain theory is also to be contrasted to most efforts at "the integration of different delinquency theories." In this essay, then, I have identified three strategies for theory construction, and I have exemplified one of them in some detail.

Note

1. This paper, I have come to realize, is, in effect, a review, elaboration, and extension of the 1965 paper listed in the References. I look forward to doing another essay on this subject in 2025.

References

Agnew, Robert. 1992. Foundation for a general strain theory of crime and delinquency. *Criminology* 30:47–87.

Cloward, Richard. 1951. Illegitimate means, anomie, and deviant behavior. *American Sociological Review* 16:653–61.

Cohen, Albert K. 1955. *Delinquent boys: The culture of the gang.* Glencoe, Ill.: The Free Press.

———. 1965. The sociology of the deviant act: Anomie theory and beyond. *American Sociological Review* 30:5–14.

———. 1990. Criminal actors: Natural persons and collectivities. *New Directions in the Study of Justice, Law, and Social Control,* prepared by the School of Justice Studies, Arizona State University. New York and London: Plenum Press.

Hirschi, Travis. 1969. *Causes of delinquency.* Berkeley: University of California Press.

Sutherland, Edwin H., and Donald R. Cressey. 1970. *Criminology,* 8th ed. Philadelphia, New York, and Toronto: Lippincott.

NIKOS PASSAS

Anomie, Reference Groups, and Relative Deprivation

Introduction

The introduction of the concept of anomie in the sociological jargon by Durkheim and Merton (Orrù, 1987) gave rise to a tradition of theoretical and empirical work that continues to this day (Passas, 1995). Because of Merton's explicit discussion of various types of deviance, his influence has been particularly strong in the field of criminology (Clinard, 1964; Cole and Zuckerman, 1964). The anomie tradition is best conceived as an evolving research program or paradigm that keeps generating theoretical elaborations, research puzzles, and policy ideas by drawing attention to the consequences of structural problems (Cole, 1975; Merton, 1995; Passas, 1988, 1995). The general gist of anomie tradition is that whenever the guiding power of conventional norms is weakened, high rates of deviant behavior can be expected. There are several specific hypotheses as to what causes anomic tendencies (i.e., a loosening of social controls), what social forces shape the patterns of deviant conduct, what influences individual or collective choices under conditions of strain, and how such choices in turn shape the social structure and culture in given contexts.

Despite considerable amendments to Merton's theory of anomie, in particular, there is room for further development. An important limitation is that the "bearing of others' experience—their strains, their conformity and deviance, their success and failure—on ego's strain and consequent adaptations is comparatively neglected" (Cohen, 1965, p. 6).

More recently, anomie theory was rejected partly for the following reasons:

Finally, human behavior seems to depend, at least to some extent, upon people's personalities, the things they have learned, the kinds of social groups with which they are affiliated, and unusual provoking or activating circumstances, regardless of objective goals and means. Whether people conform or not seems to depend, particularly, on the accuracy with which they perceive reality, since relative deprivation (of the means) seems to be as potent as objective deprivation. However, none of this is built into anomie theory, and as a result, the best that it can claim is that a goals-means strain is one thing that may, under some circumstances, lead to deviance. (Tittle, 1995, p. 5)

In addition, references to "common symbols of success" and the assumption that the greater pressures toward deviance should be felt by those in the lower social strata have contributed to a perception that anomie theory is static, implies a monolithic image of culture, and is "class biased" (Thio, 1975).

This essay aims at rectifying the problem of neglecting the experience and influence of "others" and the "class bias" by linking the theory to reference-group analysis and the concept of relative deprivation with anomie theory. I argue that an analysis of social-interaction processes is logically required by Merton's theoretical framework; social interactions do affect people's adoption of particular goals and the means to attain them. Yet, such an analysis has not been systematically attempted. Ironically, Merton has never related his reference-group analysis to his theory of anomie although he called for research into the extent to which people in different social positions have indeed assimilated the same cultural goals and norms, and the social mechanisms that minimize strains produced by socially restricted access to means toward these goals (Merton, 1968, p. 177). Once this connection is achieved, the implications of anomie theory about relative levels of ambition according to social position would be quite different (see Downes and Rock, 1982, p. 105; Passas, 1990; Runciman, 1966, pp. 27–28).

I first outline the connections between anomie theory, reference-group theory, and relative deprivation on a general level. I discuss the implications of the consolidation of these theories separately, following on Merton's analytical distinction between the cultural level—that of the cultural goals and normative values regulating behavior—and the social level. I then focus on the issue of "rising expectations" in affluent societies and the social distribution of deviance. Finally, to highlight new possibilities for making micro-macro links, I consider processes conducive to deviance and anomie in conjunction with the concept of "anomia." This elaboration not only revises anomie theory in the light of empirical findings that challenge some of its original hypotheses, but it also provides fresh research puzzles.

Reference Groups and Anomie Theory

Reference-group theory emphasizes that people relate to groups of which they are or are not (but wish to be) members. The concept was coined by Hyman (1942) in an analysis of how individuals form a conception of their status in society. People's attitudes and overt behavior are influenced and oriented in terms of both membership and nonmembership groups and individuals who are selected as points of reference and comparison. The referents may be "positive" or "negative," depending on whether people want to emulate and associate themselves with them or dissociate themselves from them (see Newcomb, 1950). Furthermore, the referent is not necessarily a group; it may also be an individual, a "reference idol," or even an abstract idea (Eisenstadt, 1954, p. 213; Shibutani, 1955, p. 565; Turner, 1956, p. 328; Merton, 1968, pp. 353 and 356–58; Hyman, 1968, 1975; Sztompka, 1986, p. 230).

There is an important distinction between normative and comparative reference groups. The normative reference group denotes a group that lays down standards (group norms) for the individual who wishes to gain or maintain acceptance in it. By contrast, the comparative reference group denotes a group (a referent) that is used by the person as a yardstick in making self-evaluations or in judging others. Although the two may overlap in practice, it is analytically essential to keep them apart, as they make explicit the two main aspects of reference-group theory: the motivational and the perceptual (Kelley, 1952).

Anomie theory, on the other hand, deals with potential and patterned outcomes of discrepancies between culturally promoted goals and socially structured access to opportunities for attaining them, and a disjunction *within* culture, that is, between these goals and the cultural norms regulating the ways of attaining them. The former problem is what usually is described in the criminological literature as "strain" theory; the latter is the element of anomie theory that Messner and Rosenfeld (1993, this volume) have elaborated.

Two points are to be underlined here. First, for deviance to occur, it is essential that people *themselves* perceive the whole situation as problematic. This is because deviance is not assumed to happen automatically or in a deterministic way. Criminologists are often unhappy about anomie theory's lack of specificity and point out that not all those exposed to the same problems respond in the same way. One response is that the business of sociological theories is to explain *rates* or *patterns* of deviance in different contexts, rather than its *incidence* (Merton, 1968). Of course people do not respond in exactly the same way; anomie theorists adopt a probabilistic rather than deterministic view of humans (Merton, 1995). The structuring of probabilities is the main concern in contemporary work within the anomie tradition (see essays in this volume by Cullen and Wright; Hagan and McCarthy; Rosenfeld and Messner; and Vaughan; see also Cullen, 1984).[1] Another response is that not everyone *perceives* the situation in the same way. It is one thing to have in a social group or society an objective and readily observable ends-means disharmony, but it is quite another to have a group or society where people are aware of an ends-means discord, that is, subjectively feel or even, to some extent, imagine a discord. It may also be the case that a real and discernible discord of this type is not perceived as such in comparatively rigidly stratified societies. This raises the question of the mechanics and degree to which social structures may lead to *patterned perceptions*.

The implications are of paramount importance as far as the strains toward anomie and deviance are concerned. It seems obvious that the more the discrepancy is felt as such by the people involved, the higher the degree of strain in a group or society. On the other hand, the subjectively experienced gravity of such discrepancies depends on one's specific goals and actual position in the social structure. These goals depend in turn on the frame of reference within which they are conceived.

This brings us to the second point: what people desire and strive for, as well as the ways they envisage to acquire it, is not conceived in a social vacuum but depends on people's interaction and partial or full identification with others. This suggestion seems reasonable in light of the empirically corroborated thesis that people's attitude development reflects the way in which they relate to particular reference groups (Newcomb, 1952). Psychological and sociological research has found that "the major sources of the individual's weighty attitudes are the values or norms of the groups to which he relates himself, that is, of his reference groups" (Sherif, 1969, p. 286). Turner (1964, pp. 129–30) has pointed out that reference groups affect a person's ambition, playing an important role both in the selection of particular goals and the setting of standards. That is, reference-group analysis helps clarify processes by which a goal (e.g., material success) is adopted, and the level of attainment is set (e.g., how much wealth). These considerations are crucial for anomie theory, which has appeared to some "to assume a zero-sum relation between aspirations and social class: All members of the society feel the same pressures to succeed" (Hirschi and Selvin, 1967, p. 259).

This assumption, therefore, is not inherent in anomie theory. The present elaboration, thus, is in accord with empirical data that refute this assumption.

The level of aspiration implies some evaluation of available means. Turner (1964, p. 130) has noted that "persons who have immediate contact with other people who have achieved a given level are more likely to feel that they understand how to get there and consequently are willing to set their standards accordingly." This is not to deny that in a process of social interaction people also choose their reference groups according to their own values and norms. It is, rather, to emphasize that significant others are not selected at random or idiosyncratically but are to a considerable degree influenced by the social structure. The selection of referents is largely shaped and patterned by one's established social relationships.

A contribution of reference-group theory is to direct attention to nonmembership reference groups. This means that there may exist significant and varied social distance between a person and her/his referent. A consequence of such a social distance may be the incitement to lofty aspirations and goals for the realization of which there are no legitimate means available, given a particular individual's comparatively low position in the social structure. The selection of one's referent affects (may attenuate, aggravate, or indeed create), therefore, the disjunctions between cultural goals and socially available means that are so central to the conceptual framework of anomie theory.

Further, the more socially remote (upwardly) and the fuller the identification with one's referent, the more arduous will be the attainment of the goals because of limited opportunities. From this it follows that the higher (up to a certain point of remoteness) the referent is located in the social structure and the more the referent operates as an anchoring agent, the more low status and discontent will be produced (Hyman, 1968, p. 165).

Relative Deprivation

The concept of relative deprivation has been used in various ways, often signifying very different things. Following Runciman's definition,

> we can roughly say that A is relatively deprived of X when (i) he does not have X, (ii) he sees some other person or persons, which may include himself at some previous or expected time, as having X (whether or not this is or will be in fact the case), (iii) he wants X, and (iv) he sees it as feasible that he should have X. (Runciman, 1966:10)

Relative deprivation, then, means that people might feel deprived although they are not "objectively" deprived, in the sense of demonstrably lacking something vital. It also means that the sense of deprivation is a result of a comparison with the real or imagined situation of a referent. This highlights the need to distinguish between normative and comparative reference groups. As noted above, there may be overlaps between the two; but it is mainly the latter that is linked with relative deprivation. Because normative reference groups typically involve the adoption of certain values or outlooks and leave out the crucial aspect of comparison, relative deprivation can scarcely ensue. Where a reference group is comparative, however, comparisons are typically generated and, if unfavorable, can lead to relative deprivation.[2]

As the concept of relative deprivation refers to an individual or collective feeling of deprivation (Williams, 1975) and involves a comparison, it must be distinguished clearly from two types of "nonrelative" or "absolute deprivation." The first sort of absolute deprivation refers to objectively ascertained needs, which may or may not be felt as such by the people concerned. To use Runciman's example, "we might wish to speak of a Mexican village as absolutely deprived of sanitation even if its inhabitants refuse the offer of it." The other type of absolute deprivation is a felt need not dependent on comparison with some other person or group (e.g., hunger), an "affective deprivation, whereby people are only deprived (even nonrelatively) if they feel that they are" (Runciman, 1968, p. 71).

Further, it is essential to underline the difference between relative deprivation and observable conditions of inequality. Of course, objective inequality can lead to patterned perceptions and relative deprivation feelings. In such cases, the two would overlap to a great extent. Nevertheless, this is often not the case, chiefly as a result of cultural factors. For this reason, we should not uncritically operationalize the one to measure the other (some studies use unequal structural conditions as measures of relative deprivation). A negative consequence of failure to keep the two concepts separate is that relative deprivation becomes restricted to individual or collective feelings obtaining only in lower classes. Inequality may lead to relative deprivation and discontent only when it is perceived as such by the people concerned:

> Discontent is a product of *relative*, not absolute deprivation. . . . Discontent occurs when comparisons between comparable groups are made which suggest that unnecessary injustices are occurring. If the distribution of wealth is seen as natural and just—however disparate it is—it will be accepted. An objective theory of exploitation, or even a history of increased exploitative cultures have existed for generations without friction: it is the *perception of injustice*—relative deprivation—which counts. (Lea and Young, 1984, p. 81; emphasis in original)[3]

So, the concept of relative deprivation forges micro-macro links by connecting subjective feelings of individuals with culturally and socially patterned comparisons made through the selection of reference groups. The psychological dimension of relative deprivation notwithstanding, there are two important sociological dimensions. The first is related to relative deprivation within the group of which they see themselves as a member; the second has to do with people's satisfaction with the (perceived) position of their group in the social structure in general (Runciman, 1968, p. 72).

To the degree that inequalities and injustices do occur and conditions favoring awareness of them through the encouragement of social comparisons do obtain, the origin of feelings of relative deprivation must be sought in the specific sociocultural environment. Having reviewed a body of empirical studies on relative deprivation, Williams noted that "the more universalistic the normative structure of a society (or other collectivity), the greater the likelihood of relative deprivation" and that "an achievement-oriented system tends to generate feelings of relative deprivation" (Williams, 1975, p. 364).

Anomie theory points to deviance caused by a cultural overemphasis on success combined with structurally limited opportunities. Reference-group theory and relative deprivation can help in further specifying how the American Dream (which promotes such cultural overemphasis) and, more generally, egalitarian discourses affect people differently situated in the social structure. Egalitarian ideologies influence the way in which people define success, what means they see as appropriate, whether/how they perceive unfairness, and how they experience gratification or frustration. In this way, anomie theory explicitly takes into account the perception of structural inequalities by the actors.

The consequences of structural inequalities of opportunity are likely to be very different depending on whether they are experienced as such by individuals. For anomie and deviant behavior to occur, these inequalities must be judged by actors as undesirable or unjustified. Actors may or may not perceive them as such. They may attribute their failure to live up to culturally induced standards not only to the social structure but also to other factors, such as bad luck, lack of necessary contacts in high places, or personal shortcomings. Their adaptations in terms of the Mertonian typology would differ accordingly. Still, such failures involve disagreeable comparisons, leading to feelings of relative deprivation.

The Cultural Component

Merton's theory suggests that society, its culture, and its social organization pose characteristic problems of adjustment for people at each position of the system. Available means for coping within the framework of particular sets of institutionalized norms, however, may be insufficient. The incumbents of low-level positions may be so disadvantaged that they cannot benefit from available means. In such cases, they would tend to reject those aspects of the culture that contribute to the creation of the problems or the barriers to their solution and to substitute them with ambitions and norms they can live with more comfortably.

According to Durkheim, the less one has, the less one aspires to; the less limited one feels, the more intolerable any and all limitations appear to be (Durkheim, [1930], 1983, p. 282). As the horizon of the lower strata is limited by those above them, their desires are restricted (Durkheim, [1930], 1983, p. 287). By contrast, the American Dream ideology, to the extent that it is internalized, widens the horizon of all strata by inculcating or even imposing high ambitions, aspirations, and expectations for all Americans regardless of their social position. The cultural value of success and material wealth is open to all members of the American society and often considered as a duty. Consequently, all are encouraged to participate in an endless race toward monetary success.

The capitalist economic system in the United States and the way it interacts with the American Dream are also important and should not be neglected (Passas, 1990; Messner and Rosenfeld, 1993). The American Dream and the cultural dictates that are embodied in it cannot be considered in the abstract and in isolation from their wider socioeconomic and historical context. An advantage of broadening the scope of the analysis is that interesting and telling interconnections may be brought out. Elements of the American Dream may be intrinsic not only to contemporary America but also to other societies. Indeed, the encouragement of high levels of aspiration and ambition corresponds to specific socioeconomic demands and is part of process making for social integration or for discrepancies and contradictions. As Urry ([1973], 1978, p. 71) has observed,

> The whole thrust of contemporary western capitalist societies is upon industrial growth; and this has two implications. The first is that in some sense or other, economic expansion provides an increasing supply of goods and services to most individuals so that their welfare is enhanced. The second is that to bring about such expansion, it is necessary for individuals to widen their aspirations and to seek to acquire greater and greater supplies of such goods and services. Thus the contradiction that the latter is necessary to bring about the former which is only necessary because of the latter.

Further, an analysis of "Law and Order" issues in Britain has connected the incitement to lofty aspirations via comparisons with the capitalist system and modes of its legitimation:

And a major source of one's making comparisons—or indeed the feeling that one should in the first place "naturally" compete and compare oneself with others—is capitalism itself. We are taught that life is a racetrack: that merit will find its own reward. This is the central way our system legitimates itself and motivates people to compete. (Lea and Young, 1983, p. 95)[4]

An egalitarian ideology that does not distinguish among various strata in society, according to which all can "make it" and all should incessantly try to make it, paves the way for comparisons virtually with any other member of the society. It can be maintained that certain (status or other) similarities are thus encouraged to become bases for comparisons whereas others are played down (see Merton, 1968, pp. 296–97fn.), so that referents are selected out of broader fields such as "collectivities" and "social categories" (Merton, 1968, pp. 353–54). In this way, the referent may often be some "other," with whom one is not in sustained social relations.

Runciman (1968, p. 73) has remarked that "it may be that only where opportunity is believed to be equal do higher strata come to be taken as positive referents." To the extent that this proposition is correct, egalitarian ideologies enlarge significantly the range of possible reference individuals and groups one may adopt. The media of mass communication have a pivotal role in this process. It does not suffice that at least some opportunities exist and that some people have made good use of them. Others must know about it, too. Moreover, it is indeed true that, if not from "the log cabin to the White House," individuals have often made it from "rags to riches." This fact, as well as the influence and the "status-conferral function" of the mass media (Lazarsfeld and Merton, 1952, p. 76), is illustrated by the following:

> Every year the American Schools and Colleges Association polls thousands of "college leaders" to select a few men for public acclaim who have risen from humble origins to great success. When the final tally discloses the names of these fortunate few, they are summoned to New York City to receive the Horatio Alger award. Great businessmen and potent industrialists interrupt their affairs to gather for the ceremony. They are tendered a banquet in the course of which each is presented with a bronze plaque testifying that he has "climbed the ladder of success through toil and diligence and responsible application of his talents to whatever tasks were his." Newspaper photographers snap their pictures, press releases are handed out, and the next day's newspapers hold up the winners and the cynosure of a nation's admiring eyes. (Wohl, 1976, p. 501)

It would be false, nevertheless, to regard the range of possible referents as unlimited. Although high ambitions may characterize large numbers of individuals as a result of egalitarianism, it does not follow that their particular goals and standards of success will be identical or that they are not shaped by specific social networks (Passas, 1990). As Aristotle pointed out many centuries ago,

> We do not compete with men who lived a hundred centuries ago, or those not yet born, or the dead, or those who dwell near the Pillar of Hercules, or those whom, in our opinion or that of others, we take to be far above us. So too we compete with those who follow the same ends as ourselves. We compete with our rivals in sport or in love, and generally with those who are after the same things; and it is therefore these whom we are bound to envy beyond all others. (Aristotle, 1942, 1388a, 8–15)

Duesenberry (1967) has argued that the American society is classless and that, as a consequence, the whole income distribution can be taken as the frame of reference relevant for each person. Urry ([1973], 1978, p. 71) has pointed out that that analysis fails to consider the normative-comparative (and audience) reference-group distinction and rightly argued that "there are both classes and status groups such that the patterning of reference orientations will be variable as between different sectors of that society." What makes Duesenberry's argument interesting, however, is that it reflects the impact and influence of the egalitarian ideology and the American Dream in American society.

It is an open question calling for more research whether a restricted frame of reference tends to reduce one's aspirations and goals, or because one's aims are limited, the referents are more restricted. It seems reasonable to suggest that it is a reciprocal process. In any event, this analysis suggests that in American society, although the success theme makes for ever-rising aspirations and facilitates wide frames of reference, the latter are not unlimited (about other contemporary societies, see Bolte and Hradil, 1984, pp. 284ff.). People's membership reference groups are still expected to play an important role. This means that those at the lower social positions may not be always comparing themselves to those very high above, thereby reducing their level of frustration and stress. On the other hand, people at higher social positions may experience just as high levels of frustration and stress because they compare themselves with peers who are better off.

The Social Component

Thus far we have concentrated mainly on the analytically distinguishable component of culture. The other component is the social: the network of

relationships in which members of the society or group are variously involved. This relates to the actual distribution of power and differentiated
access to opportunities for the realization of cultural ends.

The discord between the cultural and social components of the social
structure brings about problematic situations. Licit opportunities to achieve
cherished goals of success are not available to all members. Inevitably, many
will never be able to attain highly valued goals as they are culturally defined.
Failures are likely to give rise to tensions and frustrations. These in turn are
likely to lead to the "withdrawal of allegiance from one or another part of
prevailing social standards," which Merton has described as anomie (Merton,
1964, p. 218). Anomic situations inherent to capitalist societies continue to
be viewed as a background against which deviance and crime can be understood. "Left realist" accounts of crime in Britain today adopt, if implicitly,
the Mertonian idea of this type of disjunction:

> The values of an equal or meritocratic society which capitalism inculcates
> into people are constantly at loggerheads with the actual material inequali-
> ties in the world. And, contrary to the conservatives, *it is the well-socialized
> person who is the most liable to crime*. Crime is endemic to capitalism be-
> cause it produces both egalitarian ideals and material shortages. (Lea and
> Young, 1984, pp. 95–96; emphasis in original)

Shortcomings of the welfare state in Britain have also been studied with
the conclusion that "inner-city deprivation may thus have to be accepted as
one of the inevitable consequences of the maintenance of capitalism in Britain in this particular period of its historic evaluation" (Smith, [1979], 1985,
p. 213). The gravity and weight of anomic tensions is likely to increase to
the degree that others to whom one relates directly or indirectly have done
better. When people and groups who constitute one's referents do better, one
might feel relatively deprived. The same can occur when people are their
own referents and make comparisons by the standards they had achieved in
the past. If past-present comparisons (Taylor, 1982) are unfavorable, as in
cases of downward social mobility, loss of employment, financial losses, and
so on, people may feel relatively deprived by their own previous standards.
This is likely to happen during economic cycles of recession, which provide
a ground for testing this hypothesis on a large scale.

Merton has put forward the hypothesis that "social systems with relatively
high rates of social mobility will tend to make for widespread orientation to
nonmembership groups as reference groups" (1968, p. 359). Further, we do
know that the United States is among the countries with the highest social

mobility rates (Lipset and Zetterberg, 1967, pp. 565–70; Heath, 1981, pp. 193–223) and that the American Dream is more than just a fiction. A good deal of social mobility has been the common feature of other contemporary Western societies, too. Britain, in particular,

> showed rather more inter-generational mobility across the line between manual and non-manual labor according to survey data from around the middle of this century than other capitalist countries including the United States. Recruitment to the small elites at the top at the same time was tighter and more exclusive than in several other comparable societies, America among them (Westergaard and Resler, [1975], 1982, p. 302)

Other surveys have revealed that, although one's position in the British class structure is not fixed at birth, "silver spoons continue to be distributed" (Heath, 1981, pp. 75–77). This indicates that in some "mobile" societies the movements up and down the occupational structure are more moderate than in others. These differences in patterns of mobility may have a significant impact on one's choice of referents. Following Merton's logic, it may be hypothesized that the "social distance" between one's actual position and one's referent will tend to be longer in social systems where high rates of social mobility also involve frequent movements across the range of social structure (e.g., "rags to riches" and "riches to rags") than where these appear to occur seldom. In any event, social mobility should not cloud the existence of sharp inequalities and the fact that capitalist societies pay little more than lip service to the ideal of equal opportunity (Westergaard and Resler, [1975], 1982, p. 312).

It can be assumed that the larger the social distance between a given individual and his/her comparative reference group, the higher the likelihood and degree of his/her relative deprivation. As noted above, an egalitarian ideology leads to the selection of referents with whom a person does not interact directly; obstacles to wide-ranging comparisons are decreased or removed: "Feelings of relative deprivation are encouraged by any social process that diminishes barriers to comparison and emulation between the advantaged and the less advantaged" (Williams, 1975, p. 362). By motivating people to try and secure success and higher social positions, the American Dream favors the selection of high-range reference groups which can potentially bring about higher rates of relative deprivation.

Egalitarian discourses may thus contribute to the creation of relative deprivation which, with the strain it entails, is conducive to anomic tendencies and increasing rates of deviance (see Burton and Dunaway, 1994). A cultural context that appears "to approximate the polar type in which great emphasis upon certain success-goals occurs without equivalent emphasis upon institutional means" (Merton, 1968, p. 190) can but provide fertile ground for such a process.

Indeed, the crime problem is aggravated where "as in the United States . . . advertising through the mass media fosters the feeling of deprivation among large numbers of less affluent members of the population" (Shelley, 1981, p. 142). This is highlighted by advertising campaigns urging youths to "be like Mike"; in a different commercial, Mike also tells them how to avoid the "embarrassment" of coming second or third. Eco has stressed the "variability of interpretation" to which media messages are subject. The meaning conferred to the same message or image varies according to the codes operating in distinct "sociological situations" in which the recipients are located:

> for a Milanese bank clerk a TV ad for a refrigerator represents a stimulus to buy, but for an unemployed peasant in Calabria the same image means the confirmation of a world of prosperity that doesn't belong to him and that he must conquer. This is why I believe TV advertising in depressed countries functions as a revolutionary message. (Eco, 1987, p. 141)

Eco's last sentence points to intriguing puzzles for international, comparative inquiry. However, as indicated by his example, the argument also pertains to more limited areas of investigation, such as one country, city, or even community within which discordant interpretations can occur. Due to mass advertising, inequalities may be experienced more strongly as such by underprivileged individuals within a country. Incessant bombardment of information about the fact that other members of a group can and do enjoy higher standards of living fosters upsetting comparisons. More generally, then, mass advertising in depressed areas may act as a "revolutionary message" (Eco, 1987, p. 141). This is only meant, of course, to draw attention to the potential for "rebellious" adaptations. Smelser (1968) and Tilly (1978), among others, have pointed out that it takes more than a message for collective responses and behavior, let alone revolution. What matters for our purposes here is that mass-media messages can produce feelings of relative deprivation, strains, and deviance.

Such feelings and tensions may motivate people to increase their efforts and strive for advancement through legitimate channels. Conformity can still be expected to be widespread. Many of us perform well under pressure and strain, which brings out the best in us. The point is that many others can be expected to deviate as another consequence of widespread messages, which

(1) nurture people's awareness of material shortages and inequalities, and (2) legitimate, encourage, or create wishes and needs that cannot be met easily, if at all. People are constantly reminded of what "is missing" in their house or in their life. And, as Easterlin (1973, p. 4) has put it, individuals "assess their material well-being, not in terms of the absolute amount of goods they have, but relative to a social norm of what goods they ought to have."

The spectacular growth of credit systems of payment in contemporary societies can be cited as a symptom of situations where everyone is called upon to spend and buy beyond affordable levels. Loan advertisements and "buy now, pay later" signs are omnipresent. "Winning a car" can be an incentive for getting a housing loan. Borrowing constitutes for many people an appealing short-term solution. At the same time, the economy's growth and companies' profit requirements may be satisfied.

In the long run, however, these processes are impregnated with risks. Interest rates are frequently preposterous and make the final settlement look quite remote or sometimes impossible. For those led into debts that cannot be paid back, further borrowing may be required. This illustrates a vicious circle and an unenviable position to be in. In Britain, for example, the consumer and household debt at the end of 1987 was estimated at about "£200–225 billion, or an average of about £11.000 per household. Within this decade, household debt has risen from the equivalent of roughly six months' to a year's disposable income" (Shields, 1988, p. 48).

Significant numbers of individuals, especially the young, unemployed, and low paid, occasionally victims of exploitation, find themselves in difficult financial situations. British Inland Revenue surveys showed that younger and poorer households take on more debt with the encouragement of the government to buy council houses. The buildup of debt has "also been fed by a sharp increase in the number of households facing severe debt problems in recent years" (Dicks, 1987, p. 232).

The credit and lending boom in recent years has tempted many to borrow more than they can manage. The governor of the Bank of England (1988, p. 49) voiced his anxiety about the real personal suffering that can be involved and noted that "a number of well publicized instances in recent months . . . have quite properly given rise to concern." Massive borrowing can be interpreted as an indicator of the desire for immediate gratification. This may be achieved up to a point and for a period of time. For some people, it may work. Yet for others, the end result may be an unpleasant return to the situation from which they temporarily escaped. For many individuals, the problem is only postponed or rendered more acute. In the effort to avoid marginality, some move head-on toward it. The problem is similar in North America. Credit has been widely available and overgenerously offered to people who are burdened by huge debts.

It may be conjectured that those trapped in such situations will seek out all means likely to resolve the problems, and, given the opportunity, they might resort to deviant methods. Their responses may be expected to be not only rational or instrumental but also irrational or "retreatist." These hypotheses require further investigation.

Meanwhile, apparent support is provided by a rise in crime rates in Britain in the 1990s. Other empirical support is provided by a study on criminality and the socioeconomic structure of German cities. It found that per capita indebtedness, as well as social assistance expenditure (used as an indicator of relative poverty), are highly correlated with crime rates. "Thefts from houses" and "thefts of cars," in particular, rose with per capita indebtedness (Friedrichs, 1985, pp. 57 and 61).

Affluent Societies and the Social Distribution of Deviance

As we have seen, relative deprivation and strains toward deviance and anomie may arise in societies characterized by egalitarianism and consumerism. Both relative deprivation and anomie refer to phenomena intrinsic to developed and affluent societies. Most students of these phenomena and the process of "rising expectations" in Western societies focus on its effect on people in the lower social strata. In this section, I argue that the daily lives of the rich and powerful are also affected. The present elaboration of anomie theory allows for the study of qualitative differences in tensions and anomic strains peculiar to all structural locations. Reference-group analysis helps to clarify not only processes whereby culturally prescribed goals are actually adopted by individuals but also what these goals may be in various contexts and what they signify for different people. This mode of analysis, then, is an essential tool for the interpretation of empirical data showing that "material success" does not represent the same thing for every member of a given group or society.

The impact of secularization, affluence, mass media, and relative deprivation on deviance has been recorded long ago. As Toby (1967, p. 143) has put it, "the distribution of goods and services here and now is a more important preoccupation than concern with eternal salvation" and the mass media . . . stimulate the desire for a luxurious style of life among all segments of the population. These considerations explain why the sting of socio-economic deprivation can be greater for the poor in rich societies than for the poor in poor societies.

Shelley has argued that in agrarian society, individuals expecting to maintain a traditional lifestyle had few reasons to raise their aspirations and little opportunity to experience discrepancies between their achievements and their aims. Thus, she concluded, "anomie is a new phenomenon unique to the conditions of modern society" (Shelley, 1981, p. 11). Social problems can be identified as disjunctions between what is actually offered by a society and what wishes people have. Processes of deterioration, as well as of rising standards, may produce this effect. There is little paradox, therefore,

> in finding that some complex, industrialized societies, having a comparatively high plane of material life and rapid advancement of cultural values, may nevertheless be regarded by their members as more problem-ridden than other societies with substantially less material wealth and cultural achievement. Nor is there any longer a paradox in finding that as conditions improve in a society (as gauged by widespread values), popular satisfaction may nevertheless decline. (Merton, 1982, p. 64)

Merton has added that, as the "rising tide of expectations" advances unmatched by actual achievement, "there tends to develop a sense of collective 'relative deprivation' " (Merton, 1982, p. 64; for empirical support, he referred to a study describing urban racial disturbances as a response to "multiple deprivations and frustrations" suffered by blacks). In addition, the urbanization of industrial societies has been regarded as conducive to relative deprivation and property crime:

> The city provided increased exposure to material possessions and greater financial expectations for those who resided there. Therefore, one of the unfortunate consequences of the increasingly urbanized society was a growth of property crime as individuals attempted to compensate illegally for their perceived deprivation. (Shelley, 1981, p. 13)

Friedrichs found that higher rates of horizontal mobility and of social assistance expenditure result in increased frequency of all criminal offenses. Also, the combination of lower social control and higher poverty leads to criminality. He has thus argued that beneficiaries of social assistance have partaken unequally in society's prosperity and, on the basis of a previously better economic position, perceive inequalities more strongly (Friedrichs, 1985, p. 60).

This does not mean that deviance will be much higher in the lower social strata. The consolidation of anomie and reference-group theories enables the study of middle- and upper-class patterns of deviance (Passas, 1990). The theoretical expectation is that tensions and pressures conducive to anomie and deviance may be more evenly spread throughout the population than has been commonly assumed.

According to Heiland (1983, p. 195), for instance, the fact that central aims of affluent societies—welfare and justice—are regarded by actors as unfulfilled or insufficiently materialized accounts both for a rise in property crime and for a wider rate of such crime among members who have participated in society's prosperity. This clearly concerns relatively well-off citizens. This point implies that property crimes are also committed by people who used to belong to the middle and upper strata (Friedrichs, 1985, p. 52).[5]

German studies have pointed out differences in problems faced by people in different classes and shown how *anomic tendencies are widespread across social classes* (Klages, 1975, pp. 12, 14ff.; Klages, 1981; Klages, 1984, pp. 8–9; Klages and Herbert, 1983). Further, it has been argued that "since the last war, the growth of the Welfare State has combined with the mass media and mass secondary education to produce a steady growth in relative deprivation" and that "the phenomenon of 'over-education' is beginning to appear" (Lea and Young, 1984, p. 222). An effect of these developments in contemporary societies is thus the raising of "minimum expectations." As these expectations can be interpreted in diverse fashions, people in high social ranks may be confronted with strains and tensions (Passas, 1988, ch. 5; 1990; forthcoming).

Earlier research has suggested that "at each income level . . . Americans want just about twenty-five percent more (but of course this 'just a bit more' continues to operate once it is obtained)" (Merton, 1968, p. 190). Therefore, relative deprivation and anomic tensions should not be expected only in the lower classes. People's "problems" at the high end of the social hierarchy may be whether they can afford a second car, a car or swimming pool like the neighbor's, more power, higher income than their peers, and so on.

At this point, one might ask: How can "social class" be an "antidote" as well as a contributor to deviance and anomic tendencies?[6] Class can be regarded as an antidote in the sense that if ambitions are determined by membership reference groups, structural inequalities will have a less potent role to play. It is essential not to ignore societies where inequalities and discrepancies are accompanied by low rates of relative deprivation. Such situations can be found in societies with a great deal of traditionalism (Keller and Stern, 1968), with a rigid stratification system considered as legitimate by its members (Coser, 1965, p. 140). In this type of society, where class functions as a "cultural break" to ambition, pressures leading to deviance and anomie would be less significant.

On the other hand, social class can be seen as a cause of strains toward deviance and anomie in the sense that it constitutes structural barriers for the realization of valued goals. This is the case in societies where goals are more universalistic, cutting across classes. Where social mobility is relatively high and adoption of nonmembership referents more frequent, inequalities are likely to lead to relative deprivation and anomic situations.

These opposite types of societies are best conceived as ideal types. Although today's societies—especially U.S. society—seem to be closer to the latter type, expectations and definitions of success are largely affected by the positions held by individuals in the social structure (Passas, 1988, chs. 5, 6). Discrepancies between specific ends and available legitimate means are felt less acutely by those members of lower classes who do not compare themselves with "dukes" (Runciman, 1966). However, in an environment promoting success (however understood by different persons), competition, consumerism and immediate gratification, comparisons with not too distant— but still nonmembership—referents are likely. The urge to "get ahead" may bring with it a willingness to break from conventional standards. Multinational surveys have shown that

> Growing numbers of young people feel the need to forge ahead and deter-
> mine their own identity and future . . . most young people are content to
> accomplish this task within traditional institutional channels. A few youth,
> however, are *willing to risk achieving their goals by working outside accept-*
> *able institutional channels.* (Braungart and Braungart, 1986, p. 376; empha-
> sis added)

Matters are more complicated by recent developments. The primary goal may not always be success but rather maintenance of current standards. With the advancement of technology and continuous economic pressures for efficiency and profit, companies tend to resort to redundancies— euphemistically called "downsizing." As a consequence, employees reasonably fear that they might lose current positions and salaries (Bolte and Hradil, 1984, p. 286). These trends underline the prevalence of competition and the strains that may ensue *throughout society*. These are additional processes potentially making for anomie. People strive for different things: unemployed for satisfactory and meaningful jobs or better incomes; employed for the preservation of levels of achievement and for possible strengthening of their position; those safe in their posts, comparing themselves with more successful peers, for advancement. The potential for relative deprivation, tensions, and departures from established norms is far from unique to any single segment of the population.

I have stressed that relative deprivation is not an objective but a subjectively felt condition. Yet, structural sources of subjective feelings should not be disregarded. Beyond psychological reductionism and structural reification, this analysis is consistent with a "structure-choice-structure" ontological view (Blau, 1990; Giddens, 1979). That is, humans produce, reproduce, and change sociocultural settings, but their attitudes and actions are also influenced and constrained by these settings.

Structural features of societies or collectivities constitute a strategic site and a legitimate point of departure for sociological theorizing and research. Therefore, one can start by examining prevalent cultural ideas in designated structural contexts, patterns of inequality or injustice, and conditions favoring comparisons, perceptions of disjunctions, and feelings of relative deprivation. Then, one may try to assess the likely responses, patterns of conformity and deviance from particular values or norms, which can affect the social unit under study. Consequently, one can speak of socially "constrained comparisons" and treat relative deprivation as a "structural effect" (Williams, 1975, p. 358).

Enter Anomia

The concept of anomie refers to attitudes: a withdrawal of allegiance from one or another part of prevailing social standards. By contrast, "anomia" refers to a person's state of mind, to the "breakdown of the individual's sense of attachment to society" (MacIver, 1950, p. 84; see also Riesman, [1950], 1953, pp. 278–82; Srole, 1956a, 1956b; Merton, 1964; McClosky and Schaar, 1965). Through this psychological concept, further links can be made between reference-group analysis and anomie theory. In a condensed paragraph, Merton has described how disjunctions between cultural goals and legitimate means, anomia, anomie, and deviance are connected:

> The men most vulnerable to the stresses resulting from contradictions between their socially induced aspirations and poor access to the opportunity-structure are the first to be alienated. Some of them turn to established alternatives (Cloward's illegitimate opportunity-structure) that both violate the abandoned norms and prove effective in achieving their immediate ob-

jectives. A few others actually innovate for themselves to develop new alternatives. These successful rogues—successful as this is measured by the criteria in their significant reference groups—become prototypes for others in their environment who, initially less vulnerable and less alienated, now no longer keep to the rules they once regarded as legitimate. This, in turn, creates a more acutely anomic context for still others in the local social system. In this way, anomie, anomia, and mounting rates of deviant behavior become mutually reinforcing unless counteracting mechanisms of social control are called into play. (Merton, 1964, p. 235)

In the light of what has been said, the above paragraph can be elaborated and extended. The American Dream ideology and a relatively open class structure facilitate and foster broad orientations in terms of reference-group selection. People's referents may be sought in nonmembership groups. Consequently, the cultural goal of success is to a degree defined more uniformly across class barriers compared to other societies. Because people are unequally equipped with the means to achieve this end, those with poorer access to the opportunity are more likely to feel relatively deprived. The higher the sense of relative deprivation, the more likely it is for one's commitment to prevalent social standards to be weakened.

Members without easy access to the kinds of opportunity suggested by their referents may engage in "innovative" deviant behavior and thus develop new alternative courses of action. These new alternatives may prove to be successful (goals are attained, and deviant acts are not punished). With nonmembership reference groups and lofty goals culturally promoted, these people become "prototypes" (*comparative referents*) for others. These, although initially less vulnerable and less anomic, may now feel relatively deprived. The sense of relative deprivation increases their degree of anomia, and they no longer keep to rules they once regarded as legitimate.

In addition, the above prototypes may constitute *normative referents* for other people. A consequence of that and of the general underemphasis on the legitimacy of the methods employed is that some others may opt for existing illegitimate alternatives (Cloward and Ohlin, 1960). These alternatives involve violation of the (at least, temporarily) abandoned norms and may prove effective in the realization of the actors' objectives. Examples of this process can be found in the literature on white-collar crime, where many are socialized into particular settings and organizational contexts in which certain deviant acts are committed as a matter of course (i.e., without the experience of relative deprivation or frustrations, expedient methods are adopted whether legitimate or not).

The breakdown of culturally prescribed ways of attaining valued objectives is aggravated, giving rise to a more anomic context for still others in the local social system. It is by no means implied that only anomics engage in deviant behavior; it is merely assumed that anomics are more likely than nonanomics to do so. Further, both anomic and nonanomic individuals will engage more often in deviant behavior in contexts with a higher degree of anomie (Merton, 1964, p. 230).

The growth of patterns of deviant behavior and illicitly achieved success gradually accentuates anomic trends in society. Many who did not react to lower degrees of anomie (relaxed *attitudes* toward rules) with deviant *behavior* may do so now. Higher rates of deviance further undermine the legitimacy of conventional norms (Merton, 1956, pp. 37–38). Furthermore, the weaker the social norms, the stronger the impact of relative deprivation on deviance and crime (Friedrichs, 1985, p. 53). In this way, socially favored comparisons, relative deprivation, anomia, mounting rates of deviant behavior, and anomie reinforce each other unless effective social controls succeed in stopping this process.

I would like to reiterate the importance of normative reference groups in this process. Because of the overemphasis on success, the influence of illicitly successful referents, and easy access to illegitimate opportunities, others will turn to these alternatives without experiencing relative deprivation or other forms of strain and without considering legitimate opportunities at all. This implies the existence of a preestablished deviant subculture—formed through the processes of interaction and feedback mechanisms. Such subcultures are manifestations of anomie and represent forces maintaining or accentuating existing levels of anomie and particular patterns of deviant behavior. Recent research into Asian deviant subcultures illustrates this point. It has been found that, before youths join gangs, an indispensable intervening variable is "the affiliation with and internalization of Triad norms and values" (Kelly et al., 1993, p. 248).

As has been argued (Bernard, 1984, 1995; Cohen, this volume; Passas, 1988, 1990), anomie theory should not be categorized as a mere strain theory of deviance. It does attempt to account for deviance in terms of culturally and socially induced strains, but this is not all. The "stress component" of the theory can be distinguished from its "anomie" component as the latter refers to *deviance not preceded by overwhelming strains*. People under strain in an anomic environment will turn to deviant adaptations more easily than in a less anomic environment. It must be emphasized that in an anomic environment *strain is not required* for the adoption of deviant means. People can be expected to be less committed to prevailing values and norms when their guiding power is significantly diminished. As a result, people may commit deviant acts whenever an opportunity is offered.

An anomic environment favors the establishment of deviant normative structures and lifestyles. Through socialization and social interaction, then, people may adopt deviant normative referents and may engage in deviant practices without having experienced relative deprivation or pressures, although these possibly contributed to the creation of the deviant subculture in the first place. In such cases, we are confronted by "nonconformity," defined as "conformity with the values, standards and expectations of reference individuals and groups" (Merton, 1968, p. 413). These suggestions find empirical support in Lewis's study of the "hustle":

> We can accept Merton's notion that such behavior is deviant in that it violates legal specifications about what is and what is not a legitimate way of pursuing success goals. Structurally, the hustle is an innovator, a deviant; but it would be an error to equate this *structural deviance* (violation of the law) with the presence of deviant social meanings in the behavior. In terms of its social meanings for those who participate, hustling is more *imitative* than *innovative*. (Lewis, 1970, pp. 183–84; emphasis in original)

The Mafia family business and the way it reproduces itself is another good example of nonconformity. The mafioso-entrepreneur is someone born in a family and to a context providing a specific type of referents, and he is considered the holder of a special position in society: "this is don A's son," "this is don B's nephew" (Arlacchi, 1986, p. 122). No recourse to strain is necessary to explain how this person joins the powerful subculture:

> He soon finds a niche in some profession or career—unlike many of his contemporaries who under present conditions in southern Italy may face long years of youth unemployment. Mafia firms are family firms, and everyone gets a chance to play their part. *From adolescence onwards, he earns—and spends—a lot.* His psychological profile reveals only faint traces of the deviant and the outsider. (Arlacchi, 1986, p. 122; emphasis added)

This puts in relief the significant difference between the concepts of anomie and anomia. Merton's article "Anomie, Anomia and Social Interaction" (1964) has been perceived by Schacht (1982) as blurring this distinction and giving prevalence to anomia; that is, anomie was allegedly conceived simply as widespread anomia. My analysis, however, leaves no doubt about the primacy of the sociological concept, while not ignoring the frame of mind of individuals and their interaction. It may be added that, just as the distinction between sociological and psychological ambivalence "is sometimes obscure because the two are so often empirically connected" (Merton et al., 1983, p. 40), the distinction between the social state of anomie and its psychological counterpart are frequently hard to separate out empirically.

The above quotation also illustrates how patterns of conformity to a given set of values and norms may at the same time represent patterns of socially defined deviance. As Becker (1963, p. 8) has pointed out, "A person may break the rules of one group by the very act of abiding by the rules of another group." Bearing in mind that Merton has also argued that "what is nonconformity to the norms of one group is often conformity to the norms of another group" (Merton, 1982, p. 74), a significant convergence with the labeling perspective may emerge (see Passas, 1988, ch. 8 for further discussion and specification of Merton's concept of nonconformity). The relevance of reference-group analysis to the study of conformity, which is as problematic as deviance, is reiterated in the sociological literature. But the primary concern here is with what constitutes deviation from prevailing standards and the processes by which it is produced and reproduced.

"Innovation" is not the only response to structural disharmonies and contradictions. Shelley (1981, p. 10) has contended that "relative deprivation is not an explanation of all forms of crime but only those offenses related to property." Her remark reflects a large body of research carried out chiefly in North America that provides support for a positive association between property crime and relative deprivation—measured mainly by income inequality (Eberts and Schwirian, 1968; Danziger and Wheelers, 1975; Danziger, 1976; Braithwaite, 1979, pp. 211–20; Jacobs, 1981; DeFronzo, 1983). However, Merton's typology of responses to strain and anomie—in the making of which, relative deprivation can play a crucial role—offers a wider range of possibilities. According to my analysis, therefore, relative deprivation may be followed by a variety of responses under various circumstances, ranging from white-collar crime to "expressive" offenses.

Interesting attempts have been made to generate hypotheses on responses to individual or collective feelings of relative deprivation (Runciman, 1966, pp. 33–35; Williams, 1975, pp. 366–73). Although their suggestions can be helpful in further clarifying Merton's typology, such exercise is beyond the scope of this essay. At any rate, a comparative study of sixty-two nations has found that although property crime increases with economic development, it is not necessarily connected with income inequality. The study suggested that relative deprivation stemming from income inequality can lead to numerous alternative responses besides crime, such as alcoholism and suicide (i.e., "retreatism") or social movements aiming at the reduction of inequality (i.e., "innovation" or "rebellion") (Stack, 1984).

The results of another study also warn against a firm postulate that anomia-leads-to-innovation and to law violation. It has been found that subjective "normlessness"

> does not lead to trouble with the law among persons who also believe they are powerless to achieve their ends. It is only among persons who do not believe they are powerless—who see themselves as active and effective forces in their own lives—that normlessness is related to trouble with the law. (Ross and Mirowksy, 1987, p. 272)

In line with the analysis of these authors (Ross and Mirowsky, 1987, pp. 272–74 and 275–76) is the proposition that structural conditions and discrepancies may promote "emotional distress" or even mental ill-health (in cases of normless individuals who feel they have little control over their lives), as well as criminal activities (in cases of anomics who feel more "instrumental"). It may be further conjectured that the perception of how much power one has to achieve valued ends depends largely on one's knowledge that others have succeeded, as well as the opportunities to associate with them and to use the same means. Moreover, when the available means are illicit, their use would depend on what control theorists have called "commitment to conformity" (Briar and Piliavin, 1965; Box, 1971; Cohen, this volume, calls it "costs of deviance") and the willingness to take risks. This brings us back to reference groups (comparative and normative). It also highlights the relevance of Sutherland's theory of "differential association" that can be seen as a "special case of the more general theoretical framework of reference group theory" (Clark, 1972, p. 91).

In addition, the political situation and the perception of possible political solutions to problems may have an impact on outcomes (Stack, 1984, pp. 236, 251–52). The reactions then can be collective and "rebellious," because the means of protest may "explicitly challenge the system itself and 'its rules of the game' " (Hall, 1974, p. 271). Hall's reasoning, despite his rejection of the "Mertonian variety of theory of deviance," is quite congruent with my analysis:

> The attainment of a par excellence democratic goal (freedom of expression of political views, respect of dissenting ideologies and practices, pluralism) is, in fact, sometimes impossible if the rules laid down by democratic theory are to be followed; in other words, *access to legitimate avenues leading to the materialization of a legitimate cultural goal is structurally denied.* (Hall, 1974, p. 266; emphasis added)

The responses to such anomie-inducing conflicts (in this case, between democratic theory and practice) can be expected to be collective. This is confirmed by the observation that "the early Civil Rights movement in Northern Ireland articulated the structural discontents of the poor, disenfranchised Catholic minorities of Ulster" (Hall, 1974, p. 270).

Summarizing, cultural and material conditions of today's societies seem to have in-built tendencies toward deviance and anomie, which can lead to a wide range of outcomes determined by specific patterns of interaction. So we can expect (given specific conditions or "structuring variables" [Cullen, 1984]) anything from quiescence, fatalism, and mental illness to "discontent, and in the absence of politics, crime" (Lea and Young, 1984, p. 74). As a consequence, the dynamic processes sketchily outlined here might lead not only to the maintenance and reproduction of existing arrangements but also to social change.

Conclusion

This essay is chiefly an attempt to connect the developing anomie theory with this question: What is the impact of social interaction and the influence of others on the ways in which people differentially located in the social structure may respond to disjunctions between lofty cultural aims and socially restricted opportunities? I have outlined a dynamic process in which egalitarian ideologies, material shortages, relative deprivation, stress, anomia, deviant behavior, and anomie are interconnected.

Some theorists have argued that two distinct and independent theories can be found in Merton's writings on anomie. One is said to be at the macrolevel, dealing with structural problems and rates of deviance, whereas the other focuses on individual strain, motivations, and deviance (Agnew, 1992, this volume; Cullen, 1984; Messner, 1988). My view is that these are two interdependent components in anomie theory that feed back on each other.

I have argued that for structural strain to translate into individual deviant behavior, it is indispensable that a significant number of people experience at some point the ends-means discrepancy. This experience varies in different social locations, depending on one's comparative reference point. A macro-micro link is achieved by the realization that the U.S. culture, the ideology of the American Dream, and high rates of social mobility encourage nonmembership referents. However, not everyone succeeds in attaining the goals of their socially distant referents, due to lack of available means. This increases the likelihood of unfavorable comparisons, feelings of relative deprivation, and deviant responses. When successful deviants become normative referents for other members of the social group, *deviance without strain* is a possible consequence. The same can occur when frustrations, interactions, and deviant responses accumulate and crystallize into subcultures.

Merton's anomie theory has traditionally been used for the analysis of lower-class crime and deviance (for exceptions, see Passas, 1990; Vaughan, 1983). In addition, several studies (mostly using inequality measures) have assumed that relative deprivation leads to higher deviance rates among the lower classes. Control theory is generally regarded as the perspective with the theoretical expectation of similar rates of deviance among all social strata (Messner, 1988, pp. 39–41). In light of my elaboration, relative deprivation and anomie theory can easily contribute to the understanding of middle- and upper-class deviance and crime as well.

I have also argued that the promotion and adoption of nonmembership reference groups occur more in the United States than in other countries and more in Western societies than in somewhat rigidly stratified societies. This does not mean that everyone in the United States does so. I have not explored here the forces and contexts in which people adopt comparative reference groups close to their social rank. To the extent they do so, frustrations and strain are minimized, because people will make pragmatic adjustments as to what can be achieved. This can explain why not everyone is equally frustrated by similar problems and why not everyone engages in deviant acts. It can also explain, to some extent, why the aspirations-expectations gap is not related to crime (Burton et al., 1994). Socially close comparative reference groups offer clues as to what can be attained. So although "dreaming" is common, when it comes to setting life goals in everyday life, realism sets in and reduces the potential for strain and crime.[7]

Further, it is worthwhile inquiring into the extent to which normative reference groups, social support (Cullen, 1994), and social capital (Coleman, 1988, 1990) mitigate strains and feelings of relative deprivation or otherwise encourage *conformity* by limiting access to illicit opportunities and reinforcing social controls (Sampson and Groves, 1989).[8]

In short, the following are some of the new research puzzles generated by this elaboration of anomie theory: To what extent does the American Dream/ U.S. culture encourage the adoption of nonmembership reference groups? To what extent are these reference groups "objectively" unrealistic? To what extent does this lead to relative deprivation and strain? To what extent does this, in turn, lead to deviance? Do differences in social distance between one's social position and that of a comparative referent have any impact on these questions? How successful are people in the pursuit of *nonmonetary goals*? What is the effect of successes and failures in attaining these other goals? To what extent does the adoption of membership reference groups lead to conformity despite cultural emphases on lofty aspirations? What conditions favor the adoption of normative reference groups that encourage conformity? How do conditions giving rise to relative deprivation relate to the availability of social support and social capital (conventional or "criminal")? How do TV programs portraying violence and disruptive family situations affect young people's adoption of normative reference groups? Comparative research may look into the effect of media globalization in terms of relative deprivation and crime rates (e.g., widely distributing to Third World countries soap operas depicting rich and glamorous U.S. lifestyles, introducing the possibility of new comparative referents). Finally, the processes outlined above do not need to be examined only in relation to whole societies. Studies may be undertaken within particular communities and institutional or organizational settings.

This elaboration of anomie theory is not geared toward the claim that it can become an all-inclusive, grand theory of deviance. The project is rather to assess the possibility of building bridges among various theoretical perspectives. In this respect, the question is, To what extent could a common language improve the communication among different orientations so often juxtaposed in a belligerent mood, rather than for the purpose of peaceful and constructive dialogue?

For a more complete understanding of deviance, it is indispensable to take into account more extensively the crucial role of social control in the dynamic processes described above. We need more thorough analyses of the informal control of normative reference groups, which complements formal societal controls. The effects of social control itself on the shaping of deviant behavior and "deviancy amplification" (Young, [1971], 1982) ought also to be included. In that, the labeling and radical perspectives have much to contribute.

Notes

1. It is noteworthy that contemporary anomie theorists show a concern with both deviance and conformity and with social forces that invite (but do not determine) specific responses. All chapters in the present book offer various insights into this structuring process (Cullen, 1984). These ways can be combined toward a more complete understanding of humans coping with problems. This is possible, because, although each explores

diverse social, economic, or cultural sources of problems/strain and socially provided remedies to them, they all adopt a "structure-choice-structure" ontological view (Blau, 1990; Giddens, 1979).

2. Runciman has argued that normative reference groups may also generate relative deprivation if they embody an unfavorable comparison (Runciman, 1966, p. 12). But, when normative reference groups have this effect, we are merely confronted with situations where they also perform the comparative function; in other words, these are cases in which a referent performs both normative and comparative functions.

3. It is interesting to see how the argument of these strong critics of Merton are rendered compatible with anomie theory through this elaboration.

4. Incidentally, it becomes clear that to say that Merton did not make these connections explicit and thus failed to "explain the primacy of such ideals as symptomatic of capitalist economic structures" (Muncie and Fitzgerald, 1985, p. 408; see also Taylor et al., 1973, p. 101) does not tell against the validity of anomie theory. Rather, it applies to Merton's *exposition* of his theory (Downes and Rock, 1982, p. 105), and it describes the boundaries of the developing theory that can be expanded as indicated above (see also the elaboration of anomie theory by Messner and Rosenfeld, 1993, and this volume).

5. This brings us back to the importance of past/present comparisons.

6. This question was raised in a personal communication with David Downes.

7. Empirical researchers have assumed that anomie theory's assumptions can be tested through measures of gaps between people's aspiration levels and expectation levels. Although it is a clever way of doing empirical work and theory testing, it actually contradicts the theoretical expectations of the anomie perspective as elaborated here. In fact, if expectations are lower than aspirations, we would not expect higher rates of misconduct. Realistic adjustments should decrease the strains one might experience. To illustrate, fans are not terribly disappointed if their team loses a game to an opponent known to be formidable and virtually unbeatable. Disappointment is much stronger for the supporters of the favorite, when the favorite loses.

8. Social support, social capital, and their relevance to the developing anomie theory are elaborated in other chapters of this volume by Cullen and Wright, and Hagan and McCarthy, respectively.

References

Agnew, Robert. 1992. Foundation for a general strain theory of crime and delinquency. *Criminology* 30(1):47–87.

Aristotle. 1942. *Rhetorica*. Oxford.

Arlacchi, Pino. 1986. *Mafia business: The Mafia ethic and the spirit of capitalism*. London: Verso.

Becker, Howard S. 1963. *Outsiders: Studies in the sociology of deviance*. New York: Free Press.

Bernard, Thomas J. 1984. Control criticisms of strain theories. *Journal of Research in Crime and Delinquency* 21(4):353–72.

———. 1995. Merton versus Hirschi: Who is faithful to Durkheim's heritage. *Advances in Criminological Theory* 6:81–90.

Blau, Peter M. 1990. Structural constraints and opportunities: Merton's contributions to general theory. In *Robert K. Merton: Consensus and Controversy*, edited by J. Clark, C. Modgil, and S. Modgil, 141–55. London, New York, and Philadelphia: Falmer Press.

Bolte, K. M., and S. Hradil. 1984. *Soziale Ungleichheit in der Bundesrepublik Deutschland*. Opladen: Leske & Budrich.

Box, Steven. 1971. *Deviance, reality and society*. London: Holt, Rinehart & Winston.

Braithwaite, John. 1979. *Inequality, crime and public policy*. London: Routledge & Kegan Paul.

Braungart, R. G., and M. M. Braungart. 1986. Youth problems in the 1980s: Some multinational comparisons. *International Sociology* 1(4):359–80.

Briar, S., and I. Piliavin. 1965. Delinquency, situational inducements, and commitment to conformity. *Social Problems* 13(1):35–44.

Burton, Velmer S., Jr., and R. Gregory Dunaway. 1994. Strain, relative deprivation, and middle class delinquency. In *Varieties of Criminology*, edited by G. Barak, 79–95. Westport, Conn.: Praeger.

Burton, Velmer S., Jr., Francis T. Cullen, T. David Evans, and R. Gregory Dunaway. 1994. Reconsidering strain theory: Operationalization, rival theories, and adult criminality. *Journal of Quantitative Criminology* 10(3):213–39.

Clark, R. E. 1972. *Reference group theory and delinquency*. New York: Behavioral Publications.

Clinard, Marshall B., ed., 1964. *Anomie and deviant behavior: A discussion and critique*. New York: Free Press.

Cloward, Richard, and Lloyd Ohlin. 1960. *Delinquency and opportunity*. New York: Free Press.

Cohen, Albert K. 1965. The sociology of the deviant act: Anomie theory and beyond. *American Sociological Review* 30(1):5–14.

———. 1966. *Deviance and social control*. Englewood Cliffs, N.J.: Prentice-Hall.

Cole, J. R., and H. Zuckerman. 1964. Inventory of empirical and theoretical studies of anomie. In *Anomie and Deviant Behavior: A discussion and critique*, edited by Marshall B. Clinard, 243–313. New York: Free Press.

Cole, S. 1975. The growth of scientific knowledge: Theories of deviance as a case study. In *The Idea of Social Structure*, edited by Lewis A. Coser, 175–220. New York: Harcourt Brace Jovanovich.

Coleman, James. 1988. Social capital in the creation of human capital. *American Journal of Sociology* 94:95–120.

———. 1990. *Foundations of social theory*. Cambridge, Mass.: Harvard University Press.

Coser, Lewis A. 1965. The sociology of poverty. *Social Problems* 13(2):140–48.

Cullen, Francis T. 1984. *Rethinking crime and deviance: The emergence of a structuring tradition*. Totowa, N.J.: Rowman & Allanheld.

———. 1994. Social support as an organizing concept for criminology. *Justice Quarterly* 11(4):527–59.

Danziger, S. 1976. Explaining urban crime rates. *Criminology* 14(2):291–96.

Danziger, S., and D. Wheeler. 1975. The economics of crime: Punishment or income redistribution. *Review of Social Economy* 33:113–31.

DeFronzo, J. 1983. Economic assistance to impoverished Americans: The relationship to incidence of crime. *Criminology* 21(1):119–36.

Dicks, M. J. 1987. The financial behaviour of the UK personal sector, 1976–85. *Bank of England Quarterly Bulletin* 27(2):223–33.

Downes, David, and Paul Rock. 1982. *Understanding deviance: A guide to the sociology of crime and rule-breaking*. Oxford: Clarendon Press.

Duesenberry, J. S. 1967. *Income, saving, and the theory of consumer behavior*. New York: Oxford University Press.

Durkheim, Emile. [1930] 1983. *Le suicide*. Paris: Presses Universitaires de France.

Easterlin, R. A. 1973. Does money buy happiness? *The Public Interest* 30:3–10.

Eberts, P., and K. P. Schwirian. 1968. Metropolitan crime rates and relative deprivation. *Criminologica* 5(4):4–52.

Eco, Umberto. 1987. *Travels in hyperreality*. London: Picador.

Eisenstadt, S. N. 1954. Studies in reference group behavior, I: Reference norms and the social structure. *Human Relations* 7(2):191–216.

Friedrichs, J. 1985. Kriminalität und sozio-ökonomische Struktur von Großstädten. *Zeitschrift für Soziologie* 14(1):50–63.

Giddens, Anthony. 1979. *Central problems in social theory: Action, structure, and contradiction in social analysis*. Berkeley: University of California Press.

Governor of the Bank of England. 1988. Personal credit on perspective. *Bank of England Quarterly Bulletin* 28(1):48–50.

Hall, Stuart. 1974. Deviance, politics and the media. In *Deviance and Social Control*, edited by P. Rock and M. McIntosh, 261–305. London: Tavistock.

Heath, A. 1981. *Social mobility*. Glasgow: William Collins Sons.

Heiland, H.-G. 1983. *Wohlstand und Diebstahl*. Bremen: Skarabäus.

Hirschi, Travis, and H. C. Selvin. 1967. *Delinquency research: An appraisal of analytic methods*. New York: Free Press.

Hyman, H. H. 1942. The psychology of status. *Archives of Psychology* 269.

———. 1967. The value systems of different classes: A social psychological contribution to the analysis of stratification. In *Class, Status, and Power*, edited by R. Bendix and S. M. Lipset, 147–65. London: Routledge & Kegan Paul.

———. 1975. Reference individuals and reference idols. In *The Idea of Social Structure: Papers in Honor of Robert K. Merton*, edited by L. A. Coser, 265–82. New York: Harcourt Brace Jovanovich.

Jacobs, D. 1981. Inequality and economic crime. *Sociology and Social Research* 66(1):12–28.

Keller, S., and E. Stern. 1968. Spontaneous group references in France. In *Readings in Reference Group Theory and Research*, edited by H. H. Hyman and E. Singer, 199–206. New York: Free Press.

Kelley, H. H. 1952. The functions of reference groups. In *Readings in Social Psychology*, edited by G. E. Swanson, T. M. Newcomb, and E. L. Hartley, 410–14. New York: Henry Holt.

Kelly, Robert J., Ko-Lin Chin, and Jeffrey Fagan. 1993. Dragon breeds fire: Chinese organized crime in New York City. *Crime, Law and Social Change* 19(3):245–69.

Klages, H. 1975. *Die unruhige Gesellschaft: Untersuchungen über Grenzen und Probleme sozialer Stabilität*. Munich: Beck.

———. 1981. *Überlasteter Staat—verdrossene Bürger? Zu den Dissonanzen der Wohlfahrtgesselschaft*. Frankfurt: Campus.

————. 1984. Wohlstandsgesellschaft und Anomie. In *Wohlfahrtsstaat und Soziale Probleme*, edited by H. Haferkamp, 6–30. Opladen: Westdeutscher Verlag.

Klages, H., and W. Herbert. 1983. *Wertorientierung und Staatsbezug: Untersuchunger zur politischen Kultur in Bundesrepublik Deutschland.* Frankfurt: Campus.

Lazarsfeld, P. F., and Robert K. Merton. 1952. Mass communication, popular taste, and organized social action. In *Readings in Social Psychology*, edited by G. E. Swanson, T. M. Newcomb, and E. L. Hartley, 74–85. New York: Henry Holt.

Lea, John, and Jock Young. 1984. *What is to be done about law and order?* Harmondsworth: Penguin.

Lipset, Seymour M., and H. L. Zetterberg. 1967. A theory of social mobility. In *Class, Status, and Power*, edited by R. Bendix and S. M. Lipset, 561–73. London: Routledge & Kegan Paul.

MacIver, R. M. 1950. *The ramparts we guard.* New York: Macmillan.

McClosky, H., and J. H. Schaar. 1965. Psychological dimensions of anomy. *American Sociological Review* 30(1):14–40.

Merton, Robert K. 1956. The socio-cultural environment and anomie. In *New Perspectives for Research on Juvenile Delinquency*, edited by L. H. Witmer and R. Kotinsky, 24–50. Washington, D.C.: U.S. Department of Health, Education and Welfare.

————. 1957. Priorities in scientific discovery: A chapter in the sociology of science. *American Sociological Review* 22(6):635–59.

————. 1964. Anomie, anomia, and social interaction: Contexts of deviant behavior. In *Anomie and Deviant Behavior: A Discussion and Critique*, edited by M. B. Clinard, 213–42. New York: Free Press.

————. 1968. *Social theory and social structure.* New York: Free Press.

————. 1982. *Social research and the practicing professions.* Cambridge, Mass.: Abt Books.

Merton, V., Robert K. Merton, and E. Barber, 1983. Client ambivalence in professional relationships: The problem of seeking help from strangers. *New Directions in Helping* 2:13–44.

Messner, Steven F. 1988. Merton's "social structure and anomie": The road not taken. *Deviant Behavior* 9:33–53.

Messner, Steven F., and Richard Rosenfeld. 1993. *Crime and the American dream.* Belmont, Calif.: Wadsworth.

Muncie, J., and M. Fitzgerald. 1985. Humanising the deviant: Affinity and affiliation. In *Crime and Society: Readings in History and Theory*, edited by M. Fitzgerald, G. McLennan, and J. Pawson, 403–28. London: Routledge & Kegan Paul.

Newcomb, T. M. 1950. *Social psychology.* New York: Dryden.

Orrù, Marco. 1987. *Anomie: History and meanings.* Boston: Allen & Unwin.

Passas, Nikos. 1988. *Merton's theory of anomie and deviance: An elaboration.* Ph.D. dissertation, University of Edinburgh.

————. 1990. Anomie and corporate deviance. *Contemporary Crises* 14(3):157–78.

————. 1995. Continuities in the anomie tradition. *Advances in Criminological Theory* 6:91–112.

————. forthcoming. *Consolidating criminology.* Albany, N.Y.: SUNY Press.

Riesman, D. [1950] 1953. *The lonely crowd.* New York: Doubleday/Anchor Books.

Ross, C. E., and J. Mirowski. 1987. Normlessness, powerlessness, and trouble with the law. *Criminology* 25(2):257–77.

Runciman, W. G. 1966. *Relative deprivation and social justice: A study of attitudes to social inequality in twentieth century England.* London: Routledge & Kegan Paul.

———. 1968. Problems of research on relative deprivation. In *Readings in Reference Group Theory and Research,* edited by H. H. Hyman and E. Singer, 69–76. New York: Free Press.

Sampson, Robert J., and W. Byron Groves. 1989. Community structure and crime: Testing social-disorganization theory. *American Journal of Sociology* 94(4):774–802.

Schacht, Richard. 1982. Doubts about anomie and anomia. In *Alienation and Anomie Revisited,* edited by S. G. Shoham and A. Grahame, 71–92. Tel Aviv: Ramot.

Shelley, Louise I. 1981. *Crime and modernization: The impact of industrialization and urbanization on crime.* Carbondale and Edwardsville: Southern Illinois University Press.

Sherif, M. 1969. Reference group in human relations. In *Sociological Theory,* edited by L. A. Coser and B. Rosenberg, 283–88. New York: Macmillan.

Shibutani, T. 1955. Reference groups as perspectives. *American Journal of Sociology* 60(6):562–669.

Shields, J. 1988. Controlling household credit. *National Institute Economic Review* 125:46–55.

Smelser, Neil. 1968. Toward a general theory of social change. In *Essays in Sociological Explanation,* edited by N. Smelser, 192–280. Englewood Cliffs, N.J.: Prentice-Hall.

Smith, D. M. [1979] 1985. *Where the grass is greener: Living in an unequal world.* Harmondsworth: Penguin.

Srole, Leo. 1956a. Anomie, authoritarianism and prejudice. *American Journal of Sociology* 62(1):63–67.

———. 1956b. Social integration and certain corollaries: An exploratory study. *American Sociological Review* 21(6):709–16.

Stack, S. 1984. Income inequality and property crime. *Criminology* 22(2):229–57.

Sztompka, Piotr. 1986. *Robert K. Merton: An intellectual profile.* London: Macmillan.

Taylor, Ian, Paul Walton, and Jock Young. 1973. *The new criminology.* London: Routledge & Kegan Paul.

Taylor, M. 1982. Improving conditions, rising expectations, and dissatisfaction: A test of the past/present relative deprivation hypothesis. *Social Psychology Quarterly* 45:24–33.

Thio, A. 1975. A critical look at Merton's anomie theory. *Pacific Sociological Review* 18:139–58.

Tilly, Charles. 1978. *From mobilisation to revolution.* London: Addison-Wesley.

Tittle, Charles R. 1995. *Control balance: Toward a general theory of deviance.* Boulder, Colo.: Westview.

Toby, J. 1967. Affluence and adolescent crime. In *Task Force Report: Juvenile Delinquency and Youth Crime,* 132–94. The President's Commission on Law Enforcement and Administration of Justice. Washington, D.C.: U.S. Government Printing Office.

Turner, R. H. 1956. Role-taking, role standpoint, and reference group behavior. *American Journal of Sociology* 61(4):316–28.

———. 1964. *The social context of ambition.* San Francisco: Chandler.

Urry, John. [1973] 1978. *Reference groups and the theory of revolution.* London: Routledge & Kegan Paul.

Westergaard, J., and H. Resler. [1975] 1982. *Class in a capitalist society: A study of contemporary Britain.* Harmondsworth: Penguin.

Williams, R. M., Jr. 1975. Relative deprivation. In *The Idea of Social Structure: Papers in Honor of Robert K. Merton,* edited by L. A. Coser, 355–78. New York: Harcourt Brace Jovanovich.

Wohl, R. R. 1967. The "rags to riches" story: An episode of secular idealism. In *Class, Status and Power,* edited by R. Bendix and S. Lipset, 501–6. London: Routledge & Kegan Paul.

Young, Jock. [1971] 1982. Beyond the consensual paradigm: A critique of left functionalism in media theory. In *The Manufacture of News: Social Problems, Deviance and the Mass Media,* edited by S. Cohen and J. Young, 393–421. London: Constable.

DIANE VAUGHAN

Anomie Theory and Organizations: Culture and the Normalization of Deviance at NASA

In the scholarly quest to understand the causes of misconduct by government, corporations, athletic teams, and myriad additional organizational manifestations, culture has been an important explanatory variable. To a great extent, however, its true effects have eluded us. We have theorized about it, but we have few empirical studies. Merton's (1958) SSAT poses a single cultural imperative: economic success. The imagery matches what we intuitively know and understand about life in this capitalistic society. Some theorists, following Merton, have cited the drive for economic success at the societal level in formulating causal explanations, then theorized about how it affects organizational culture, consistently invoking competition for economic success as the dominant cultural imperative driving illegal acts in the workplace (Barnett, 1981; Braithwaite, 1989; Cohen, D.V., 1995; Coleman, 1987; Gross, 1980). The term "criminogenic" has been used to describe both industries and organizations where these factors are found (Denzin, 1977; Clinard and Yeager, 1980; Farberman, 1975). The term connotes a cultural context conducive to misconduct.

However, research has been stymied in exploring the relationship between culture and organizational misconduct by a paucity of data and research that is, by definition, retrospective. Empirical work on violative behavior in industries, across organizations, or even case studies of organizations has not been able to study culture directly but inferred its existence when competitive pressures, resource scarcity, and violations occur in conjunction. With the exception of Geis's (1967) Heavy Electrical Equipment Antitrust Case and Quinney's (1963) study of prescription violations by retail pharmacists, in which he connected occupational norms with the actions of pharmacists, we have no systematic examination of the effects of culture on individual decisions to violate.

Overall, in research and theory on misconduct in and by organizations,

scholars have assumed a trickle-down effect: the Mertonian cultural imperative at the societal level finds expression in the normative environment of
certain industries and certain organizations. From this, we presume that the
cultural imperative to achieve competitive success creates a unidimensional
culture in organizations that affects individual choice. From structural data,
we assume a theory of individual choice that is driven by a single cultural
imperative. Moreover, the conjunction of rule violations, competitive pressures, and scarcity invariably leads us to implicit and often unarticulated
assumptions about intent: a rational choice theory of individual decision
making that (typically) has managers as "amoral calculators," weighing the
costs and benefits of violative behavior and proceeding, regardless of the
social harm that might ensue (Kagan and Scholz, 1984, pp. 179–85).

However, people are carriers of culture, and our own experience, both as
individuals and as members of organizations, suggests that hanging the
causal explanation on a unidimensional cultural hook does not match reality.
A great deal of variation exists. In the literature on deviance and social
control, the long standing documentation of subcultures contradicts any assumptions about isomorphism between societal culture and the culture of
socially organized settings within that dominant culture (see, e.g., Cohen,
1955; Miller, 1958). Cultural variation also is extensively documented in the
organizations literature, where cultural dynamics, not statics, are taken for
granted, where multiple subcultures can be identified in a single organization, and where managers—and sometimes even their subordinates—
apparently can create and change culture at will.[1] Complex cultures of choice
are at work in organizations. We also know from Herbert Simon's (1957a;
1975b) work on "bounded rationality" and "satisficing" in organizations that
factors are at work consistently undermining the sort of rational choice assumption that so frequently permeates the organizational misconduct literature. Therefore, we cannot make assumptions about how culture plays out
in organizational decision making without research identifying the relevant
characteristics of a particular culture and tracing the connection between
cultural imperatives and choice—the macro-micro connection.

In this chapter, I will examine the relationship between culture and decision making in NASA's 1986 space shuttle *Challenger* tragedy. My research
on NASA's *Challenger* launch decision is part of a long-term project on organizational misconduct in which Merton's SSAT plays a major role. The project
originated in an analysis of Merton's texts, as well as analyses of them by
other theorists.[2] This examination led to my (1983) reconceptualization that
expanded the range of possible applications of SSAT to include individuals

of the middle- and upper-class strata and organizations as the units of analysis. I begin this essay with a summary of my reconceptualization and the rationale for using the Mertonian framework to examine misconduct by individuals of other social classes, as well as the misconduct of organizations. Then I will discuss my use of SSAT to guide an analysis of decision making at NASA and the *Challenger* tragedy (Vaughan, 1996).

The research is an historical ethnography: a reconstruction of structure and process using archival data as the primary data sources, supplemented by interviews. The book addresses two questions: Why, in the years preceding the disaster, did NASA continue launching the shuttle despite in-flight anomalies on the solid rocket boosters that became more frequent and more serious? And why did NASA launch the *Challenger*, despite warnings from engineers that the launch was risky? Here, I draw selectively from the full case analysis, narrowing the focus to the history of decision making from 1977 to 1985. The purpose is to use data on culture and decision making at NASA to reconsider the cultural aspects of Merton's SSAT. The discussion in the next section is condensed from Vaughan, 1983, pp. 54–104.

A Reconceptualization: Position in a Structure, Social Class, and Organizations

Merton developed SSAT to explain rates of deviant behavior by individuals. His theory, perhaps the most widely cited and tested of all theories of deviance, has received scholarly criticism for many reasons, among them its failure to address the deviant and criminal behavior of the middle- and upper-class offenders who are less likely to show up in the crime statistics. In 1938, when Merton published the first version of SSAT, the Uniform Crime Reports had been in existence since 1933. Not only did those reports initiate the construction of crime as a social problem in this country, but the kinds of crimes included—street crimes—focused attention on the crimes of the working class. This historical context, and perhaps Merton's boyhood in a working-class Philadelphia neighborhood, may explain his emphasis on the deviance of the working class. Although in later versions he discusses at some length the deviant business practices of the elite, the thrust of his argument is that the social structure exerts greater pressures toward deviation on those in the lower part of the class structure.

However, the applicability of the Mertonian framework is not restricted to the working class. It applies to people across the class spectrum and to organizations. This broader application of SSAT calls for recognition of two

heretofore underrecognized aspects of Merton's work. First, SSAT traditionally is viewed—and taught—as a theory that is "about" social class. But that
perception is only partially accurate. The theory is about *position in a structure*, a broader category that includes, but is not restricted to, social class.
Social location is the linchpin of anomie theory, not social class. Second,
resource scarcity and competition are implicit through Merton's exegesis,
although he seldom refers to them explicitly. Consequently, both socially
approved means and culturally approved success goals can be reconceptualized as scarce resources for which both individuals and organizations compete. This reconceptualization eliminates two criticisms that are often leveled
at SSAT: the theory falsely assumes a uniform, collectively held, culturally
approved goal; and that goal is economic success. Moreover, Merton's concepts of "means" and "ends" have often created research difficulty because
the empirical referents of means and ends cannot be disentangled. Recon-
ceptualizing both as scarce resources for which individuals compete eliminates this problem as well. I will expand on this overview to show first how
his paradigm extends to individuals across the class structure and then how
it applies to organizations.

BREAKING THE CLASS BARRIER

Distilled to its essence, Merton's argument is as follows: position in the social
structure allows some social actors to compete for goals and excludes others.
Those competing for goals tend to follow rules and norms, and those excluded
from the competition tend toward deviance (among other options). An un-
stated assumption is that once in the competition, actors have equal access
to goals. But what happens to those in the middle and upper class who have
the legitimate means (or opportunity structures, usually defined empirically
as education and jobs) and thus appear to have gotten into the competition?
Not all who get in the competition can win because *the resources that represent success are in scarce supply.* So, for example, having a bachelor's degree
does not guarantee getting a job; getting a job does not guarantee keeping it;
keeping it does not guarantee a promotion or raise. At each attempt to move
up the social ladder, scarce resources can block goal attainment.

Furthermore, attaining a goal does not mean that competition for scarce
resources necessarily stops. To the contrary, the societal scripts about position in a structure and success that Merton so aptly identified make us constantly vulnerable to rising expectations (Vaughan, 1983, p. 59). Having
achieved a goal, we establish a new one. The result is competition for both
access to legitimate means and culturally approved ends, even for those of

the middle and upper class who have the social and cultural capital to get into the competition. And when a competitor is threatened with loss in the competition, "innovation" may be one result. At each position in the stratification system, the resources representing success may be scarce, so that social actors must compete to elevate their status, maintain it, or prevent a downward trajectory. Thus, scarcity, competition, and rising expectations create the possibility of blocked opportunities and anomie across the class spectrum. We might hypothesize, under these circumstances, that the consequent structural strain would systematically generate innovation and the other modes of adaptation Merton specifies throughout the social structure.

SSAT AND ORGANIZATIONS

Simmel (1950) believed that the forms of interaction were the exclusive domain of sociology. The task was to explore not the discrepant and the unique but to discover the underlying uniformities across events and social settings. In Simmel's formal analysis, certain features of concrete phenomena are extracted from reality, allowing us to compare phenomena that appear radically different in concrete content yet are essentially similar in structural arrangement. Thus, the sociologist could identify martial conflict and marital conflict as essentially similar interactive forms. From this perspective, organizations are legitimate subjects of analysis for a theory originally designed to explain rates of deviance by individuals, because all deviance occurs in socially organized settings, and Merton's emphasis on position in a structure and the sources generating anomie are similar structural arrangements that apply equally to individuals and organizations. In fact, in many ways SSAT appears better suited to explain the deviant and violative behavior of formal and complex organizations than that of individuals.

Organizations also occupy positions in the social structure, are exposed to culturally approved goals, and experience blocked opportunities. Although individuals may hold other values than economic success, such as altruism or cooperation, organizations, regardless of altruistic or cooperative goals, still are subject to competitive pressures to acquire the resources necessary to survive. It is imperative that they do so. For organizations, scarcity is always a factor, regardless of position in the organizational stratification system. Those at the top must compete to secure their top standing; others compete to be upwardly mobile or maintain standing; those at the bottom compete to keep from failing altogether. Logically, organizations, too, are subject to rising expectations, that is, setting new goals once one is achieved.

The condition of anomie so essential to precipitating innovation appears to be perpetual for organizations. According to Merton, innovation is likely to be chosen as a survival strategy when support diminishes for legitimate procedures for reaching desired goals. The societal standards guiding the conduct of organizations are ambiguous and thus are ineffective at regulating organizations.[3] The formal rules promulgated by social control agents reflect this situation. They fail to regulate because most often they are *mala prohibita* rather than *mala in se*. Normatively, a fine line exists between a clever workplace decision and misconduct: often, it is not at all clear what constitutes deviance. As a result, organizations, struggling to improve their rank, maintain it, or keep from dropping out of the organizational stratification system entirely, also are subject to anomie. Whether examining individuals or organizations, the structural arrangements generating deviance appear to hold, regardless of social location.

This conclusion gains affirmation through the extension of Merton's (1968; 1995; 1997, this volume) notion of opportunity structures. Although the social structure may produce tensions for organizations to seek scarce resources by illegal methods, misconduct cannot be understood by these structural tensions alone. Opportunities must be available to obtain the sought-after resources for which organizations compete (Cloward and Ohlin, 1960). These opportunities are present and readily available to personnel in legitimate organizations in the form of organization structure, processes, and transactions (Vaughan, 1983, pp. 67–87). Created for the purpose of conducting legitimate activity, these factors also are the mechanisms by which deviant acts may be carried out. They provide legitimate means that, in the face of competition for scarce resources, can be used to achieve organization goals illegally. Organization structure facilitates misconduct as a solution to blocked opportunities by creating structural secrecy, that is, many settings where specialization, geographic distance, and division of labor minimize the risk of detection and sanctioning; organization processes facilitate misconduct by creating a normative environment—a culture—that supports individual action that conforms to organization goals; and transactions, either by their computerized or documentary form, encourage misconduct by providing difficult-to-monitor mechanisms for carrying out illegal acts that conceal rather than reveal. Combined, organization structure, processes, and transactions supply opportunities for organizations to opt for misconduct in response to the competitive environment and the pressures it generates.

The major concepts that allow the Mertonian framework to be extended both to individuals of various social classes and to organizations are position in a structure, competition, scarce resources, and opportunity structures.

Merton's original texts contain the logic for extending this reconceptualization to organizations. Not only is it theoretically appropriate and legitimate to do so, but it is advantageous. It escapes the confusion of empirical referents for means and ends. Moreover, it allows us to explore deviance and misconduct in a variety of socially organized settings, thus maximizing the possibility of a general theory.

Method

I gained the above insights about SSAT by shifting units of analysis: reconsidering a theory developed to explain rates of deviance among individuals with organizations in mind. I did it intuitively, realizing that comparison of similar phenomena in differentially organized social settings was not only consistent with Simmel's formal sociology but also an extremely productive way to theorize. As a result of this (1983) reconceptualization of Mertonian theory, I began a more systematic development of the method itself. This mode of theory elaboration (Vaughan, 1992a; 1992b) undergirds my analysis of the *Challenger* case. It can be briefly be summarized as follows.

Theory elaboration is a strategy for developing general theory about similar phenomena that occur in organizational forms that vary in size, complexity, and function. It relies on qualitative data, which can include interviews, case studies, ethnography, or historical studies. Theory can be elaborated using secondary analysis as well. By theory, I mean theoretical tools in general (theory, models, and/or concepts) rather than a more restricted formal meaning (a set of interrelated propositions that are testable and explain some phenomenon). By elaboration, I mean the process of refinement to specify more carefully the circumstances in which it does or does not offer potential for explanation. By cases, I mean organizational forms that are analyzed regarding some similar event, activity, or circumstance, for example, social control in family, nation-state, or professional association.

The goal is not to test theory, in a deductive, positivistic mode, but to use it as an heuristic device to guide the analysis. As the analysis proceeds, the guiding theoretical notions are assessed in the light of the findings. Following strictly the principles of analytic induction (Lindesmith, 1947), the researcher may find the data contradict the starting theory, reveal previously unseen inadequacies, confirm the theory, or develop new hypotheses. In general, we come up with a clearer sense of the situations in which the theory does or does not apply. This clarification occurs because the method dictates that each case be explained, making vivid similarities and differences across cases.

Perhaps the greatest benefit of this method is the possibility it creates for making macro-micro links. This comes as a result of combining qualitative analysis with the comparative study of a variety of socially organized settings. By varying social settings, we gain access to data that are perhaps unavailable if we analyzed only organizations similar in size, complexity, and function. In the case of organizational misconduct, for example, data on processes and decision making that are hard to obtain when a large, powerful corporate profit-seeker is the research target may be obtained when we examine misconduct in other organizational forms.

THE ANALYTIC FRAMEWORK, CASE SELECTION, AND THE MACRO-MICRO LINK

My analysis of NASA's decision to launch the *Challenger* was begun as part of a project to elaborate a general theory of organizational misconduct. My working definition of organizational misconduct (also susceptible to redefinition as part of the method) was violation of laws, regulations, or rules by acts of omission or commission by individuals or groups of individuals acting in their organization roles in behalf of organization goals.

Prior to the *Challenger* disaster, I had already chosen police misconduct and family violence as two cases for comparison and was looking for an example concerning a large, complex organization that was not a corporate profit-seeker. My chief interest was in the macro-micro connection: How do competitive pressures, opportunity structures, and normative environments affect the action of individuals? Making this connection required linking environment, organization, and individual choice. For use as a heuristic guide for organizing the data in the case analyses, I reduced my detailed causal model (1983) to the following skeletal analytic framework, built around SSAT as the major conceptual apparatus:

Competitive Environment: The Structural "Push." Competition, scarce resources, and norms create structural pressures to violate laws, rules, or regulations (1983, pp. 54–66).

Organization Characteristics: Opportunity Structures. When resource scarcity blocks opportunities, organization structure, processes, and transactions provide legitimate opportunities to respond to competitive pressures with misconduct (1983, pp. 67–87).

Regulatory Environment: Structural Barriers to Effectiveness. The above two conditions are necessary but not sufficient to explain misconduct. The regulatory environment plays an important role in determining individual choice. The structure of regulatory relations is characterized by autonomy and interdependence, which present obstacles to social control. Autonomy and interdependence between regulator and regulated organizations tend to create obstacles at all phases of the social-control process and systematically to mitigate regulatory effectiveness. By virtue of its ineffectiveness, the regulatory environment also contributes to organizational misconduct (1983, pp. 88–105).

I chose the *Challenger* disaster as the third case comparison because post-tragedy evidence suggested that the conditions typical of other examples of organizational misconduct existed. First and paramount, NASA personnel appeared to have violated both industry rules and internal NASA rules designed to assure safety. People committing violations to achieve the goals and interest of the organization to which they belong is what makes misconduct "organizational." Second, the conditions stipulated by the Mertonian paradigm were obvious. Competitive pressures and resource scarcity originating in the environment were widely acknowledged to have created production pressure at NASA. The number of scheduled flights per year was increasing without adequate resources to meet that schedule, creating a strain on the organization. Thus, the safety rule violations suggested that NASA decision makers knowingly risked safety to keep the shuttle flying and to meet the production goals. Third, organization characteristics appeared to have facilitated wrongdoing by providing opportunities for misconduct: structure obscuring what was happening from insiders and outsiders alike; an organization culture described as "success-oriented," "can-do," and "a pressure cooker"; a transaction system for the exchange of information that became a mechanism for concealing rather than revealing technical problems. And, finally, in parallel with other cases of misconduct, safety regulatory ineffectiveness was well documented.

CULTURE AND DECISION MAKING AT NASA: A COMPLEX CHOICE ENVIRONMENT

Overall, the case suggested that NASA had a normative environment, or culture, where production concerns had priority over safety. The implication, based on rule violations, economic strain, and production pressures occurring in conjunction, was a rational choice theory: NASA middle managers acted as amoral calculators, knowingly violating safety rules and proceeding with the *Challenger* launch despite engineering warnings that it was risky to do so. Production concerns had corrupted the former R&D agency's technical culture, impacting on decision making. The macro-micro link—exploring the possible connection between scarcity and competition originating in the environment and rule-violating behavior by NASA managers—was a major focus of my inquiry. The advantage of this much-publicized case was that data were available to connect structure with agency. In addition to the extensive media coverage, the Presidential Commission (1986) published five volumes, and the U.S. House Committee on Science and Technology (1986) published three. All original documents collected by the Commission are available at the National Archives, as well as transcripts of 160 interviews collected by official investigators assisting the Commission. However, as I went deeper into original sources than the Presidential Commission's Volume I (an extensive summary of its findings, but a summary nonetheless), I discovered that many of my beginning assumptions about the case were wrong.

After a year of examining the extensive archival records, a critical turning point came when I found that two of NASA's well-publicized "rule violations" were not rule violations but actions that conformed to NASA rules (Vaughan, 1996, pp. 56–62).[4] Two things were clear: (1) these controversial NASA actions that outsiders defined as deviant after the accident were not defined as deviant by insiders at the time the actions took place; and (2) my beginning hypothesis of organizational misconduct was based on rule violations, and I hadn't found any yet. Apparently—and in addition to whatever political factors were driving the investigation—the Commission's Volume I was not based on a thorough understanding of the NASA culture, as evidenced by the mistaken conclusions about the rules and procedures that guided decision making. These discoveries alerted me to the importance of an ethnographic approach to the case that would reveal more about NASA culture prior to the accident and the meaning of actions to insiders at the time those actions were taken (Geertz, 1973). NASA culture was available to me in the historic record: technical diagrams and documents, memos and letters, NASA formal language and everyday expressions, rules and procedures, and both verbatim and paper trail descriptions of how people in this agency behaved in the 1970s and 1980s.

As a consequence, I expanded the research focus from the launch decision itself to the history of decision making about the solid rocket booster joints from the beginning of the shuttle program in 1977. I felt this was necessary, because the official reports suggested that rules had been violated from the early design and development period of the shuttle throughout the program. To investigate each of these alleged rule violations (a strategy necessary to my starting hypothesis), I started over. I reconstructed events chronologically, examining the social context of each launch decision. The history of decision making, 1977–85, produced two important discoveries:

1. *A five-step decision-making sequence in which the working engineers redefined each incident of technical deviation of the solid rocket booster (SRB) joints as an acceptable risk in their official launch recommendations.* This sequence was repeated, becoming a pattern. Each time tests or flight experience produced signals of potential danger, the risk of the SRBs was negotiated between NASA and Thiokol working engineers. Each time the working engineers produced an engineering analysis indicating the SRBs were an acceptable risk. This pattern indicated the existence of a *work group culture* in which the managers and engineers working on the SRB problems constructed beliefs and procedural responses that became routinized. The dominant belief, grounded in a three-factor technical rationale, was that the SRB joints were not a threat to flight safety. From the early development period until the eve of the *Challenger* launch, the work group's cultural construction of risk of the O-ring problem became institutionalized. Despite dissensus about what should be done about the problem, the working engineers who assessed risk—obviously worried, as memos indicated— nonetheless *initiated* recommendations that the SRB joints were an acceptable flight risk in official decisions.

2. *Decision making in the work group conformed to NASA rules.*[5] With all procedural systems for negotiating risk in place and adhering to the requirements of those systems, NASA managers made a disastrous decision. Rule violations are a key aspect of the definition of organizational misconduct. But the finding that the work group responsible for decision making about the SRBs conformed to NASA rules and guidelines indicated that the *Challenger* tragedy was not an example of misconduct, at least as I had defined it in my working definition. What became interesting about the case, then, was not rule violations. Rather, it was the normalization of deviance. By "normalization of deviance," I mean that technical incidents that the work group initially interpreted as deviant were, after engineering analysis, reinterpreted as within the norm for acceptable joint performance. Gradually—*and fatally*—over time the working engineers and managers systematically expanded the bounds of acceptable risk, making an incremental descent into poor judgment.

Because theory elaboration relies on qualitative case analysis, explaining a particular case may lead us to elaborate theory in unexpected directions. In the NASA case, culture turned out to be a major explanatory variable.

The case exposed the process by which deviant incidents were repeatedly normalized and the factors that contributed to insiders' definition of the situation as SRB problems occurred. Gradually, a work-group culture developed that blinded people to the harmful consequences of their actions. This work-group culture shows how individuals in organizations, interacting about a task, initiate a culture that then influences subsequent decision making. Importantly, this work-group culture was sustained by macrolevel cultural meaning systems that overlapped. Competition, resource scarcity, and norms in the competitive environment played a major role in decision making, but that role was very different than in most postdisaster interpretations: these factors altered the culture, affecting managers and engineers alike, resulting in the normalization of deviance prior to the *Challenger* launch.

The institutional forces and ethnographic data necessary to document the case fully cannot be presented in an essay-length discussion. The following summarizes the history of decision making from 1977 to 1985. I will discuss some of the data and some of the findings about culture that this case provided. Additional factors (e.g., organization structure) contributed importantly to the outcome; therefore, interested readers should refer to Vaughan, 1996.

Risk, Culture, and the Normalization of Deviance

The *Challenger* tragedy was not the result of a single decision—or even the several decisions—made on the eve of the launch. It was choice in which the past played a determining role. The launch decision cannot be understood without understanding that preexisting construction of risk of the SRB joints, its origin, and persistence. In the history of decision making, a cultural construction of risk developed that became a part of the worldview that many participants brought to the 27 January 1986 teleconference. From 1977 to 1985, people in the work group assigned to the SRBs normalized the technical deviation they discovered, so that it became normal, acceptable, and nondeviant to them (Vaughan, 1996, pp. 77–195). At the macrolevel, a multilayered and complex culture of production perpetuated the normalization of deviance at the microlevel (1996, pp. 196–237).

Engineering culture—in the aerospace industry and at NASA—was an important institutional context that contributed to the normalization of deviance in the work group. Flight anomalies were a taken-for-granted part of the space shuttle program from its inception. Problems were common in all innovative aerospace designs, because engineering calculations, tests, and experiments could not duplicate the forces of nature that each mission would experience. Moreover, the shuttle design was unprecedented. In addition, damage due to the forces of nature was expected on each flight, requiring complete assessment and extensive refurbishment of the vehicle before the next mission. Consequently, problems were expected, and risk assessment was carried out on a daily basis. But the shuttle program was based on the assumption that after everything that could be done to remove and control risk had been done, some residual risk would remain.

The guidelines for determining risk prior to each launch were set out in NASA's "Acceptable Risk Process" (Hammock and Raines, 1981). This risk-assessment procedure at NASA mandated that any deviation from expected performance during tests or flight be treated as a signal of potential danger, requiring engineering hazard analysis and corrective action, if necessary, to meet the engineering standards of risk acceptability. The determination of technical risk at NASA was the responsibility of work groups: the managers and engineers at Level IV and Level III of the NASA launch-decision chain who were assigned to do the technical work for each shuttle component. Thus, risk assessment was a bottom-up process. In the aftermath of the *Challenger* tragedy, the official investigations and other postaccident analysts reacted to and publicly defined as deviant behavior NASA's repeated launching with "acceptable risk" and "acceptable erosion" of the SRB joints. However, these analysts focused on outcomes and managers, ignoring bottom-up hazard analysis at NASA and the routine research processes and decision making among rank-and-file working engineers prior to the *Challenger* incident.

Also contradicting public understanding after the disaster, the practice of accepting risk was normative in the NASA culture: in assessing flight readiness, working engineers had to determine whether or not every component was an acceptable risk and present a technical rationale to back their decision. In flight readiness documents for all components, not just the SRB joints, the words "acceptable risk" appear. Following the guidelines of the Acceptable Risk Process, contractor and NASA engineers and managers at Level III and Level IV worked closely on a day-to-day basis assessing risk. Two weeks prior to each launch, risk assessment was formalized in a hierarchical review process known as Flight Readiness Review (FRR), which pulled together hundreds of people of varying specializations in all parts of the NASA/contractor system in the prelaunch decision process (Presidential Commission, 1986, pp. 82–83).

In FRR, each level of the NASA management hierarchy had to certify in writing to the flight readiness of the various shuttle elements to the level above it. At every level, FRR was adversarial. The presentation of engineering analysis, conclusions about flight readiness, and recommendations about flight were subject to harsh criticism in open meetings that were described as a "fishbowl" atmosphere so harsh that NASA manager Lawrence Wear said, "I've seen grown men cry" (personal interview, 2 June 1992). The purpose of the adversarialism was to ferret out flaws in the engineering analysis. Standards for technical arguments were rigorous. No recommendation of flight readiness was acceptable unless it was backed by a solid technical argument (Vaughan, 1996, pp. 90, 221, 342).

The launch-decision process began with Level IV contractor engineers, who made a formal determination of risk and flight readiness of their component for the upcoming mission, based on tests, calculations, and flight experience. They then reported their conclusions about flight readiness and risk acceptability to their counterparts (NASA Level IV managers and working engineers) who challenged their technical arguments and conclusions to assure the engineering analysis was rigorous. This process was repeated at the Level III FRR, chaired by the NASA Project Manager for that particular technical component. The Level III Project Manager was responsible for reporting and defending the work-group recommendations and conclusions about risk acceptability up the hierarchy in the Level II and Level I FRRs. The risk assessments and launch recommendations finally accepted by top administrators were based on initial recommendations and conclusions of the working engineers at the bottom of the FRR process.

THE SOLID ROCKET BOOSTER WORK-GROUP CULTURE

Early in the shuttle program, an unexpected problem developed in the SRB, which was the responsibility of Level III and IV managers and engineers at NASA's Marshall Space Flight Center (Huntsville, Alabama) and Level III and IV managers and engineers at the SRB contractor Morton Thiokol, Inc. (Wasatch, Iowa). Test results indicated that the SRB joint deviated from the performance predicted by the design. Because no precedent existed for the joint design, no precedent existed for responding to the problem. The shuttle was not yet flying, thus the test evidence presented no immediate threat to flight safety. However, the Acceptable Risk Process required that every unpredicted incident be treated as a signal of potential danger. The SRB work group—defined as the Level IV Marshall and Thiokol managers and engineers responsible for the SRB joints—responded to this first technical deviation of the joint, assessing the consequences of the new technical information for flight safety. The following events occurred in sequence:

1. Signals of potential danger
2. Official act acknowledging escalated risk
3. Review of evidence
4. Official act indicating the normalization of deviance: accepting risk
5. Shuttle launch

As Level IV and Level III Marshall and Thiokol engineers and managers negotiated the risk of the SRB joints in this five-step decision sequence, the work group normalized the deviant performance of the SRB joint. Once this first challenge to field joint integrity was resolved, management's definition of the seriousness of the problem and the method of responding to it (correct rather than redesign) became a collectively constructed cultural reality, incorporated into the worldview of the work group. The work group brought their construction of risk and their method of responding to the SRB joints to the next incident when signals of potential danger again challenged the prevailing construction of risk. Risk had to be renegotiated. The past—past problem definition, past method of responding to the problem—became part of the social context of decision making.

The significance of the above sequence of events lies not in its initial occurrence but in its repetition. Decision making became patterned (Vaughan, 1996, pp. 77–195). Many times in the shuttle's history, tests or flight performance deviated from expectations. Each time, the above sequence occurred. The connection between some incident in the past and the present is demonstrated when it is repeated. Patterns of the past—in this case, decision-making patterns pertaining to technical components—constitute part of the social context of decision making in the present. This decision-making pattern indicates the development of norms, procedures, and beliefs that characterized the work-group culture.

A culture is a set of solutions produced by a group of people to meet specific problems posed by the situations that they face in common. These solutions become institutionalized, remembered, and passed on as the rules, rituals, and values of the group (Van Maanen and Barley, 1985). With no formal rules to guide them initially about how to respond to technical deviation of the SRB joints, Level IV and III Marshall and Thiokol engineers and managers responsible for the SRB joints evolved a set of solutions to a problem they faced in common. That the initial solutions became a part of the work-group culture is indicated by its repetition: the work group generated norms, beliefs, and procedures relevant to its task. The importance of the shuttle launch concluding the sequence must be emphasized: The postflight engineering analysis of the SRB joint performance reinforced the engineering analysis and conclusions that went into the construction of risk prior to launch. Initially without guidelines, the work group evolved an unobtrusive normative structure that was reinforced over time and did, in fact, guide. A fundamental sociological notion is that choice creates structure, which in turn feeds back, influencing choice in a way that again feeds into structure, tending to affirm it (Giddens, 1979). In the history of decision making about the SRBs, we see this principle at work, as work-group participants in inter-action created a cultural construction of risk that, once created, influenced subsequent choices.

A culture is generally typified by a dominant worldview or ideology. Even as engineering concerns grew, the belief that the SRB design was an accept-able risk dominated the worldview of the work group. A technical analysis affirming that the primary and secondary O-rings worked as a redundant system was the basis of the work group's construction of the O-ring problem as an acceptable risk. Engineering analysis based on a three-factor technical rationale confirmed that, erosion notwithstanding, the primary O-ring would seal the joint, and if, under a rare and unexpected worst case condition, it should not, the secondary O-ring would act as a backup. Certainly there was dissent. Any culture encompasses many ways of thinking, feeling, and behaving that often conflict. Engineering controversy is normal, especially when a technologically innovative product is involved. And between Marshall and Thiokol working engineers, the "hands-on" people evaluating and con-structing risk each time a shuttle returned from space, disagreement about the dynamics of the joint began in the earliest phases of the shuttle program and persisted through the fateful teleconference on 27 January 1986.

But that dissent did not alter the work group's collective belief that the SRB joints were not a threat to flight safety from 1977 to 1985. Throughout the many controversies embedded in the history of the O-ring problem, this belief prevailed. It survived many challenges. It prevailed to the extent that it became institutionalized: encoded in NASA and Thiokol documents and the belief systems of work-group participants. Even in 1985, when two sig-nals of potential danger finally attracted sufficient attention that both Thiokol and NASA began funneling resources into a design modification, the belief that the design was an acceptable risk led working engineers repeatedly to recommend that space flight continue while they worked on the fix (Vaughan, 1996, pp. 153–95). Throughout 1985, the work group—and this included the Thiokol engineers who, on 27 January 1986, so vigorously voiced their objections to the *Challenger* launch—continued to recommend launching shuttles, based on the three-factor technical rationale that supported their decision to proceed with flight.

MICROLEVEL FACTORS AND CULTURAL PERSISTENCE

We must ask why the work group's cultural construction of risk persisted despite the fact that SRB joint in-flight anomalies continued and, on some flights, grew more serious. Decision making in organizations takes place in a social context that lends meaning to actions and incidents. Emerson (1983) notes the influence of "holistic effects" on decision making: the tendency for workers to process cases (or, at NASA, technical issues) not independently of others, but in ways that take into account the implications of other cases for the present one, and vice versa. The tendency to evaluate a problem in relation to some larger problem set is especially keen in situations of uncertainty and when the task is to assess the seriousness and priority of the problem in order to treat or control it. To understand the persistence of the work group's cultural construction of risk through the end of 1985, we must examine *how patterns of information affected risk assessments as the problem unfolded.*

One important aspect of the immediate decision context was that there *were* numerous other problem sets: having problems was normal at NASA. Many other technical problems existed, both on the SRBs and on other shuttle parts. SRB joint anomalies were occurring in a workplace environment where problems were normal and expected—and occurring—on every element of the space shuttle (Vaughan, 1996, pp. 79–82). This situation was not indicative of deviance at NASA but exemplifies normal technology. Wynne (1988) refers to it as "unruly technology": the inevitable uncertainties and ambiguous decision-judgment problems that exist in developing expert knowledge about technological systems. Every FRR report for every shuttle component identified numerous "Unsatisfactory Conditions," "Discrepancies," and "Anomalies" that had to be resolved before the next launch. Further, flying with these problems was normal and expected. Residual risk could not always be eliminated, but risk was acceptable (as the Acceptable Risk Process specified) if a hazard were corrected and/or sufficient technical rationale existed to believe that an anomaly was not a threat to flight safety. To correct and fly was the accepted method of dealing with anomalies. The existence of these other problem sets and the method of responding to them were important characteristics of the NASA culture that contributed to the normalization of deviance in the SRB work group.

Work-group decision making also took place in a context shaped by other decisions on the *same* problem. I call this the decision stream: the sequence of decisions made about a given case, or issue. At NASA, the production schedule created a circumstance where risk assessment of each technical artifact had to be made prior to each launch, creating a decision stream, or sequence, for each technical object. The working engineers were evaluating each deviant incident on its own merits and within a larger organizationally determined whole consisting of the decision stream for the SRB joint problems. Patterns of information affected the working engineers' definition of the situation. In summary, the microlevel factors contributing to cultural persistence were as follows:

1. technological uncertainty, lack of decision-making precedent, and absence of particularistic rules to guide decision making about the problem;

2. the temporal pattern of anomalies and the diverse possible causes made the problem ill-structured;

3. problem resolution had a "learning by doing" character, wherein the work group incrementally developed engineering rules to guide decision making as it went along;

4. deadlines cut into continuous risk assessment processes, requiring working engineers to convert uncertainty to certainty to give an official construction of risk in FRR;

5. the first decisions to accept deviance in the early development period established precedents for subsequent decisions;

6. decision making was sequential and interdependent, taking into account organizationally relevant problem sets;

7. the risk of each in-flight anomaly was assessed by analytic calculations, a variety of test results, subsequent flight experience. As a result of postflight engineering analysis, signals of potential danger were redefined in ways that made them acceptable: (a) some because they lost their salience in the hazard assessment process, (b) some because they were weak signals, (c) some because they were mixed, and (d) some, repeatedly conforming to predictions, became routine;

8. each decision to accept deviance was affirmed in numerous formal, public, adversarial reviews that reduced ambiguity and reinforced commitment to a line of action;

9. each decision to accept deviance had peer support (in the work group) and elite support (upper level NASA administrators);

10. each decision to accept deviance was reinforced after a flight when engineers compared their preflight predictions to joint flight performance. Thus, flight "success" reinforced all the engineering theories, procedures, beliefs, and practices that went into the work group's cultural construction of risk for that flight and all previous flights;

11. each decision was shaped by the preexisting construction of risk and the engineering theories, methods, and procedures on which it was based.

Collectively, these factors contributed to the normalization of deviance in the work group. Proceeding with launches under these circumstances was nothing more nor less than "normal engineering" within the culture.

MACROLEVEL FACTORS AND CULTURAL PERSISTENCE

The social context of decision making extends beyond the daily negotiation about the task in the workplace, however. People bring to their choice situations a variety of cultural scripts and meaning systems derived from the broader environment. The normative structure of the culture of production played an equally important role in the normalization of deviance by the work group (Vaughan, 1996, pp. 196–237). The culture of production was comprised of the institutionalized belief systems of the engineering profession, the aerospace industry, and the NASA organization. This institutional environment contributed to the persistence of the work group's cultural construction of risk—and thus the repeated decisions to accept risk and fly.

What was the role of the competitive environment—competition, scarce resources, and norms—on launch decision making during those years? Competitive pressures were brought into the organization through the actions of elites. Those actions altered the preexisting culture (i.e., norms and formal actions, as well), converting the R&D agency into a production-oriented concern. Rather than the single cultural imperative of economic success that Merton posited, however, NASA culture was permeated by a triumvirate of conflicting cultural imperatives: NASA's original technical culture, a strong bureaucratic culture, and a schedule-oriented production culture. This triumvirate originated in the external environment. NASA's original technical culture, developed during the Apollo program, derived from the culture of aerospace engineering as a profession. It materialized at NASA, and particularly at Marshall Space Flight Center, as conservatism, stringent adherence to engineering methods and standards for technical arguments, and professional accountability, which deferred to the authority of working engineers. According to McCurdy (1989) and Romzek and Dubnick (1987), this original technical culture *did not die out* during the shuttle program. It continued to exist, but it coexisted with other cultural imperatives that made its practices *more difficult to carry out*.

The original technical culture was forced to coexist in a culture that was redefined by the actions of political elites. These elite actions resulted in altering the culture of decision making at the bottom of the hierarchy by joining bureaucratic accountability and political accountability to NASA's original technical culture. The seeds for a production-oriented political accountability were in the engineering profession as an occupation located in technical production systems. Political accountability was joined to NASA's original technical culture by the actions of Congress and the Executive Branch, which jointly developed the policy that the space shuttle should provide routine, economical space flight, but then failed to provide the resources commensurate with achieving that goal; and the actions of NASA top administrators who sought to live up to this policy, despite the budget constraints, by pushing the launch schedule to ensure the survival of the agency and their own power base (Vaughan, 1996, pp. 17–32; 212–15). Bureaucratic accountability also had an external point of origin—in the culture of engineering as a profession educated for work in technical production systems, where rules are necessary to engineering analysis and to coordinate activities in the large, highly specialized firms where engineers often work. Bureaucratic accountability was elaborated at NASA by a preoccupation with bureaucratic proceduralism and hierarchical authority relations during the shuttle program that grew out of contracting out practices and the need to regulate an expanding, unwieldy system, as well as regulatory changes implemented during the Reagan administration (Vaughan, 1996, pp. 204–12).

The pressure that existed on the SRB work group was not just production pressure that was a response to the competition generated by scarce resources but *performance pressure that compelled them to conform to all three cultural imperatives*. Significantly, the work group struggled to conform to all three, including the meaning system developed in relation to the SRB joints in the work group. Indeed, the work group's definition of the SRB joint performance as normal and acceptable was reinforced by the *fact* of its conformity to the rules and norms of these various overlapping meaning systems: members of the group were assured in the correctness of their actions, because in all their technical and procedural choices they "went by the book" and "did everything we were supposed to do." Even in 1985, when working engineers at Thiokol expressed concern and attempted to get extra resources to resolve the problem, their rigorous conformity to the cultural beliefs and practices of the microlevel and macrolevel decision-making context reinforced their belief in the SRB joint's acceptable risk.

Most certainly, this was a system that predisposed certain kinds of choices over others. Production pressure in NASA's shuttle program was well documented after the disaster. Because Thiokol and Marshall working engineers originated all launch decisions with their risk assessments, we might justifiably ask if this was a system that pushed working engineers and managers alike to make decisions collusively, repeatedly, and knowingly that gave priority to the launch schedule over mission safety from 1977 to 1985? Consider, first, that the production schedule and launch safety were interrelated. Avoiding harmful technical incidents and disasters was a significant precept in the cultural meaning systems of engineering work, engineering as a bureaucratic profession, and in the NASA organization. Indeed, the history of decision making in the shuttle program indicates that delaying the production schedule for safety reasons was institutionalized at NASA. In the period between the Level I FRR and completion of countdown, only eight of twenty-five launches had no delays; the rest averaged two delays each.[6] Although the American press castigated NASA for incompetence every time launch was delayed, the reality was that NASA's launch delays were based on decision making in work groups concerned about safety and unwilling to allow a launch to proceed unless certain conditions were met.

The centrality of safety concerns to organization goals notwithstanding, both macrolevel cultural meaning systems and the SRB work group's own history of decision making were obstacles to changing the decision-making pattern. *As long as quantitative, rigorous, scientific analysis assured acceptable risk (original technical culture) and all rules were followed (bureaucratic accountability), then engineering concerns and intuitions were not enough to interrupt the schedule (political accountability).* For the work group members to reverse themselves at any point prior to the 1986 *Challenger* launch teleconference would have required a rejection of the engineering theories, methods, and procedures that they had previously advanced in FRR for all previous launches. To do so was an occupational risk, jeopardizing their professional integrity, causing them to lose face: they were either wrong then or wrong now.[7] But prior to the *Challenger* teleconference, reversing themselves was not an option they considered. To delay or halt the launch production schedule, as Marshall's SRB Project Chief Engineer Jim Smith pointed out, "You have to be able to show you've got a technical issue that is unsafe to fly" (personal interview, 8 June 1992). But that was not what the working engineers had. Indeed, they had the opposite: a cultural belief system in risk acceptability, based upon a now longstanding, experientially based, three-factor technical rationale justifying acceptable risk.

Initially, what were signals of potential danger lost their salience through engineering analysis, tests, and corrective actions; they had signals that were mixed, weak, and routine. These signals, occurring incrementally, diagnosed as the result of odd, localized deviant events that were resolved each time, could not justify a reversal of the engineering stand. At the heart of their commitment to risk acceptability was the technical analysis that convinced them that it was safe to fly in the years preceding the *Challenger* launch. The working engineers (including Marshall's Leon Ray, Thiokol's Al McDonald, Roger Boisjoly, and Brian Russell, to name only a few in the work group who became known for their integrity after the tragedy) believed the design was an acceptable risk.[8] As Wiley Bunn, director of reliability and quality assurance at Marshall, said of the years preceding the *Challenger* teleconference,

"Why didn't we lay down in front of the truck? Because when you read the analysis and the rationale as to why you could fly like that, it made sense. There wasn't anything worse than that going to happen. You could expect the kind of events that had occurred to happen, but you need not expect anything worse to happen. And there was margin (of safety) even if it did happen worse. And people really believed that. There wasn't any truck—the truck wasn't even coming" (interview transcript, Marshall Space Flight Center files, National Archives, Washington, D.C., 3 April 1986, p. 27).

By continuing to recommend launches, the working engineers assigned to the project were not being deviant, in their view. They were conforming to the overlapping meaning systems of the work group, of engineering as a craft, engineering as a bureaucratic profession, and the NASA organization. On the basis of their interpretation of the signals they had, to argue officially for delay in FRR (which they never did, recommending for launch even in the *Challenger* FRR two weeks before the launch) would have been deviant within each of the nested cultural meaning systems that constituted the social context of decision.

Theoretical Implications: The Normalization of Deviance in Organizations

What is important in the foregoing analysis is that continuing to launch with damage on O-rings, which outsiders saw as deviant after the disaster, was normal and acceptable to insiders as the problems were unfolding. Even though Marshall and Thiokol engineers were concerned, they continued to come forward with recommendations to accept risk and fly, gradually increasing the bounds of acceptable risk. In the history of decision making from 1977 to 1985, there is no evidence that supports organizational misconduct and amoral calculation by the SRB work group. The Level III and Level IV managers and engineers at Marshall and Thiokol were not violating safety rules to achieve organizational goals and thus using illegitimate means to desired ends. Instead, they conformed, using legitimate means to desired ends.

Certainly risks were calculated, for hazard assessment was fundamental to daily activity in the work group, but instead of violative behavior, the workgroup decision making conformed to rules and norms. The extensive archival record of documents created from 1977 to 1985 and interviews (including interviews with whistle-blowers) indicate that proceeding with flight with a design that deviated from performance expectations was legitimate and acceptable behavior within the work-group culture. Moreover, this line of action conformed to the expectations of the culture of production, as it was manifested in the NASA organization. Within the various cultural meaning systems affecting choice in the work group, continuing to launch was acceptable behavior and, thus, nondeviant in its view.

The engineering position changed on the eve of the *Challenger* launch, however. Contrary to most postdisaster interpretations, it was Thiokol engineers who were being deviant that night, not NASA managers. Thiokol engineers were unwilling to conform to the organizational mandates that had shaped their behavior prior to the *Challenger* launch decision. The striking irony is that having created a cultural construction of risk in the years preceding the accident, the engineers themselves could not overturn it.

A thorough reconsideration of Merton's SSAT in light of this analysis requires a systematic discussion of his conceptual scheme, as reconceptualized, that is not possible in these pages.[9] Even when painted in broad strokes, however, these data affirm the appropriateness of SSAT for organizational analysis. The NASA case shows how competition, resource scarcity, and norms, originating in the environment and responded to by people in positions of power, resulted in actions that altered the culture of the organization, trickling down to impact the environment of decision in the work group. These actions added production pressures that affected the decisions of all concerned in subtle and insidious ways that even the participants could not identify. The cultural mandates narrowed the range of choices that participants deemed rational as the SRB problems unfolded. In addition, the data demonstrate the complexity of culture as a choice environment. Rather than the unilateral trickle-down assumptions that a single cultural imperative, economic success, affects choice in the workplace, in this case culture was not a single-faceted phenomenon, but multifaceted and dynamic, linking environment, organization, and individual interaction. Decision making was a product of interaction, history, and precedent, which led to a work-group culture. It was reinforced by a macrolevel culture of production that encompassed the original technical culture, bureaucratic accountability, and political accountability. The case allows us to see the macro-micro connection, demonstrating how the structure of competition was transformed into organizational mandates.

Although the case deals with science-based decision making about a particular technical artifact, it suggests how organizational processes can convert unexpected and deviant incidents to accepted, normal, and routine events. This finding has extensive implications for theory. It demonstrates how institutionalized cultural meaning systems shape the menu of choices that are perceived as rational at a given moment (DiMaggio and Powell, 1983; Powell and DiMaggio, 1991). Moreover, it demonstrates how incrementalism, conformity to rules and norms, precedent, and informational and social context (both immediate and far-ranging) congeal in a process that can create a worldview that neutralizes deviant events, making them acceptable and nondeviant.

Nested cultural meaning systems, although invisible, were influential in molding common understandings at NASA. It is often said that a way of seeing is simultaneously a way of not seeing. Although the normalization of deviance can be functional for an organization, reducing uncertainty and/or enabling problem resolution by defusing a kind of "crisis mentality" that might interfere with action, it also can lead to a neutralization of signals of danger that can lead to mishap, mistake, and, as in the *Challenger* incident, disaster. Moreover, the processes of deviance normalization revealed in this case may play a role in facilitating rule violations and misconduct in other organizational forms.

Much research and theory has emphasized the role of normative environments conducive to deviance and misconduct (Cohen, 1955; Merton, 1968; Sutherland, 1940; Quinney, 1963; Ermann and Lundman, 1978; Denzin, 1977; Farberman, 1975). In tracing the evolution of a work-group culture, this research shows how people created a normative environment in which deviance was normalized. It shows how, once created, the norms, beliefs, and procedures of that culture constrained subsequent choices. Further, it demonstrates the *process* by which deviant incidents were converted to acceptable, nondeviant behavior in group interaction. It suggests the role of conformity in choice, leading to the obvious but ironic insight that for participants in the culture in question, it may not be deviance that is learned (as some scholars traditionally have viewed it) but *conformity* to group rules and norms (Sutherland, 1949). We see evidence of the role of conformity in the deviant outcomes described in such works as Hannah Arendt's (1964) *Eichmann in Jerusalem* and Herbert Kelman and Lee Hamilton's (1989) *Crimes of Obedience*. Building on this tradition, the NASA research illuminates the longitudinal microlevel processes and dynamic interactions in which participants came to see their own actions from 1977 to 1985—obviously deviant to outsiders after the disaster—as normal and acceptable.

Most certainly, the *Challenger* incident is unique in a number of ways that must limit the generalizability of the findings. Nonetheless, the analysis also has implications for social control that deserve consideration. Typically, strategies for controlling deviance and misconduct focus on the individual actor, assuming a rational choice model, wherein individuals calculate costs and benefits of deviant actions. In this model, the individual is calculating the cost of getting caught violating some law or rule in advance of the misconduct. The rational choice perspective, focusing on the individual as the worthy unit of analysis in deviance and misconduct, quite naturally focuses on the individual as the target for social control. Consequently, both the deterrence perspective and, in the case of organizational deviance, business ethics are logical strategies to alter individual choice because both target individuals. However, the rational choice perspective does not allow for the fact that people construct their realities or that those realities are shaped by cultural meaning systems that are based on the individual's historical and social location in a variety of forms of social organization.

Instead, it posits an individual isolated from social/contextual influences that affect choice—an individual who knows he or she is about to engage in some harmful act or wrongdoing—and can be deterred either by contemplating punishments and costs or/and ethical considerations concerning self and community. Cultural meaning systems constrain choice, narrowing the possible options that will appear rational at a given moment. Shared cultural understandings facilitate interaction, yet because they exist at a prerational level, present problems of control. How influential can the deterrent effects of punishment/costs or business ethics be when cultural belief systems and organizational processes shape understandings so that actors do not view their behavior as unethical, deviant, or having a harmful outcome?

Notes

1. For excellent analyses of this extensive literature, see Trice and Beyer, 1993, and Martin, 1992.

2. Among the texts I analyzed, the principal ones were Merton, 1964, pp. 213–42; Merton, 1968; Merton, 1975, pp. 21–52; Stinchcombe, 1975, pp. 11–34.

3. For an insightful discussion of the structural evolution of this situation, see Arthur L. Stinchcombe, 1965, pp. 169–80.

4. These well-publicized rule violations were the waiver of the Criticality 1 status of the SRB joint design and the lifting of the launch constraint by Level III Marshall management.

5. In a two-article series in the *New York Times*, Stuart Diamond reported many rule violations at NASA ("NASA Wasted Billions, Federal Audits Disclose," *New York Times*, 23 April 1986: A-1; "NASA Cut of Delayed Safety Spending," *New York Times*, 24 April 1986: A-1). My inquiry focused only on those rules allegedly violated by Level III and IV managers and engineers in the Solid Rocket Booster Project work group. Procedural guidelines proliferated at NASA, with revisions of rules replacing revisions that replaced still other revisions. Moreover, in the interest of safety, redundancy was built into the rules system to assure that problems got flagged, recorded, reported, and so forth. This created some overlaps between rule systems for various subunits. I found that work-group decision making was consistently governed by adherence to the rules, many of which were not understood by the official investigators. In some cases, when investigators believed a rule promulgated at NASA headquarters had been violated, work-group participants were conforming to a Marshall rule system. In two instances, I found deviation from established rules. These rules were violated by working engineers, not managers in the SRB Project. In both cases, the rules were defined as red tape that increased work, and in both cases, the circumvention of these rules was recorded (following procedures, and thus conforming, even so).

6. For a listing of delays on each launch and the technical causes, see Gurney and Forte, 1988.

7. For discussions about how making decisions public commits decision makers to a line of action, see Ross and Staw, 1987, p. 277; Staw and Fox, 1977, pp. 431–50.

8. My conclusion here is drawn from analysis of interview transcripts stored at the National Archives, Washington, D.C. The interviews were legal depositions conducted by a team of investigators that assisted the Presidential Commission investigating the disaster. (See W. Leon Ray, interview transcript, Marshall Space Flight Center files, National Archives, Washington, D.C.: 25 March 1986; Allan McDonald, interview transcript, Morton Thiokol Inc. files, National Archives, Washington, D.C.: 19 March 1986; Brian Russell, interview transcript, Morton Thiokol Inc. files, National Archives, Washington, D.C.: 19 March 1986; Roger Boisjoly, Morton Thiokol Inc. files, National Archives, Washington, D.C.: 2 April 1986.) The conclusions drawn from these transcripts are also verified in

numerous personal interviews with Ray and Boisjoly over the years and with other personnel, as well as documents.

9. A book-length manuscript, *Theory Elaboration: The Heuristics of Case Analysis*, is in progress.

References

Arendt, Hannah. 1964. *Eichmann in Jerusalem: A report on the banality of evil*. New York: Viking Press.

Barnett, Harold. 1981. Corporate capitalism, corporate crime. *Crime and Delinquency* 27:4–23.

Braithwaite, John. 1989. *Crime, shame and reintegration*. Cambridge: Cambridge University Press.

Clinard, Marshall B., and Peter C. Yeager. 1980. *Corporate crime*. New York: Free Press.

Cloward, Richard A., and Lloyd E. Ohlin. 1960. *Delinquency and opportunity*. New York: Free Press.

Cohen, Albert K. 1955. *Delinquent boys: The culture of the gang*. Glencoe, Ill.: Free Press.

Cohen, Deborah Vandiver. 1995. Ethics and crime in business firms: Organizational culture and the impact of anomie. In *The Legacy of Anomie Theory*, edited by F. Adler and W. S. Laufer, 183–206. New Brunswick, N.J.: Transaction.

Coleman, James W. 1987. Toward an integrated theory of white-collar crime. *American Journal of Sociology* 93:406–39.

Denzin, Norman K. 1977. Notes on the criminogenic hypothesis: A case study of the American liquor industry. *American Sociological Review* 42:905–920.

DiMaggio, Paul J., and Walter W. Powell. 1983. The iron cage revisited: Institutional isomorphism and collective rationality in organizational fields. *American Sociological Review* 48:147–60.

Emerson, Robert M. 1983. Holistic effects in social control decision-making. *Law and Society Review* 17:415–55.

Ermann, David M., and Richard J. Lundman, eds. 1978. *Corporate and governmental deviance*. New York: Oxford University Press.

Faberman, H. A. 1975. The criminogenic market structure: The automobile industry. *Sociological Quarterly* 16:438–57.

Geertz, Clifford. 1973. *The interpretation of cultures*. New York: Basic Books.

Giddens, Anthony. 1979. *Central problems in social theory: Action, structure, and contradiction in social analysis*. Berkeley: University of California Press, 1979.

Gross, Edward. 1980. Organization structure and organizational crime. In *White-Collar Crime: Theory and Research*, edited by G. Geis and E. Stotland, 52–76. Beverly Hills, Calif.: Sage.

Gurney, Gene, and Jeff Forte. 1988. *Space shuttle log: The first 25 flights*. Blue Ridge Summit, Pa.: AERO/TAB Books.

Hammack, J. B., and M. L. Raines. 1981. Space shuttle safety assessment report. Houston, Tex.: Johnson Space Center Safety Office.

Kagan, Robert A., and James T. Scholz. 1984. The criminology of the corporation and regulatory enforcement strategies. In *Enforcing Regulation*, edited by K. Hawkins and J. M. Thomas, 67–96. Boston: Kluwer-Nijhoff.

Kelman, Herbert C., and V. Lee Hamilton. 1989. *Crimes of obedience*. New Haven: Yale University Press.

Lindesmith, Alfred E. 1947. *Opiate addiction*. Bloomington, Ind.: Principia.

Martin, Joanne. 1992. *Cultures in organizations: Three perspectives*. New York: Oxford University Press.

McCurdy, Howard E. 1989. The decay of NASA's technical culture. *Space Policy* (November): 301–10.

Merton, Robert K. 1964. Anomie, anomia, and social interaction: Contexts of deviant behavior. In *Anomie and Deviant Behavior: A Discussion and Critique*, edited by M. B. Clinard, 213–42. New York: Free Press.

———. 1995. Opportunity structure: The emergence, diffusion, and differentiation of a sociological concept, 1930s–1950s. In *The Legacy of Anomie Theory*, edited by F. Adler and W. S. Laufer, 3–80. New Brunswick, N.J.: Transaction.

———. 1968. *Social theory and social structure*. Glencoe, Ill.: Free Press.

———. 1975. Structural analysis in sociology. In *Approaches to the Study of Social Structure*, edited by P. M. Blau, 21–52. New York: Free Press.

Powell, Walter W., and Paul J. DiMaggio. 1991. *The new institutionalism in organizational analysis*. Chicago: University of Chicago Press.

Presidential Commission on the Space Shuttle *Challenger* Accident. 1986. *Report to the president by the Presidential Commission on the Space Shuttle Challenger Accident*. 5 vols. Washington, D.C.: Government Printing Office.

Quinney, E. Richard. 1963. Occupational structure and criminal behavior: Prescription violation by retail pharmacists. *Social Problems* 11:179–85.

Romzek, Barbara S., and Melvin J. Dubnick. 1987. Accountability in the public sector: Lessons from the *Challenger* tragedy. *Public Administration Review* 47:227–38.

Ross, Jerry, and Barry M. Staw. 1986. EXPO '86: An escalation prototype. *Administrative Science Quarterly* 31:274–97.

Simmel, Georg. 1950. *The sociology of Georg Simmel*. Edited and translated by K. H. Wolff. New York: Free Press.

Simon, Herbert A. 1957. *Models of man: Social and rational*. New York: John Wiley.

———. 1976. *Administrative behavior*, 3d ed. New York: Free Press.

Staw, Barry M., and Frederick Fox. 1977. Escalation: Some determinants of commitment to a previously chosen course of action. *Human Relations* 30:431–50.

Stinchcombe, Arthur L. 1965. Social Structure and Organizations. In *Handbook of Organizations*, edited by J. G. March, 169–80. Chicago: Rand McNally.

———. 1975. Merton's theory of social structure. In *The Idea of Social Structure: Papers in Honor of Robert K. Merton*, edited by L. A. Coser, 11–34. New York: Harcourt Brace Jovanovich.

Sutherland, Edwin H. 1940. White-collar criminality. *American Sociological Review* 5:1–12.

———. 1949. *White-collar crime*. New York: Holt, Rinehart, and Winston.

Trice, Harrison M., and Janice M. Beyer. 1993. *The cultures of work organizations*. Englewood Cliffs, N.J.: Prentice Hall.

U. S. Congress. House. Committee on Science and Technology. 1986. *Investigation of the Challenger accident: Hearings*. 2 vols. Washington, D.C.: Government Printing Office.

————. 1986. *Investigation of the Challenger accident: Report*. Washington, D.C.: Government Printing Office.

Van Maanen, John, and Stephen Barley. 1985. Cultural organization: Fragments of a theory. In *Organization Culture*, edited by P. J. Frost, L. F. Moore, M. R. Lewis, C. C. Lundberg, and J. Martin, 31–54. Beverly Hills, Calif.: Sage.

Vaughan, Diane. 1983. *Controlling unlawful organizational behavior*. Chicago: University of Chicago Press.

————. 1992a. The macro/micro connection in "white-collar crime" theory. In *White-Collar Crime Reconsidered*, edited by K. Schlegel and D. Weisburd, 124–49. Boston: Northeastern University Press.

————. 1992b. Theory elaboration: The heuristics of case analysis. In *What Is a Case: Exploring the Foundations of Social Inquiry*, edited by C. Ragin and H. S. Becker, 173–201. New York: Cambridge University Press.

————. 1996. *The Challenger launch decision: Risky technology, culture, and deviance at NASA*. Chicago: University of Chicago Press.

Wynne, Brian. 1988. Unruly technology: Practical rules, impractical discourses and public understanding. *Social Studies of Science* 18:147–67.

JOHN HAGAN & BILL MCCARTHY

Anomie, Social Capital, and Street Criminology

Robert Merton's work on anomie is part of a more general theoretical formulation that is often unrecognized in criminology. This strain-and-opportunity-structure paradigm is meant to explain patterns of social life that extend far beyond crime, including phenomena as disparate as marriage and the development of science (see Merton, 1995; Passas, 1995). The purview of this theoretical approach therefore includes the development of a science of crime and calls attention to the ways in which anomie theory has been influenced by changes in U.S. society over the past century.

We suggest that socioenvironmental strains and opportunities in American society and criminology influenced the development of anomie theory in the first half of this century. In the 1950s and 1960s a new social and economic optimism about solving problems of poverty and crime established the theory's prominence and provided fertile ground for important theoretical revisions and extensions. However, in the ensuing years, transformations in the U.S. economy and the concurrent ascendancy of an American "school criminology" discouraged interest in anomie theory; thus, anomie theory was developmentally dormant for much of the post-1960s period. Even Travis Hirschi (1989, p. 45), a trenchant critic of the anomie tradition, noted this neglect and observed that this theoretical approach deserves renewed attention (see also Agnew, 1995; Savelsberg, 1995).

Recently, a handful of scholars have offered several innovative extensions and reformulations that have revitalized anomie theory (e.g., Cullen, 1984; Agnew, 1985, 1992; Bernard, 1987; Messner and Rosenfeld, 1994). We propose an additional elaboration, introducing the work of one of Merton's most prominent students, James Coleman. Coleman's (1988, 1990) social-capital theory has several links to the anomie tradition, and when combined these two theories enhance our understanding of the effects of economic and social conditions and opportunities on crime and delinquency. We illustrate the contributions of this union through a discussion of our research with home-less street youth in Toronto and Vancouver (Hagan and McCarthy, 1996a). Our thesis is that a renewed criminology of the streets focused around Cole-man's concept of social capital can promote new opportunities for Mertonian insights into the causes of crime.

A Century of Crime Theory

Concerns about poverty and its effects on families, especially children, were defining features of American criminology in the first quarter of this century. These issues remained prominent through the Great Depression and into the post–World War II period. Although frequently connected to the work of the Chicago School (e.g., see Thrasher, 1927; Shaw, 1929), the lack of opportu-nities and the urgent economic circumstances of the second quarter of this century also set the stage and provided important motivation for the early growth and development of Merton's anomie theory (see Merton, 1995). Clearly not an economic determinist, Merton (1938, p. 678) nonetheless em-phasized the relationship between economic conditions and opportunities, suggesting that the effects of anomie would be most severe among those with low incomes and from the unskilled class.

The Postwar Boom, sometimes called the Golden Era, brought better times to America. A surge in economic growth sparked confidence in American society's capacity to solve many problems, including those of poverty and crime. During the New Frontier and Great Society years of the Kennedy and Johnson presidencies, it was even possible to imagine waging a successful War on Poverty, in part with the goal of reducing America's growing crime problem.

These developments provided a unique set of opportunities for the evolu-tion of American criminology, particularly anomie-inspired theory. Building on the efforts of several schools of thought, Cohen (1955) extended Merton's theory to incorporate collective adaptations to the strain that arose from the disjunction between economic goals and opportunities. Half a decade later, the concern with poverty that characterized the Kennedy and Johnson years coincided with Cloward and Ohlin's (1960) elaboration of anomie theory. Cloward and Ohlin's focus on differential opportunities advanced Merton's insights and drew attention to the importance of legitimate and illegitimate opportunity structures. During the 1960s, Cloward and Ohlin's work gained special prominence and played a significant role in encouraging social programs that were central to the War on Poverty during the Johnson presidency (Moynihan, 1969).

In the 1970s and 1980s the economic fortunes of many Americans continued to improve in an economy that was expanding at record rates; however, property and violent crime also rose, and doubts developed that economic adversity was fueling this growth. The American public became increasingly uncertain about the role economic disadvantages played in the causation of crime, and criminologists began to hedge their bets, weakening their claims about the effects of class on crime.

These reservations culminated in Travis Hirschi's (1969) classic book, *The Causes of Delinquency*. Hirschi challenged the prominence of anomie, offering a well-argued critique on prevailing assumptions about the effects of economic adversity. Rejecting anomie and class as significant determinants of delinquency, he articulated a class-neutral control theory that focused on young people's weakened social bonds to families and schools. Using self-report surveys conducted in the schools of Richmond, California, Hirschi found that measures of anomie were unrelated to adolescent delinquency and that the effect of father's socioeconomic position was weak and therefore uncertain.

Kornhauser (1978) added to Hirschi's work, and these influential critiques of strain theory discouraged interest in Merton's (1938) pioneering attempt to explain why impoverished groups experienced disproportionate amounts of crime. Thus, the class-crime connection receded into a shadow of doubt, reducing opportunities for the advancement of anomie theory.

Meanwhile, other theories also encouraged reservations about the class-crime relationship. Differential-association theory argued that intervening definitional processes and not economic circumstances must be the causal forces of concern (Sutherland and Cressey, 1966). More radical in its approach, labeling theory boldly suggested that crime was actually the product of police and court biases that single out the poor for selective mistreatment (Becker 1963, 1964).

None of these theoretical developments excluded the possibility of a connection between class and crime, or that economic disadvantages were a source of crime; rather, each perspective provided a different emphasis on alternative or intervening factors. It is doubtful that these theoretical developments alone would have dramatically diminished American criminologists' interest in economic adversity and class. However, a change did occur when these theoretical developments coincided with a methodological shift—

signaled most successfully in Hirschi's research—to a survey approach that focused on self-reported activities of students.

School studies provided unique opportunities for enterprising criminologists to experiment with newly developing quantitative research methods on a virtually captive population. However, these school-based surveys focused on the children of relatively stable parents who infrequently had employment problems and other economic difficulties associated with seriously disadvantaged class circumstances. These studies also shifted attention from serious crimes to conventional acts of delinquency commonly perpetrated by high school adolescents. Not surprisingly, the more American criminologists studied these relatively privileged youth, the more doubtful they became about links between poverty and crime.

As this methodologically sophisticated school criminology reached its pinnacle in the 1970s and 1980s, the U.S. economy was again changing, experiencing more moderate and inconsistent growth. A "dual economy" increasingly characterized American life, intensifying the division between a "core or primary labor market" with its better paying and more stable jobs, and a "periphery or secondary labor market" in which wages and job security were substantially reduced (Averitt, 1968; Hodson and Kaufman, 1982). The slower economic growth, intermittent recessions, and "split" or "segmented labor markets" reduced expectations that problems of poverty would abate; at the same time, problems of crime and violence continued to escalate. In criminology, self-report studies of students remained dominant; yet the more persistently these methods convinced school criminologists that class was unimportant, the more others looked to the increasingly polarized social and economic conditions that surrounded them and questioned the usefulness of these studies for reaching conclusions about class and crime (e.g., Braithwaite, 1989; Sullivan, 1989; Hagan, 1992).

Essentially, American criminology was confronting contradictions similar to those found in the sociological study of social stratification and race relations. In this field, an earlier interest in race and poverty gave way to a focus on the roles of education and status in the process of occupational attainment among samples of people with jobs. Consequently, social scientists increasingly neglected the conditions of inner city life, particularly unemployment, at a time when problems of poverty and crime were becoming more apparent. As Wilson (1987) convincingly demonstrates, social scientists are woefully shortsighted to ignore the presence and significance of urban poverty and a growing underclass.

On the Streets

Today, some of the most serious and persistent problems of crime and economic adversity are found among youth who spend much of their time on the street, without a permanent place to live. In developed and developing countries, youthful homelessness, poverty, and despair are increasingly common. Recent figures indicate that approximately 100 million children and adolescents live on the streets of cities worldwide, with an estimated two fifths of the world's street youth living in Latin America (UNICEF, 1989). In the United States, figures suggest that the street youth population has reached one and a half million (Shane, 1989), and for much of the past decade in Toronto—one of the locations of our research—annual estimates of the number of street youth have ranged from ten to twenty thousand (Janus et al., 1987). North American experiences with homeless youth are surprisingly similar to those in other countries—from the nations of Europe (see Mingione and Zajcyk, 1991; Martinez, 1992) to those in South and Central America (see Campos et al., 1994). Wright, Wittig, and Kaminsky (1993, p. 90) make this unsettling point in a recent comparison between street youth in the United States and those from one of the poorest nations in the Western hemisphere, Honduras:

> Homeless street children suffer the burdens of disorganized and estranged family life—in Honduras *and* the United States. Homeless street children show exceptional levels of physical illness and mental anguish—in Honduras *and* the United States. Homeless street children are often underfed if not clinically malnourished—in Honduras *and* the United States (Wright, 1991). Homeless street children abuse drugs, prostitute themselves, scavenge for sustenance in the garbage, and become involved in crime—in Honduras *and* the United States. . . . Homelessness and extreme poverty are far more decisive in setting the conditions of life for children than national context or cultural differences. When we hold the situation of street children in Honduras up to the mirror, we see . . . ourselves.

The implications of these findings are shocking, as is the reluctance of academic criminologists to focus on street youth in their research. Yet, our intent is not to diminish a school criminology based on self-report techniques, or to disparage the development in this century of several important traditions of criminological theory. Instead, our goal is to build on recent methodological innovations while simultaneously resurrecting anomie theory's concern with changing social and economic contexts. An important avenue for this project involves the renewal of a street criminology that focuses on the ways in which youth come to the streets and on the consequences of street life.

A street criminology can take advantage of several theoretical traditions introduced earlier, particularly as these approaches are integrated through an application of social-capital theory. Social-capital theory adds to the economic emphasis in earlier interpretations of Merton's work by broadening our focus to include social processes that give force and form to the structural opportunities made available through the family, schools, and in community and work settings (Bourdieu, 1986; Coleman, 1988, 1990; Sampson, 1992; Hagan, 1994, ch. 3). Our approach does not abandon self-report survey techniques but reapplies them in an effort to learn about the lives of youth living on the streets. Thus, we argue that a self-report survey methodology can be used with the concepts of social-capital theory to provide new Mertonian-inspired insights into the causes of crime.

Anomie and Social-Capital Theories of Crime

Social-capital theory is concerned with the ways in which individuals socially organize their activities over the life course to improve their circumstances and attain cultural goals. This focus on the acquisition and accumulation of resources over time provides a theoretical grounding for attention to the place of delinquency and crime in life-course development (Elder, 1985; Hagan and Palloni, 1988; Sampson and Laub, 1993).

As Merton (1995, p. 23) recently notes, the concept of "social capital" is a reflection of an earlier anomie-connected emphasis on the ways in which opportunities may or may not be nurtured. Merton (p. 28) adds that the anomie-inspired concept of "differing access to opportunities" is also equivalent to the Weberian notion of "life chances." Social capital is, therefore, the key to understanding how the organization of social groups influences their ability to access opportunities for obtaining cultural goals and improving life outcomes. Although the concept of social capital is at the heart of the strain-and-opportunity-structure paradigm, Merton (1995, p. 23) observes that "the powerful concept of social capital remained . . . unformulated back in the 1940s, thus providing us with another conceptual example of what has been identified in the sociology of science as a 'postmature scientific discovery.' "

The theoretical evolution and application of the concept of social capital requires an elaboration of its constitutive components and an explanation of how this type of capital is obtained. Social-capital theory begins with the premise that we acquire at birth and accumulate through our lives unequal shares of various types of capital that alter and determine our life chances. We obtain access to and amass capital through several processes, including those that Dannefer (1984) refers to as sociogenic—structurally and culturally shaped processes—as well as those he describes as ontogenetic—individually and developmentally determined processes. Several kinds of capital are involved, and it is important to understand how social capital develops and evolves in ways that are analogous to more familiar resources, including physical, human, and cultural capital.

Physical capital typically refers to tools, machinery, and other productive equipment that form the foundation of economic relations. Economists have added to this concept, introducing the idea of human capital. Human capital refers to the abilities, skills, and knowledge acquired by individuals through inheritance, education, and training (Schultz, 1961; Becker, 1964). The capital that is embodied in humans is somewhat less tangible than that in tools or machinery, but both involve the accumulation of resources or power through a transformative process. As Coleman (1990, p. 304) notes: "Just as physical capital is created by making changes in materials so as to form tools and facilitate production, human capital is created by changing persons so as to give them skills and capabilities that make them able to act in new ways."

Pierre Bourdieu's (1986) concept, cultural capital, explicitly connects one aspect of human capital to the cultural conditions from which it originates. According to Bourdieu, cultural capital involves a unique type of culturally valued knowledge associated with music, art, literature, and other esteemed areas of cultural life. Like other human capital, cultural capital is influenced by training and education; moreover, access to and accumulation of this type of capital often is predicated on and productive of wealth and social position.

Although social capital may be less tangible than physical, human, or even cultural capital, its creation involves analogous processes that are no less real and probably even more important. According to Coleman (1990), social capital refers not to a single entity but to a variety of resources. These resources originate in the socially structured relations that connect individuals to families and to aggregations of other individuals in neighborhoods, churches, schools, and so on. Social capital is therefore embodied in relations between people, and it includes the knowledge and sense of obligations, expectations, trustworthiness, information channels, norms, and sanctions that these relations engender. Most important, social capital facilitates purposive action.

Coleman (1990, p. 305) introduces the process of social capitalization with a simple triangular figure, in which the end points or nodes of the triangle represent the accretion of human capital by two parents and a child. Coleman reasons that for the parents to further the accumulation of human capital through the cognitive development of the child, there must be capital in the nodes and the links of the diagram. That is, the most effective means of transmitting the human capital of the parents to the child is through the social capital represented in all the connecting links between both parents and the child. Coleman refers to this as a form of social closure of the social network of the family. This closure is important, however, not just in the family, but in other social groups, such as those connecting parents and children to other parents, neighbors, and teachers in several settings including schools, neighborhoods, and communities (see Cullen, 1994). Social groups can maximize their contributions to the development of various forms of capital when they have this characteristic of closure.

Individuals vary in their access to social capital, and they must continually adapt to changing structures and opportunities that characterize the circumstances they inherit and inhabit. Adaptations to these conditions are expressed through various formations of human and particularly cultural capital. Parents who are well situated within secure and supportive social networks may be inclined or driven—by their capital positions—to endow their children with forms of social, human, and cultural capital that increase the likelihood of success in school and later life. When social capital is abundant in the community and family, cultural adaptations often include the amassing of credentials of higher education and even involvements in high culture, for example, including participation in the arts that significantly enhances life chances (see DiMaggio, 1982; 1987).

However, in less advantaged community and family settings, parents who lack abundant social and cultural capital are less able to endow or transmit opportunities to their children. Survival itself may be a struggle, and children and families must adapt to the diminished circumstances and opportunities they encounter. Moreover, children of less advantageously positioned and less driven and controlling parents may more often drift or be driven by harsh circumstances along less promising paths of social and cultural adaptation and capital formation (Hagan, 1991).

Capitalizing the Street

The street youth we recently studied disproportionately come from families with diminished social capital. Many of these youth come from surplus population families headed by an unemployed parent; from families in which one or more family members has a history of criminal involvement; and from disrupted families in which one or both biological parents are absent from the home. These conditions are often linked: youth from surplus population families are in part more likely to be on the street because of difficulties and disruptions in their families. This connection represents an important illustration of Merton's argument that the strain-and-opportunity-structure paradigm significantly points to both economic and social sources of nonnormative behavior. Coleman's conceptualization is especially useful in broadening this focus of attention by conceiving both work and family problems as sources of diminished social capital.

The limited social capital available to the children of surplus population and disrupted families is a reflection of factors emphasized in both Hirschi's (1969) version of control theory and in Agnew's (1985, 1992, 1995) recent formulation of a social-psychological version of strain theory. The importance of control theory is apparent in street youth's limited levels of parental involvement and control, whereas the significance of strain theory is evident in increased levels of coercion in the form of parental abuse. As a result of both kinds of experiences, these youth are less likely to be attached to their parents or committed to school work, and they are more likely to report conflict with teachers. These problems distance youth from the traditional sources of social, human, and cultural capital that they need to improve their life chances.

The downward spiral in the capital of young people who take to the street is intensified by the conditions that characterize homelessness. These include a release from any family and school control that these youth may have experienced, as well as new sources of strain encountered on the street. The latter reflects the crises of day-to-day survival that young people experience and includes problems of finding shelter, food, and work. We found consistent evidence that several of these problems are related to crime, independent of a range of other kinds of variables known to cause criminal behavior. For example, hunger leads street youth to theft of food; hunger and the lack of safe shelter encourage further involvement in more serious types of theft; and problems finding shelter and employment increase involvement in prostitution. Thus, although some youth come to the streets with individual backgrounds and experiences that encourage persistent involvement in crime, other youth are swept and pushed into crime by the sociogenic circumstances they encounter on the street. These findings are important examples of strain-

and-opportunity linked sequences that follow from the absence of social capital.

The nature of street life has other implications for understanding the structural and life-course processes that lead street youth into crime. For example, recall that social capital accumulates not only among individuals but also within communities. We found that Toronto and Vancouver differed considerably in the social capital they made available to young people on the street. Although Toronto could be characterized as having a social welfare orientation, reflected in the provision of overnight shelters and support services to street youth, Vancouver operated more within the confines of a crime-control model, providing fewer resources or support services. More often left to find their own means of survival, Vancouver youth were more exposed to the hardships of the street, as well as to opportunities to become involved in crime. These community differences did not differentiate street youth in terms of involvement in violent crime, a kind of crime that likely has more ontogenetic origins; however, it notably increased the participation of Vancouver street youth in nonviolent forms of crime, such as drugs, theft, and prostitution. These findings imply that the absence of social capital in the form of services and support encouraged Vancouver youth to capitalize on the opportunities they encountered on the street: opportunities for involvement in theft, prostitution, and the drug trade. This is precisely the kind of "innovation" that Merton's strain-and-opportunity paradigm emphasizes.

Thus far, social-capital theory has provided a useful means for considering the pathways by which youth come to the streets together with the strains and opportunities that encourage street crime. This theoretical framework's attention to the closure of social networks also alerts us to a process of embeddedness that sustains street youth's involvement in several types of street crime. To illustrate the role of networks, we first explain how social embeddedness operates in more conventional circumstances. In many peoples' lives, the personal contacts of individuals, friends and families, and the networks of relations that flow from these contacts, are important sources of social capital used in finding jobs and making job changes (Granovetter, 1974, 1985; Coleman, 1990). People in advantaged circumstances are more likely to have acquired the social capital that derives from being "socially embedded" in job networks, and these contacts increase the prospects of getting a job and enhance occupational mobility.

Connections with street people and embeddedness in street life act in a converse way, increasing the probability of unemployment and downward life trajectories. Street peers involved in crime are more likely to integrate young people into the criminal underworld than into referral networks of legal employment, and these relations further distance youth from school and job contacts that can provide opportunities and develop legitimate pathways in the life course.

The process of criminal embeddedness results from exposure to offenders encountered on the street. These offenders operate as mentors and tutors and transmit a type of human capital that constitutes a criminal form of cultural capital. This "criminal capital" includes knowledge, information, and skills related to crime and represents an important resource that youth often define as essential for survival on the street. We found that, net of background ontogenetic measures of predispositions or propensities, embeddedness in crime networks and the subsequent acquisition of criminal capital play important roles in street youth's capitalizing on opportunities to participate in some types of street crime. The closure of mentoring and tutoring networks around these opportunities for involvement in crime can be thought of as a process through which street youth recapitalize their limited life prospects.

Lacking the social capital of conventional families or peers, it is not surprising that many street youth become involved with groups of other similarly situated young people. Although these groups are sometimes confused with gangs, they tend not to be distinctively male, territorial, or criminal—salient characteristics of the groups emphasized in the criminological literature on gangs. Instead, the youth we studied were more likely to think of themselves as being members of street families. These groups coalesced around issues of mutual support and safety, and they addressed needs of security and survival. This pattern was especially true for female street youth and for youth in Vancouver, who experienced gender and city specific strains of living on the street.

We anticipated that street families might enhance the social capital of their members, especially by improving their sense of emotional well-being; however, this was not borne out in our research. Although street families seem to form an important part of the lives of many street youth, these pseudofamily structures appear to be neither the source of, nor the solution to, the persistent emotional and survival problems of youth on the street.

We also found that the negative life-course effects of spending time on the street can be compounded further by being officially labeled and known as a criminal. In a downside version of the sense in which Merton (1948) spoke of self-fulfilling prophecies, street youth with backgrounds of parental abuse were especially sensitive to the stigmatizing effects of police sanctions. That is, these youth were at an especially high risk of intensifying their involvement in crime after being arrested and officially sanctioned. This criminal amplification may result from a compounding sense of shame and embarrassment that links earlier intense feelings of parental rejection and abuse with later police contacts. Labeling theorists (see Scheff, 1988; Scheff and Retzinger, 1991; Sherman, 1993) note that these highly charged emotional experiences can lead to defiant spirals or sprees of secondary deviance that in turn lead to increased levels of criminal embeddedness and greater opportunities for acquiring criminal capital. Moreover, police stigmatization may reduce access to traditional sources of social capital when those stigmatized are avoided and rejected in the larger society.

Further exploring the effects of labeling, we discovered an intragenerational effect of sanctioning that operates uniquely with gender (Hagan and McCarthy, 1996a). We found that male street youth with fathers or mothers (but especially fathers) who have been arrested were significantly more likely to intensify their criminal involvement after being arrested. In contrast, girls who were charged on the street and whose mothers or fathers had been arrested were less likely to become involved in later crime sprees. These findings suggest that for males, sanctioning experiences were more likely to produce a defiant transition into a persistent trajectory of secondary deviance, whereas females were apparently deterred and not spurred into subsequent involvement in crime. The stigmatization that accompanies intragenerational sanctioning has a further effect, reducing access to traditional sources of social capital, particularly for young men.

Clearly, our application of social-capital theory in this research is not a source of optimism about the life-course prospects of street youth. The focus of this theory on limitations imposed by disrupted family backgrounds and the hazards of embeddedness in criminal networks is not encouraging for the futures of young people on the street. However, social-capital theory points to employment as at least one potential avenue of escape from street life (see also Sampson and Laub, 1993; forthcoming). As social-capital theory's focus on social embeddedness makes clear, legal employment is a starting point in the process of acquiring social capital that can lead to more promising life outcomes. Furthermore, the notion of embeddedness usefully identifies competing conventional and street domains between which some street youth are able to move successfully. Finding and keeping a job is often a key to traversing the gap between these settings and to shifting the emphasis from street life to legitimate employment.

Over the course of the summer that we tracked street youth in Vancouver and Toronto, we discovered that although most of the work that street youth found was in the secondary labor market, these jobs offered some hope of establishing a life apart from the street. For example, youth who were able to find employment spent less time hanging out, panhandling, searching for food and shelter, using drugs, and stealing with other street youth. They also reported less individual involvement in several kinds of criminal activities. Youth who found jobs were not usually enamored of the employment they found; nonetheless, they viewed these jobs as a place to begin the transition to more conventional lives apart from the street.

Some Conclusions

Social-capital theory offers a powerful tool in the development of a science of crime. An important feature of this theoretical approach is that it allows a broadening and lengthening of explanatory attention to factors that cause crime and delinquency. Social-capital theory broadens our explanatory attention by revitalizing the Mertonian insight—only partially developed in the anomie tradition—that strains and opportunities derive from social as well as economic sources.

Travis Hirschi (1989, p. 45) has noted the narrowness of many applications of Mertonian anomie theory, observing that

> strain theory . . . remains alive, in spite of decades of pounding by research and general neglect by those who might make something more of it. It could be said with justification that the apparent failure of strain theory was the major motive behind the integrationist movement. With strain theory gone, those who accepted the idea that crime has its own motives were left with no place to begin. They therefore revived strain theory and placed it to the extreme left of their models, where it appears to remain today. Put another way, integrationists have patronized strain theory, but they have not contributed to its development. It may deserve more attention than it is now getting.

Hirschi's point about the "extreme left" presumably refers to the place integrationists assign to economic sources of strain, usually in the form of parental class position (e.g., Wiatrowski et al., 1981). Coleman provides a means of reinvigorating Merton's broader purposes. Extending Coleman's work, we use the concept of social capital to represent causal forces involving strains and opportunities that derive not just from the class position of families of origin but also from a variety of institutional sources—including work, family, school, neighborhood, and community—that contribute to the explanation of crime and delinquency. Social-capital theory therefore broadens the study of crime by emphasizing a wide range of structural causes.

Social-capital theory further lengthens the explanatory focus of contemporary criminology by drawing attention to the ways in which social capital accumulates, is conserved, and/or diminished over the life course. Despite an implicit awareness of the importance of life-course factors in delinquency as well as crime, most theories are rather static, concentrating on either delinquency or crime to the exclusion of the other and confining attention to rather brief periods of the life span. A social-capital theory of crime moves beyond this tendency, focusing on longer term development of capital accumulations and its consequences. By emphasizing the cumulative significance of critical events and transitions in the life course, social-capital theory further lengthens the study of crime.

It remains to be seen how our findings will influence the larger criminological research agenda. We maintain there is an important place for a reconstituted street criminology that supplements the more prominent school-based one. For example, school and street studies can be combined to investigate the effects of important causal variables usually lacking sufficient variation in school studies. In contrast to the results of most school studies, we found that adverse class backgrounds play an important role in crime through their effect on leaving home; in turn, foreground class conditions channel involvement in crime through the harsh socioeconomic situations street youth encounter on the street.

Studies that focus exclusively on street youth also have merit in that variation in the background and foreground experiences of street youth are reflective of fundamental causal processes that lead to crime. Many street youth do not become heavily involved in street crime, and finding out why some of these young people offend, whereas others do not, can significantly advance our theoretical understanding of crime. This understanding may depend in part on research that connects our highly developed knowledge of the background causes of crime with a more probing exploration of foreground experiences. Social-capital theory provides a useful framework for this merger, and the experiences of street youth are a valuable source for such research.

Of course, we should exercise caution in generalizing from our study of young people living on the streets of two Canadian cities to homeless youth in other parts of the world. There are reasons to expect differences as well as similarities. Some of the most important differences may arise from the ways street youth in different settings relate to their families of origin. Many of the street youth we studied moved back and forth from their families, or fragments of these families, before taking to the streets for extended periods. In this sense, these youth retained some connections to their families of origin.

However, many of these relationships were fraught with conflict and were usually highly unstable. Researchers in the developing countries of Central and South America also emphasize familial relationships and often distinguish youth "in" the street from youth "of" the street (Campos et al., 1994). The former live with their families of origin, and although they make their livelihood in the streets, they usually return home at the end of the day; the latter work, eat, and sleep and make their home on the street. We know little about how this variation in ongoing family contact and relationships influences the nature and degree of street youth's involvement in crime and, therefore, are uncertain about the theories that may be required to account for different orientations to the street.

We also know that the experience of being on the street can be quite different in the developing countries of Central and South America than in North America, at least in the sense of threats to the safety of these young people. In Central and South America, merchants and the police are known to use violence in their attempts to eliminate problems they associate with the presence of street youth. There are recurrent stories of organized killings of street youth, sometimes in substantial numbers. In contrast, street youth in North America have more to fear from adults and other youth who also live on the street, or from adults who come to the streets to victimize young people. Again, we know less than we should about the nature and degree of these differences and of how they might inform the theoretical approaches we should use to understand the experiences of street youth in various settings.

As we move rapidly into the next century, criminology remains a science that is predominantly connected to the national settings where it is undertaken. We have lacked research designs and imperatives that encourage an understanding of differences and similarities in national crime problems. Yet the problems of street youth and crime clearly pose a set of issues that invite international cooperation. Our research on street youth represents a modest attempt to reach beyond a single research setting by including two cities, albeit in the same country, in its design. We found important differences between these settings and suggest that an anomie-inspired conception of social capital provides a flexible theoretical framework for examining these differences as well as the similarities. Far more is required if we are to broaden both our understanding of street life and the international implications of the crimes perpetrated by many of these troubled young people.

References

Agnew, Robert. 1985. A revised strain theory of delinquency. *Social Forces* 64:151–67.
———. 1992. Foundation for a general strain theory of crime and delinquency. *Criminology* 30:47–87.

————. 1995. The contribution of socio-psychological strain theory to the explanation of crime and delinquency. In *Advances in Criminological Theory. Vol. 6: The Legacy of Anomie*, edited by Freda Adler and William S. Laufer. New Brunswick, N.J.: Transaction.

Averitt, Robert. 1968. *The dual economy*. New York: W. W. Norton.

Becker, Gary. 1964. *Human capital*. New York: National Bureau of Economic Research.

Becker, Howard. [1963], 1973. *Outsiders: Studies in the sociology of deviance*. New York: Free Press.

Becker, Howard, ed. 1964. *The other side: Perspectives on deviance*. New York: Free Press.

Bernard, Thomas. 1987. Testing structural strain theories. *Journal of Research in Crime and Delinquency* 24:287–90.

Bourdieu, Pierre. 1986. The forms of capital. In *Handbook of Theory and Research for the Sociology of Education*, edited by J. G. Richardson. New York: Greenwood Press.

Braithwaite, John. 1989. *Crime, shame and reintegration*. Cambridge: Cambridge University Press.

Campos, Regina, Marcela Raffaelli, and Walter Ude. 1994. Social networks and daily activities of street youth in Belo Horizonte, Brazil. *Child Development* 65:319–30.

Cloward, Richard, and Lloyd Ohlin. 1960. *Delinquency and opportunity: A theory of delinquent gangs*. New York: Free Press.

Cohen, Albert. 1955. *Delinquent boys: The culture of the gang*. Glencoe, Ill.: Free Press.

Coleman, James. 1988. Social capital in the creation of human capital. *American Journal of Sociology* 94:S95–S120.

————. 1990. *Foundations of social theory*. Cambridge, Mass.: Harvard University Press.

Cullen, Francis. 1984. *Rethinking crime and deviance theory*. Montclair, N.J.: Rowman & Allanheld.

————. 1994. Social support as an organizing concept for criminology. *Justice Quarterly* 11:527–60.

Dannefer, Dale. 1984. Adult development and social theory: A paradigmatic reappraisal. *American Sociological Review* 49:100–116.

DiMaggio, Paul. 1982. Cultural capital and school success: The impact of status culture participation on the grades of U.S. high school students. *American Sociological Review* 47:189–201.

————. 1987. Classification in art. *American Sociological Review* 52:440–55.

Elder, Glen, Jr. 1985. Perspectives on the life course. In *Life Course Dynamics: Trajectories and Transitions, 1968–80*, edited by Glen Elder Jr. Ithaca, N.Y.: Cornell University Press.

Granovetter, Mark. 1974. *Getting a job: A study of contacts and careers*. Cambridge, Mass.: Harvard University Press.

————. 1985. Economic action and social structure: The problem of embeddedness. *American Journal of Sociology* 91:481–510.

Hagan, John. 1991. Destiny and drift: Subcultural preferences, status attainment and the risks and rewards of youth. *American Sociological Review* 56:567–82.

————. 1992. The poverty of a classless criminology. *Criminology* 30:1–20.

————. 1994. *Crime and disrepute*. Thousand Oaks, Calif.: Pine Forge Press.

Hagan, John, and Bill McCarthy. 1996a. *Mean streets*. New York: Cambridge University Press.

————. 1996b. Intergenerational sanction sequences and trajectories of street crime amplification. In *Trajectories and Turning Points*, edited by Ian Gotlieb and Blair Wheaton. New York: Cambridge University Press.

Hagan, John, and Alberto Palloni. 1988. Crime as social events in the life course: Reconceiving a criminological controversy. *Criminology* 26:87–100.

Hirschi, Travis. 1969. *Causes of delinquency*. Berkeley: University of California Press.

———. 1989. Exploring alternatives to integrated theory. In *Theoretical Integration in the Study of Deviance and Crime*, edited by Steven F. Messner, Marvin D. Krohn, and Allen E. Liska. Albany, N.Y.: State University of New York Press.

Hodson, Randy, and Robert Kaufman. 1982. Economic dualism: A critical review. *American Sociological Review* 47:727–39.

Janus, Mark-David, Arlene McCormack, Ann Wolbert Burgess, and Carol Hartman. 1987. *Adolescent runaways: Causes and consequences*. Lexington, Mass.: Lexington Press.

Martinez, Celorrio. 1992. Captive marginality and despicable poverty: Careers of deculturation among homeless youth. *Revista Internacional de Sociologia* 3:113–39.

Merton, Robert K. 1938. Social structure and anomie. *American Sociological Review* 3:672–82.

———. 1948. The self-fulfilling prophecy. *Antioch Review* (Summer): 193–210.

———. 1995. Opportunity structure: The emergence, diffusion, and differentiation of a sociological concept, 1930s–1950s. In *Advances in Criminological Theory*. Vol. 6: *The Legacy of Anomie*, edited by Freda Adler and William S. Laufer. New Brunswick, N.J.: Transaction.

Messner, Steven F., and Richard Rosenfeld. 1994. *Crime and the American dream*. Belmont, Calif.: Wadsworth.

Mingione, Enzo, and Francesca Zajczky. 1992. The new urban poverty in Italy: Risk models for the metropolitan area of Milan. *Inchiesta* 22:63–79.

Moynihan, Daniel P. 1969. *Maximum feasible misunderstanding*. New York: Free Press.

Passas, Nikos. 1995. Continuities in the anomie tradition. In *Advances in Criminological Theory*. Vol. 6: *The Legacy of Anomie*, edited by Freda Adler and William S. Laufer. New Brunswick, N.J.: Transaction.

Sampson, Robert. 1992. Family management and child development: Insights from social disorganization theory. In *Advances in Criminological Theory*, Vol. 3: *Facts, Frameworks, and Forecasts*, edited by Joan McCord. New Brunswick, N.J.: Transaction.

Sampson, Robert, and John Laub. 1993. *Crime in the making: Pathways and turning points through life*. Cambridge, Mass.: Harvard University Press.

———. Forthcoming. Socioeconomic achievement in the life course of disadvantaged men: Military service as a turning point, circa 1940–1965. *American Sociological Review*.

Savelsberg, Joachim J. 1995. Crime, inequality, and justice in Eastern Europe: Anomie, domination, and revolutionary change. In *Crime and Inequality*, edited by John Hagan and Ruth D. Peterson. Stanford, Calif.: Stanford University Press.

Scheff, Thomas. 1988. Shame and conformity: The difference-emotion system. *American Sociological Review* 53:395–406.

Scheff, Thomas, and Suzanne Retzinger. 1991. *Emotions and violence: The role of shame-rage*. New York: Free Press.

Schultz, Theodore. 1961. Investment in human capital. *American Economic Review* 51:1–17.

Shane, Paul. 1989. Changing patterns among homeless and runaway youth. *American Journal of Orthopsychiatry* 59:208–14.

Shaw, Clifford R. 1929. *Delinquency areas*. Chicago: University of Chicago Press.

Sherman, Lawrence. 1993. Defiance, deterrence, and irrelevance: A theory of the criminal sanction. *Journal of Research in Crime and Delinquency* 30:445–73.

Sullivan, Mercer. 1989. *Getting paid: Youth crime and work in the inner city*. Ithaca, N.Y.: Cornell University Press.

Sutherland, Edwin, and Donald Cressey. 1966. *Principles of criminology*. 7th ed. Philadelphia: J. B. Lippincott.

Thrasher, Frederick M. 1927. *The gang: A study of 1,313 gangs in Chicago*. 2d rev. ed. Chicago: University of Chicago Press.

UNICEF. 1989. *Annual Report*. New York: UNICEF.

Wiatrowski, Michael, David Griswold, and Mary Roberts. 1981. Social control and delinquency. *American Sociological Review* 46:525–41.

Wilson, William J. 1987. *The truly disadvantaged*. Chicago: University of Chicago Press.

Wright, James. 1991. Health and the homeless teenager: Evidence from the national health care for the homeless program. *Journal of Health and Social Policy* 2:15–35.

Wright, James, Martha Wittig, and Donald Kaminsky. 1993. Street children in North and Latin America: Preliminary data from Projecto Alternativos in Tegucigalpa and some comparisons with the U.S. case. *Studies in Comparative International Development* 28:81–92.

SCOTT MENARD

A Developmental Test of Cloward's Differential-Opportunity Theory

Robert K. Merton (1938) proposed a theory of deviant behavior in which social structural and cultural patterns led to individual adaptations, which in turn resulted in differential individual and aggregate rates of crime and other forms of deviance. Once a dominant theoretical perspective in criminology, Merton's anomie theory was subsequently modified (Cloward, 1959; Cloward and Ohlin, 1960), criticized as being empirically unsupported (Kornhauser, 1978), and more recently defended (Bernard, 1984; Bernard, 1987; Menard, 1995) as not having been adequately tested. In an early response to Merton's theory of anomie, Cloward (1959) and Cloward and Ohlin (1960) attempted to consolidate the anomie tradition of Durkheim (1951) and Merton (1957) with two related theoretical traditions that emerged from the University of Chicago Sociology Department in the 1930s and 1940s: the social disorganization perspective of Clifford R. Shaw and his associates (Shaw, 1930; Shaw, 1931; Shaw and McKay, 1942) and the differential-association theory of Edwin H. Sutherland (Sutherland, 1937, 1947, 1949). The earlier paper by Cloward (1959) consolidated the anomie and Chicago traditions to explain illegal and other deviant behavior by individuals in general (not for any specific ethnic, gender, or other social category). Cloward and Ohlin (1960) used Cloward's consolidation of anomie, social-disorganization, and differential-association theories as part of their differential-opportunity theory of "how delinquent *subcultures* arise, develop various law-violating ways of life, and persist or change" among "*adolescent males* in *lower-class areas* of *large urban centers*" (Cloward and Ohlin, 1960, p. 1, emphasis added).

My purpose in this study is to extend an earlier test of Merton's anomie theory to incorporate the extensions to that theory proposed by Cloward (1959). In an earlier paper (Menard, 1995), I used longitudinal data to test Merton's (1968) anomie theory of illegal behavior. Arguing that previous attempts at testing Merton's anomie theory oversimplified the theory by looking only at social class or goals-means discrepancies as predictors of illegal behavior, my test of the theory included consideration of both macrosocial and microsocial elements of the theory and included not only discrepancies between goals and means but also the mode of adaptation as predictors of illegal behavior. I found that the results of testing the full theory for early (age 11–14), middle (age 14–17), and late (age 17–20) adolescent respondents supported the theory, more so for late and middle adolescence than for early adolescence. In the present essay, the same techniques are applied to Cloward's differential-opportunity theory, an extension of anomie theory.

Merton's Anomie Theory

Anomie, according to Merton (1968), exists when there are both *universally prescribed success goals* (whether those goals are universally *accepted* or not) and *inequality of legitimate opportunity to attain culturally prescribed success goals*. Anomie is a social-structural condition, not a characteristic of individuals. As Bernard (1987) correctly observed, anomie may properly be regarded as a variable only when societies or social systems are being compared across space or time. For a particular society at a particular time, *anomie is a constant*. The effects of anomie, however, may vary by location within the social structure. According to Merton (1968), it may be felt more strongly among lower-class individuals who have internalized the culturally prescribed success goals than among individuals who either have not internalized those success goals or have, by virtue of their higher social status, greater access to the culturally approved or legitimate means for fulfilling the culturally prescribed success goals. This does not mean that anomie itself varies within the social structure. Instead it means that the effects of anomie may be felt differently by individuals with different positions in the social structure.

Whether anomie, the social-structural condition, leads an individual to commit crimes depends on how that individual responds to the condition of anomie. That response, in turn, depends on the social-structural location of the individual in American society. According to Merton, the effects of anomie are most likely to be felt among lower-class individuals who have internalized the culturally prescribed goal of success. For these individuals and for others, regardless of social class, who experience blocked opportunities for success, the structural condition of anomie is manifested at the individual level as *anomia* (Merton, 1964, pp. 225–28). Anomia may involve the recognition that one lacks the culturally approved means to achieve the culturally prescribed goal or the realization that the culturally approved means to which one has access will not be effective in attaining the culturally prescribed goal of success.

Whether blocked opportunities result in deviant behavior at the individual level depends on whether the individual rejects either or both of the culturally prescribed goals or the constraints dictating culturally approved means of attaining those goals. Different combinations of acceptance of goals and means result in different *modes of adaptation*: conformity, ritualism, innovation, retreatism, and rebellion, as detailed by Merton (1968, p. 194).[1] Innovation, retention of the goal but rejection of "the institutional norms governing ways and means for its attainment" (Merton, 1968, p. 195), is the most likely of the five modes of adaptation to result in illegal behavior. By contrast, ritualism, the relinquishing of the goals but continued adherence to cultural norms regarding means, may, according to Merton (1968, pp. 238–41), produce *overconformity* and may result in the lowest rates of deviance among the five modes of adaptation.

According to Merton (1968, pp. 203–9), differences in adaptation depend at least in part on differential socialization. (Implicitly, this opens up the possibility that the patterns of acceptance of goals and means may arise in response to conditions other than anomie, rather than to anomie alone.) The modes of adaptation are also linked to social class. According to Merton (1968, p. 237), conformity tends to be the modal response even among individuals in the most stressful position. Given choices among the adaptations other than conformity, innovation is more likely to be associated with lower-class status and ritualism with middle-class status (Merton, 1968, pp. 203–9). Retreatism seems most likely to occur among individuals in the lowest social strata (Merton, 1968, p. 242). Merton also indicated that the modes of adaptation are not stable personality traits, but may vary over time, with different sequences for different individuals (Merton, 1968, p. 242).

The principal elements of Merton's anomie theory are diagrammed in Figure 1. At the cultural level (the left column), success goals, norms regulating means to success, social stratification, and differential access to legitimate means, which results from social stratification, are represented. The combination of the cultural and social-structural variables is felt at the individual level, differentially by social status (gender, ethnicity, socioeconomic status), in the form of differences in perceived access to legitimate means for success, all represented in the center column. Excluding the part of Figure 1 that is in the rightmost column (this is Cloward's contribution to the theory), these differences in perceived access to legitimate opportunities lead to anomia,

FIGURE 1. *Anomie-Opportunity Theory*

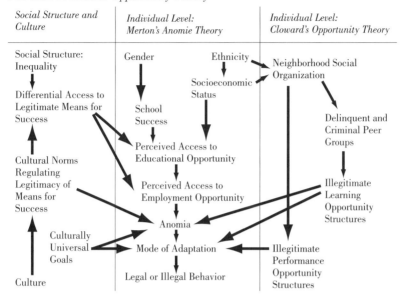

which in turn leads to a choice among modes of adaptation. The mode of adaptation is the most direct and important influence on illegal behavior, according to the theory. Note that this is not a "path diagram" in the technical sense in which that term is sometimes used (Agresti and Finlay, 1986). Instead, the arrows in Figure 1 only indicate a general causal flow. It is entirely possible that variables farther back in the causal order may have effects on variables later in the order (for example, gender may have a direct effect on mode of adaptation), but these details are left out of Figure 1. Also, the influences from the structural level (left column) to the rest of the model cannot be tested in the context of a single society. Given data from a single society, only the individual level relationships can be tested.

Differential-Opportunity Theory

According to Cloward (see also ch. 6 of Cloward and Ohlin, 1960), Merton's anomie theory focused on differences among individuals or social groups with respect to access to legitimate means of achieving culturally prescribed goals but largely ignored differences in access to *illegitimate* means of achieving those same goals. In effect, access to illegitimate means was treated as though it were unlimited and nonproblematic. In both the social disorganization and differential-association traditions, by contrast, access to illegitimate means was implicitly treated as limited and problematic and access to legitimate means was largely taken for granted. Cloward argued that access to both legitimate and illegitimate means was both limited and problematic and that criminal behavior could be explained better by a theory that combined consideration of both legitimate and illegitimate opportunity (access to means) than by a theory that included one but not the other.

According to Cloward, opportunity or access to (legitimate or illegitimate) means involves access to both *learning* and *performance* structures. In learning structures, the individual learns both techniques (how to burglarize a house and get away with it) and values, attitudes, and beliefs (it is all right to steal, or at least to steal from rich people—because they probably have insurance—or to steal from people who deserve to be ripped off because they rip off you and your friends) that are supportive of illegal behavior. This closely parallels Sutherland's (1947) statement of differential-association theory: "When criminal behavior is learned, the learning includes (a) techniques of committing the crime, which are sometimes very complicated, sometimes very simple; and (b) the specific direction of motives, drives, rationalizations, and attitudes."

In performance structures, the individual has the opportunity to implement those techniques and to apply those beliefs, attitudes, and values by performing illegal acts. Performance structures appear to correspond closely to "opportunity" in the routine activities/lifestyle/opportunity theoretical perspective described by Cohen and Felson (1979), Felson and Cohen (1980), Hindelang et al. (1978), and Cohen, Kluegel, and Land (1981). Although the social-disorganization and differential-association theories do not explicitly specify (a) presence of willing perpetrators, (b) presence of vulnerable victims, and (c) absence of capable guardians as elements of opportunity to commit offenses, these elements are implicit in some of the work of the social-disorganization theorists, especially Shaw and McKay (1942).

As Cloward noted, Sutherland suggested the distinction between learning and performance structures as early as 1944. Insofar as a distinction may be made between learning and performance structures, both appear to be rooted in the community, but learning structures and not performance structures explicitly involve interpersonal interactions in small face-to-face groups. Performance structures appear to refer more to the physical and social environment of the willing perpetrator.

Cloward (1959, p. 164) regarded his consolidation of anomie theory with social-disorganization and differential-association theories as an extension of anomie theory. Cloward and Ohlin (1960, p. x) commented that, to explain delinquent subcultures, "The task of consolidating them required that we redefine the unique contributions of each, that we reconceptualize elements of both, and that we develop linking concepts. The result is what we call the theory of differential opportunity systems." For reasons to be described below, the focus of this essay is more on Cloward's explanation of individual deviance than on Cloward and Ohlin's explanation of delinquent subcultures. The term "differential-opportunity theory" will be used to refer to Cloward's (1959) theoretical statement, both by itself and as it is incorporated in the analysis of Cloward and Ohlin (1960).

Cloward's contribution to differential-opportunity theory is represented by the elements in the rightmost column of Figure 1. The overriding concept is access to illegitimate opportunity. Delinquent peer group bonding and neighborhood disorganization are indicators of illegitimate opportunity, to be discussed below. Once again, although illegitimate opportunity is portrayed as influencing mode of adaptation, the model will also be examined for direct influences on illegal behavior. Also, social status generally may be regarded as influencing access to illegitimate opportunity.

Differences between Cloward (1959) and Cloward and Ohlin (1960)

Cloward (1959) attempted to explain *individual* criminal behavior within its cultural and social-structural context. He emphasized a concern with "stable criminal roles to which persons may orient themselves on a carreer [*sic*] basis, as in the case of racketeers, professional thieves, and the like" (Cloward, 1959, p. 170, n. 15). Cloward and Ohlin (1960) attempted to explain the onset, persistence of, and changes in *delinquent subcultures* or (as suggested in their subtitle) *delinquent gangs*, not individual delinquency. Cloward and Ohlin, moreover, limited their theory to adolescent males in lower-class areas of large urban centers. Cloward (1959) placed no such limitations on his theoretical statement. He considered white-collar crime as well as "street crime" in his application of differential-opportunity theory, and he considered variations in illegitimate opportunity based on social class, race, ethnicity, gender, and kinship (Cloward, 1959, pp. 172–73) within the context of the theory. No group was excluded from consideration. Cloward (1959) and Cloward and Ohlin (1960) thus differ both on what is being explained (individual illegal behavior or delinquent subcultures) and for whom it is being explained (everyone or only adolescent males in lower-class areas of large urban centers).

In addition to the rather pronounced distinctions in what is explained and for whom, there are subtle differences in the explanations offered by Cloward and by Cloward and Ohlin. For example, in his analysis of the work of Clifford Shaw, Cloward (1959, p. 170) concluded, "In other words, access to criminal roles depends upon stable associations with others from whom the necessary values and skills may be learned." The corresponding passage in Cloward and Ohlin (1960, p. 154, emphasis added) reads:

> Thus the "big shots"—conspicuous successes in the criminal world—become role-models for youth, much more important as such than successful figures in the conventional world, who are usually socially and geographically remote from the slum area. Through *intimate and stable* associations with these *older* criminals, the young acquire the values and skills required for *participation in the criminal culture*.

Although both statements are similar in orientation, Cloward's is broader in its implications. Cloward and Ohlin stress the importance of *older* criminals as role models in the maintenance of the criminal *subculture*. Cloward's description includes this pattern but is not specifically limited to it, and it is open to the inclusion of interactions with not-so-much-older individuals, including companions of about the same age, as teachers of skills and socialization agents for values. The point here is that for Cloward and Ohlin, it appears that contact and integration between adolescent delinquents and adult criminals is necessary for a *delinquent subculture* to persist. For Cloward, contact with other individuals (age and other characteristics unspecified), from whom criminal values and skills may be learned, is necessary for *individual illegal behavior* to persist in a stable pattern.

In emphasizing the differences between the theoretical statements of Cloward and Ohlin (1960) and Cloward (1959), there is no suggestion that they are in any way incompatible or contradictory. Quite the opposite: they are complementary applications of the same general perspective, differential-opportunity theory (a consolidation of anomie, social-disorganization, and differential-association theories) to the explanation of two distinct but related phenomena (individual illegal behavior and delinquent subcultures) for two populations, one of which is a subset of the other (the general population and adolescent males who live in lower-class areas of large urban centers). To the extent that the theoretical statements appear different, the difference may be explained by the differences in what is explained and for whom it is explained. The theory itself remains consistent in both statements.

These distinctions between Cloward (1959) and Cloward and Ohlin (1960) are commonly overlooked in the criminological literature. Most often, the earlier paper by Cloward is ignored altogether, and attention is focused exclusively on Cloward and Ohlin (1960). Attempts at testing Cloward and Ohlin's theory have often treated it as a theory of individual behavior rather than as a theory of adolescent subcultures or gangs (see the review by Bernard, 1987) or focused on whether the types of gangs predicted by Cloward and Ohlin are, in fact, present in a particular city or community (see the review by Covey et al., 1992). Bernard (1987) has been sharply and correctly critical of the misapplication of empirical data to Cloward and Ohlin's theory and has provided useful guidelines for an appropriate test of Cloward and Ohlin's theory of differential-opportunity structures.

Here, *there is no attempt to test Cloward and Ohlin's (1960) theory of differential-opportunity structures.* The concern is with the explanation of delinquent behavior at the individual level, *not* with the rise, persistence, or change in delinquent subcultures or gangs. Insofar as differences exist between Cloward (1959) and Cloward and Ohlin (1960), Cloward's (1959) statement of differential-opportunity theory is more directly applicable to the goal of explaining individual-level variations in illegal behavior. In the present analysis, therefore, the attempt is made to operationalize and test Cloward's (1959), not Cloward and Ohlin's (1960), version of differential-opportunity theory.

One consequence of testing Cloward's formulation of differential-opportunity theory, instead of Cloward and Ohlin's formulation, is that variables that might have been important to a test of Cloward and Ohlin's theory are excluded from the present test. The issue of internal as opposed to external blame for failure, described in Cloward and Ohlin (1960, pp. 108–24) as an explanation for the evolution of delinquent subcultures, is not part of Cloward's formulation of the theory. More generally, in an attempt to be faithful to Cloward's (1959) theory of individual-level illegal behavior, the subcultural elements of Cloward and Ohlin's theoretical statement have been excluded from the operationalization of differential-opportunity theory, except insofar as they are reflected in illegitimate opportunity structures.

Data and Variables

Data are taken from the National Youth Survey (NYS), a national probability sample of adolescents who were 11–17 years old in 1976, the first year for which data were collected. The NYS is described in detail elsewhere (Elliott and Ageton, 1980; Elliott, Ageton, Huizinga, Knowles, and Canter, 1983;

Elliott et al., 1985). In the present study, data from waves 1 through 5, for the years 1976–80, were used.

The earlier operationalization of Merton's anomie theory (Menard, 1995) can be directly incorporated into the operationalization of Cloward's differential-opportunity theory. Cloward, as noted above, viewed his theory as an extension of Merton's anomie theory, produced not by altering anomie theory but by adding to it the concept of illegitimate opportunity structures. Merton (1959), in turn, viewed Cloward's theoretical statement favorably, as a reasonable and appropriate extension of his anomie theory. Correspondingly, the operationalization of Cloward's differential-opportunity theory requires no modifications to the operationalization of Merton's anomie theory, other than the addition of indicators of illegitimate opportunity structures to Merton's anomie theory.

The dependent variables are the frequencies of minor delinquency, index offending, marijuana use, and polydrug use. Minor and index offending are scales from the NYS, described in Elliott et al. (1989). Both include offenses that are illegal whether the offender is an adolescent or an adult, and the index offending scale includes offenses parallel to those offenses included as FBI Index offenses: sexual assault, robbery, aggravated assault (including gang fighting), burglary, theft of more than $50, and motor vehicle theft. Neither scale includes illicit drug use. The other two offenses involve illicit substance use: marijuana use and polydrug use (any combination of heroin, cocaine, hallucinogen, barbiturate, and amphetamine use; almost always accompanied by marijuana and alcohol use). We may expect to find that innovators have the highest rates of minor and index offending, but that retreatists have the highest rates of marijuana and polydrug use. Because of the skewness of the frequency data, a logarithmic transformation, ln(frequency + 1), is applied before analyzing frequency of illegal behavior.

Sex was coded as male or female. Race was coded as white or nonwhite. The size of the sample (1,725 at wave 1; just under 1,500 at wave 5) does not permit the analysis of subgroups by age with any finer distinctions within the nonwhite category. Socioeconomic status is measured by the Hollingshead two-factor index (Bonjean, Hill, and McLemore, 1967), a continuous scale with a range from 11 (high status) to 77 (low status). For the adolescent respondents in this study, socioeconomic status of the parents, rather than the respondents, was used. Self-reported grade point average (GPA) was used as a measure of academic success. GPA may be expected to affect perceptions of educational opportunities, which may in turn affect economic opportunities (Farnworth and Leiber, 1989). For respondents who were not in school (dropouts or graduates), the most recently reported GPA was used.

Educational opportunity was operationalized as a question that asked, "What do you think your chances are for completing a college degree?" Economic opportunity was measured in terms of occupational opportunity: "What do you think your chances are for getting the kind of job you would like to have after finishing school?" The use of occupational opportunity is justified based on the use of occupational success as a cultural goal in Merton (1968, pp. 190–92, 199, 226–28), as discussed above. Both educational and economic opportunity were originally measured on a three-point scale (Good/Fair/Poor), but responses in the "Poor" category were too few for analysis of subgroups. The "Fair" and "Poor" categories were therefore collapsed for the present analysis.

The perception that legitimate means were inadequate to achieve desired goals was measured as a subset of the peer, family, and school normlessness scales discussed in Elliott et al. (1983; 1985). The NYS normlessness scales were designed to tap the concept of normlessness as described by Seeman (1959, p. 788, italics in original): "Following Merton's lead, the anomic situation from the individual point of view, may be defined as one in which there is a *high expectancy that socially unapproved behaviors are required to achieve given goals*." As is evident from Seeman's discussion of normlessness, the concept is a specific and deliberate attempt to measure individual-level anomie, or anomia. The specific items used in the combined scale (hereafter called anomia) were all measured on a five-point Likert scale ranging from "Strongly Agree" (5) to "Strongly Disagree" (1). The items were

a. Sometimes it is necessary to lie to your parents in order to keep their trust;

b. It may be necessary to break some of your parents' rules in order to keep some of your friends;

c. In order to gain the respect of your friends, it's sometimes necessary to beat up on other people;

d. You have to be willing to break some rules if you want to be popular with your friends;

e. To stay out of trouble, it is sometimes necessary to lie to teachers;

f. At school, it is sometimes necessary to play dirty in order to win.

Reliability for the additive scale used to measure anomia was .75–.81 (Cronbach's alpha) for the first five waves of NYS data. Each of the items indicates that to achieve a desired goal, compliance with norms regarding legitimate means leads to failure.

Modes of adaptation were constructed based on two variables. The first was a measure of aspirations: "How important is it to you to have a good job or career after you've finished school?" Again, for reasons detailed above, occupational aspirations are used as the measure of economic goals. This question was originally measured on a three-category scale (very important/somewhat important/not important at all), but with 80–90 percent of respondents for the first wave in the first (very important) category, the other two categories were collapsed to form a single category, which represented rejection of the culturally prescribed goal of economic success. The second variable was a belief scale described in Elliott, Huizinga, and Menard (1989) and Elliott et al. (1985), in which respondents were asked how wrong it was (very wrong/wrong/a little bit wrong/not wrong at all) to commit a variety of delinquent acts. For purposes of the present study, individuals who responded either "very wrong" or "wrong" to every item were regarded as having accepted the norms that proscribe illegal behavior. Anyone who answered "a little bit wrong" or "not wrong at all" was classified as not having accepted norms against illegal behavior and, in effect, regarding illegitimate means as acceptable, if less than ideal, methods of achieving goals.

Measuring Illegitimate Opportunity

Both learning and performance structures for illegitimate opportunity are, according to Cloward and according to the theoretical traditions that emerged from the University of Chicago, located within the neighborhood. Learning structures are interpersonal in nature: "access to criminal roles depends upon stable associations with others from whom the necessary values and skills may be learned" (Cloward, 1959, p. 170). Sutherland's theory of differential association is cited as focusing on illegitimate learning structures (Cloward, 1959, pp. 168–71). Following these two leads, *delinquent peer group bonding* (DPGB), the product of association with delinquent friends and involvement with friends, is included as the indicator of illegitimate learning opportunities. This variable consists of involvement with peers (how much time you spend with friends on weekday afternoons, weekday evenings, and weekends) multiplied by the extent to which friends are involved in illegal behavior, the latter centered at the five-year mean for 1976–80, so that a negative score indicates lower than average delinquency, and a positive score indicates higher than average delinquency, on the part of one's friends.

There are several reasons for the selection of this indicator. First, delinquent peer group bonding has face validity as an indicator of stable association with others from whom illegal values and skills may be learned. Second, this measure has been used in the past to operationalize Sutherland's differential association (or social-learning theories, more generally) in tests of an integrated strain, control, and learning theory model (Elliott et al., 1989; Menard and Elliott, 1994; Roitberg and Menard, 1995). Because Cloward draws upon the work of Sutherland in defining illegitimate learning structures, a previously used indicator, based on Sutherland's differential-association theory, is appropriate here. Third, although it would be desirable to include measures of association with delinquent siblings, parents, or other adults, such measures are not directly available from NYS data. (It is worth noting that nothing in the NYS questions regarding the illegal behavior of friends precludes respondents from describing the behavior of *adults* whom they regard as friends; it is, therefore, possible, but not by any means certain, that the NYS may be picking up some influence of adult criminals on adolescent behavior.) It seems unlikely, however, that an adolescent would have extensive involvement with adult criminals, absent extensive involvement with delinquent peers. Indeed, the descriptions in Cloward (1959) and Cloward and Ohlin (1960) suggest that the adolescents with substantial contact with adult criminals are a subset of those adolescents who are heavily involved in delinquent peer groups.

Fourth, the inclusion of a measure of DPGB is consistent with Merton's anomie theory, of which Cloward's differential-opportunity theory was intended as an extension. In his analysis of Cohen's (1955) work on the emergence of delinquent subcultures, Merton (1968, pp. 232–33) noted that anomie theory could not explain all aspects of delinquent behavior:

> It seems to be the case, however, that the "versatility" and "zest" with which some boys are observed to pursue their group-supported deviations are not directly accounted for by the theory of social structure and anomie. For the sources of these properties of the deviant behavior, one must presumably look to the social interaction among these likeminded deviants who mutually reinforce their deviant attitudes and behavior which, in the theory, results from the more or less common situation in which they find themselves.

Although "versatility" and "zest" are not clearly defined, they appear to refer to the variety or eclecticism and to the frequency with which delinquent boys commit their offenses. Insofar as differential-opportunity theory is an extension of Merton's anomie theory, it seems entirely appropriate to include a measure that Merton himself acknowledges may account for some delinquent behavior that is not fully accounted for by anomie theory.

Performance structures, as described by Cloward, are also linked to neighborhood characteristics but not to interpersonal interactions. Performance structures for *stable* criminal-role performance are linked by Cloward (following Kobrin 1951) to the degree to which carriers of criminal and conventional values are integrated in the community. The presence or absence of such integration, however, as described by Cloward (1959, pp. 171–73) and Kobrin (1951), seems to affect not *whether* or *how much* illegal behavior occurs in the community but *what kind* of illegal behavior—organized career crime associated with stable criminal roles or disorganized, situational crime, "the absence of systematic and organized adult activity in violation of the law, despite the fact that many adults in these areas commit violations" (Kobrin 1951, pp. 657–58). This point is further developed in Cloward and Ohlin's discussion of differences among delinquent subcultures. Similarly, differences in class, ethnicity, gender, and other social characteristics may have an impact on performance structures but more on what kind of crime is committed (white-collar crime, prostitution, organized racketeering) than on whether or how much crime is committed.

At this point, it is desirable to make a minor departure from Cloward's (1959, p. 170, n. 15) focus on stable criminal roles and to move to a more broadly inclusive consideration of illegal behavior, whether it is committed in the performance of a stable criminal role or not. First, the stability of a criminal role is a continuous variable, not an all-or-nothing dichotomy. Following Blumstein et al. (1986), a criminal career may be as brief as two successive offenses or may continue over an extended period of time and a large number of offenses. Any division between "stable" and "unstable" criminal roles is necessarily arbitrary.

Second, the concern here is with illegal behavior in adolescence, which may or may not lead to the development of stable criminal roles in adulthood. Whether illegal behavior in adolescence does or does not stem from or lead to a stable criminal role cannot adequately be determined on the basis of adolescent delinquency alone but must take into account adult illegal behavior, which is beyond the scope of the present study.

Third, the interest in this essay is in explaining illegal behavior generally, not with differences in types of crime and not just with career criminality associated with stable criminal roles. This consideration is especially important when we consider the test of differential-opportunity theory in the context of other tests of Merton's anomie theory, control theory, and learning theory. For different theories to be properly compared, they should be tested on the same behavior. Finally, at a more pragmatic level, we lack the data in the NYS to determine the extent to which carriers of deviant and conventional values are integrated in the neighborhoods within which NYS respondents reside. This effectively precluded a full analysis of organized as opposed to unorganized criminal behavior at the neighborhood level.

Based on these considerations, it seems that the best indicator of the stability of criminal roles *over a one-year time span* (the measurement period for which the NYS data were collected) is the use of *frequency* rather than prevalence of illegal behavior. Given a fixed time span, higher frequency of illegal behavior (all other things being equal) indicates a more stable criminal role than a lower frequency of illegal behavior. It remains to be seen whether differential-opportunity theory is applicable only to stable criminal roles, or whether it applies to unorganized, casual, or situational delinquency as well, but to the extent that frequency of delinquency is indicative of a stable delinquent or criminal role, we will have captured Cloward's concern with stable delinquent roles.

The departure from Cloward's original theoretical statement is minor, because the issue of stable criminal careers is addressed (albeit not as well as we might wish) by the use of frequency of illegal behavior as an outcome measure. This departure is justifiable, because of the broader concern with developing tests of anomie, learning, and control theories and comparing the theories with one another in terms of their explanatory power and the degree to which they are confirmed. Also, the concern here is with adolescent delinquency, for which the notion of a stable criminal (or delinquent career) may have less applicability than for adult crime. In addition, although Cloward was concerned with stable criminal roles, it is reasonable to ask whether his theory might have broader applicability.

The broadening of the scope of Cloward's differential-opportunity theory becomes problematic only if the theory fails to provide a better description of illegal behavior than anomie theory. If differential-opportunity theory *fails* to improve on the explanatory power of anomie theory, then the failure may be either because the theory was wrong or because it was misapplied to a domain (noncareer delinquency) for which it is inappropriate. If, on the other hand, differential opportunity does provide a better explanation of delinquency than anomie theory, then the theory is supported (perhaps for a broader domain of behavior than that to which it was thought applicable), and the question remains whether it would provide an even better explanation of stable criminal roles as described by Cloward. This latter question, insofar as it focuses on differences in the *kind* of delinquency committed (rather than whether or how much delinquency is committed), is beyond the scope of the present research.

As a result of broadening the inquiry from Cloward's concern with only stable criminal roles to the present concern with both stable, organized illegal behavior and sporadic, unorganized illegal behavior, the integration of carriers of deviant and conventional values in the neighborhood is no longer relevant. The opportunity to perform illegal acts, however, remains relevant. As the indicator of opportunity to perform illegal acts, an index of social disorganization or vulnerability to illegal behavior at the neighborhood level is used. This index consists of six items, combined in an additive scale: whether (yes or no) assaults and muggings, robberies and thefts, vandalism and property damage, winos and junkies, abandoned houses, and run-down property are problems in the neighborhood, according to the parents of the respondents in 1976 and according to the respondents in 1980. This index of neighborhood social disorganization has a reliability (Cronbach's alpha) of 0.70.

These measures are taken from the parent interview schedule for wave 1 (1976) and the respondent interview schedule for wave 5 (1980) of the NYS. Data on these items are unavailable for 1977–79, so the measures of neighborhood social disorganization that are closest in time to the measures of illegal behavior are used. For 1976–77, therefore, the temporal order is correct, but for 1979–80, neighborhood social disorganization is measured contemporaneously with illegal behavior. In effect, it is assumed that neighborhood social disorganization is stable from 1979 to 1980. To the extent that this assumption is incorrect, we should find differences between the effects of neighborhood social disorganization on illegal behavior for ages 14–17, depending on whether those effects are measured for 1976–77 or for 1979–80. The alternative would have been to assume stability in both place of residence and degree of neighborhood social disorganization for a longer time period, 1976–79, and to use only 1976 neighborhood social disorganization in the model.

Analytical Procedures

The variables identified by strain theory are a mix of continuous variables, categorical variables that reflect an underlying continuous scale, and categorical variables measured on a nominal scale. It would be most difficult to cast these variables into a structural equation or path model without seriously compromising either the theory or the assumptions of the model. The inclusion of mode of adaptation in a path model would be especially problematic, because it is inappropriate to use dummy (or nominal) variables as dependent variables in regression and path analysis (Agresti and Finlay, 1986). Accordingly, analysis of variance and covariance (ANCOVA) and logistic regression analysis are employed to separately test different components of the theory. The theory is tested for four subsamples: 11–14 year olds in wave 1 (1976), 14–17 year olds in wave 1 and wave 4 (1979), and 17–20 year olds in wave 4. The use of 14–17 year olds allows us to examine the tested models for consistency over time, and the use of three periods of adolescence—early (11–14), middle (14–17), and late (17–20)—allows us to detect possible developmental trends.

All of the models are time-ordered cross-sectional models (Menard, 1991) in which predictors are measured in wave 1 or wave 4 and response (dependent) variables are measured one year later, in wave 2 (1977) or wave 5 (1980). The disadvantages to this are that the separate components of the model cannot be arranged end-to-end in a semblance of a path model with multiple time periods, and indirect effects cannot properly be calculated. The advantages are that each component of the model is valid for the same time and age spans, and although the strength of indirect effects cannot be precisely calculated, the existence of indirect effects may reasonably be imputed from the separate components of the models.

In logistic regression, it is not variance in a continuous dependent variable but the odds of membership in a category of a (usually dichotomous) categorical variable that the model attempts to explain. It is therefore technically questionable to speak of "explained variance" in a logistic regression model. Still, several analogues to the R^2 statistic for the linear regression and ANCOVA model have been proposed for the logistic regression model. Hosmer and Lemeshow (1989) and Knoke and Burke (1980) recommended a measure that treats the likelihood ratio X^2 as a sum of squares that may be partitioned into a total X^2 (the likelihood ratio X^2 with only the intercept in the model, analogous to the sum of squares based only on the grand mean in ANCOVA), the unexplained X^2 (the likelihood ratio X^2 with all predictors in the model), and the explained X^2 (the model chi-square, equal to the difference between the likelihood ratio X^2 with only the intercept and the likelihood ratio X^2 with all predictors in the model). This pseudo-R^2 measure is calculated and included in each of the tables based on logistic regression analysis to compare the relative ability of anomie theory to predict dichotomous responses across age groups. The statistical significance of the model X^2 is also considered.

Causal Ordering

Neighborhood social disorganization is, in one sense, an exogenous variable that should not be affected by the individual characteristics of the respondents. In another sense, however, whether a person lives in a neighborhood that is perceived as socially disorganized is a function of her or his socioeconomic status and ethnicity, with nonwhite and lower status individuals being more likely to live in more socially disorganized neighborhoods (Shaw and McKay, 1942). An adolescent's grade point average, delinquent peer group bonding, and perceived opportunities are unlikely to have a substantial impact on neighborhood social disorganization, but based on Cloward (1959), Cloward and Ohlin (1960), and the social disorganization tradition on which their theory is partially based (Shaw and McKay, 1942), neighborhood social disorganization may have an impact on school performance, patterns of association, and perceived opportunities. Neighborhood social disorganization is, therefore, placed causally subsequent to ethnicity and social class but prior to the other variables in the model.

According to the logic of the preceding paragraph, delinquent peer group bonding should be placed causally subsequent to neighborhood social disorganization and to the sociodemographic characteristics (sex, ethnicity, socioeconomic status) of respondents. According to Cloward's theory, it should be placed causally prior to the mode of adaptation. Its location with respect to other variables in the model, however, is not clearly specified in differential-opportunity theory, either by Cloward (1959) or Cloward and Ohlin (1960). At issue is the causal ordering of delinquent peer group bonding with respect to (a) grade point average, (b) perceived access to legitimate opportunity (both educational and occupational), and (c) anomia. Arguments can be made for both causal directions, and for a reciprocal pattern of causation, for all these variables. Absent clear guidance from Cloward (1959) or Cloward and Ohlin (1960), it becomes necessary to rely on the work of others in the anomie/strain and differential-association theoretical traditions.

For the present analysis, delinquent peer group bonding is placed causally subsequent to grade point average and causally prior to perceived access to educational opportunity, perceived access to occupational opportunity, and anomia. According to Cohen (1955), school failure leads to involvement in delinquent peer groups or subcultures. One could also argue that involve-

ment in delinquent peer groups or subcultures suppresses school performance, but Cohen's formulation, which is part of the same anomie/strain
tradition as Cloward (1959), Cloward and Ohlin (1960), and Merton (1968),
is more consistent with differential-opportunity theory. From the perspective
of differential-association theory, upon which differential-opportunity theory
is partially based, attitudes and beliefs (such as anomia and perceived access
to legitimate opportunity) are formed in the process of interaction that occurs
in intimate, face-to-face, primary groups. This suggests that delinquent peer
group bonding should be placed causally prior to perceived college chance,
perceived job chances, and anomia. Again, alternative causal orderings are
possible. For example, Elliott et al. (1985) suggest that lack of access to
legitimate opportunity and the negative attitudinal response to lack of access
to legitimate opportunity lead to delinquent peer group bonding, but for a
test of differential-opportunity theory, the causal ordering suggested by differential-association theory is more appropriate.

It is important to keep the issue of the causal ordering of delinquent peer
group bonding in perspective. The principal concern in this analysis is with
how well differential-opportunity theory explains illegal behavior. Whether
school performance has an indirect effect on illegal behavior via delinquent
peer group bonding, or delinquent peer group bonding has an indirect effect
on illegal behavior via school performance, is a comparatively minor concern.
Neither result would provide strong evidence for or against differential-
opportunity theory as formulated by Cloward (1959). Should differential opportunity prove useful in explaining illegal behavior, the relationships among
the intermediate variables in the model can be explored in more detail; if
not, the question is moot. The causal order involving delinquent peer group
bonding is the one that seems most consistent with differential-opportunity
theory, but future research should include a consideration of alternative
causal orderings.[2]

Conditional Relationships Involving Mode of Adaptation and Illegitimate Opportunity

Individuals may respond to a lack of access to legitimate opportunity for
achieving culturally prescribed goals either by rejecting the constraints on
legitimate means and becoming innovators, by rejecting the culturally prescribed goals and becoming ritualists, or by rejecting both and becoming
retreatists or rebels (Merton 1968). A fourth, presumably unstable alternative, is to continue to play the game and to play it by the rules, even though

there appears to be no hope of winning, that is, to continue to accept both cultural goals and normative constraints on legitimate means and to be a conformist. The relationship between legitimate opportunity and mode of adaptation is thus subject to individual choice, probabilistic not deterministic.

The relationship between illegitimate opportunity and mode of adaptation is also probabilistic in nature. Individuals may have access to illegitimate opportunity, but because they also have access to legitimate opportunity, may choose conformity over innovation or retreatism. Others may choose ritualism, playing by the rules but not really in the game, not expecting to succeed, rather than rejecting the constraints on legitimate means. Some individuals who do not have access to illegitimate means may nonetheless become innovators, possibly setting themselves up for the double failure that Cloward (1959) suggested as a path toward the retreatist mode of adaptation.

For individuals who choose a conforming (conformist or ritualist) mode of adaptation, access to illegitimate opportunity should be relatively unimportant because of their unwillingness to use illegitimate means to achieve their goals. For individuals who choose a nonconforming adaptation (innovator or retreatist), access to illegitimate opportunity should have a major impact on the frequency of offending. The relationship between illegitimate opportunity (as represented here by neighborhood social disorganization and delinquent peer group bonding) and illegal behavior is thus *conditional*; it varies depending on the mode of adaptation. Conversely, the impact of choosing a conforming as opposed to a nonconforming mode of adaptation is conditional on access to illegitimate opportunity. The choice of a nonconforming mode of adaptation may not result in a high frequency of illegal activity for individuals who lack access to the learning and performance structures for illegal behavior. In other words, some individuals may have the will but not the ability, and others may have the ability but not the will, to engage in high-frequency illegal behavior. The conditionality of the relationships of mode of adaptation, neighborhood social disorganization, and delinquent peer group bonding to illegal behavior implies that a complete model of Cloward's differential-opportunity theory should include interaction terms involving illegitimate opportunity and mode of adaptation.

It is not clear, however, how much these interaction terms should contribute to the overall explanatory power of the model. To the extent that mode of adaptation is influenced by access to illegitimate opportunity (or to put it another way, to the extent that the choice of illegitimate means is rationally based on availability of illegitimate means), the interaction terms should add little to the explanatory power of the model. In addition, there are some offenses that require very little learning and that may easily be performed in a variety of contexts. Such offenses include petty theft, minor assault, and public disorder, offenses of the type found in the minor offending scale of the NYS.

Because it is not clear whether conditional relationships involving mode of adaptation and illegitimate opportunities should play a major or minor role in explaining illegal behavior, separate tests are performed for these conditional relationships. To the extent that such conditional relationships exist, they reflect a mismatch between opportunity and orientation, between the desire to take advantage of illegitimate means and access to illegitimate means. If individuals exercise a sort of bureaucratic rationality and take the path of least resistance, the interaction terms should be small and perhaps not statistically significant. If individuals exercise value rationality (Weber, [1920], 1947) and free will in the face of pressures to do otherwise, and to the extent that some opportunity for learning and performance either enables (is necessary) or facilitates (makes it easier) committing illegal acts, we should find statistically and substantively significant interactions between the effects of social disorganization and delinquent peer group bonding with the mode of adaptation on illegal behavior.

As suggested above, for purposes of testing interaction effects, modes of adaptation are best divided into conforming (conformist, ritualist) and non-conforming (retreatist, innovator). A second, more practical consideration suggesting this division is that the number of retreatists and ritualists, as predicted by Merton (1968), is small, making it difficult to support analyses as complex as those involved in the assessment of interaction effects in a multiple regression or ANCOVA model. For the analysis of conditional effects (and *only* for that analysis), therefore, mode of adaptation is dichotomized into conforming and nonconforming modes of adaptation, then multiplied by DPGB for one interaction term and by social disorganization for the other. The interaction terms are then tested for substantive and statistical significance in the model for differential-opportunity theory.

Influences on Illegitimate Opportunity, Legitimate Opportunity, and Anomia

Table 1 presents the ordinary least squares regression results of the analysis for social class, social disorganization, grade point average (GPA), and delinquent peer group bonding (DPGB). Sex was not included as a predictor of social class, because males and females are equally likely to be born into high- or low-status families, but ethnicity explains about 8 percent of the variance in social class. Ethnicity, but not social class, is predictive of living in a socially disorganized neighborhood. There is an anomalous, just barely statistically significant relationship between being female and living in a socially disorganized neighborhood for 17–20-year-old respondents. Because there are four tests of this relationship (two age groups in each of two periods), the probability of obtaining a relationship this strong (at the 0.046 level for a single test) is actually 0.17, so random sampling variation is one plausible explanation for this result. Another possibility is that women in late adolescence are more likely than men to perceive a neighborhood as socially disorganized, all other things being equal. It is also worth noting that sociodemographic background factors (ethnicity, sex, class) are weakest in their ability to predict the social disorganization of the areas in which respondents live in late adolescence.

Grade point average is weakly explained in early and middle adolescence, but like neighborhood social disorganization, its explained variance declines in late adolescence. Neither ethnicity nor (except for an anomalous result for 14–17-year-old respondents in 1979–80) neighborhood social disorganization is a particularly good predictor of GPA, but females and higher-status individuals consistently have higher grade point averages than their male or lower-class counterparts, a result consistent with the general literature on school performance (for example, Boocock, 1980). Considering that it is one of four tests, the anomalous result for social disorganization and GPA for 14–17-year-old respondents in 1979–80 has a combined, four-test probability of 0.07, not quite statistically significant at the 0.05 level.

Delinquent peer group bonding is not well explained in early adolescence ($R^2 = 0.04$) but better explained in middle and late adolescence ($R^2 = 0.10$ to 0.12). Male respondents and respondents with low grade point averages consistently have higher levels of DPGB than female respondents or respondents with high GPAs. Social disorganization does not appear to matter for 1976–77, but it does for 1979–80. This may be a period effect, or a result based on the difference between parents' reports and respondents' reports of neighborhood social disorganization. There is also an anomalous, statistically significant relationship between ethnicity and DPGB (nonwhites are less likely to be involved in delinquent peer groups) for 14–17-year-old respondents in 1979–80, but this relationship is questionable, because it does not occur elsewhere, particularly for 14–17-year-old respondents in 1976–77.

Table 2 presents the logistic regression results of the analysis for perceived college and employment chances. Perceived college chances are best ex-

TABLE 1. *Grade Point Average (GPA) and Socioeconomic Status*

Dependent Variable (Age group, wave of survey)	$R^2(p)$[a]	Standardized regression coefficients (significance)[b]				
		Ethnicity (nonwhite)	Sex (female)	Lower class	Disorganization	GPA
Lower Class (11–14, W1; 14–17, W4)	.082 (.000)	.29 (.000)				
Lower Class (14–17, W1; 17–20, W4)	.083 (.000)	.29 (.000)				
Disorganization (11–14, W1)	.047 (.000)	.22 (.000)	.01 (.771)	−.03 (.367)		
Disorganization (14–17, W1)	.041 (.000)	.21 (.000)	.03 (.305)	−.02 (.504)		
Disorganization (14–17, W4)	.041 (.000)	.19 (.000)	.01 (.843)	.02 (.552)		
Disorganization (17–20, W4)	.028 (.000)	.16 (.000)	.07 (.046)	−.03 (.395)		
GPA (11–14, W1)	.086 (.000)	.03 (.433)	.19 (.000)	−.23 (.000)	−.00 (.927)	
GPA (14–17, W1)	.108 (.000)	−.03 (.394)	.18 (.000)	−.25 (.000)	−.02 (.503)	
GPA (14–17, W4)	.070 (.000)	.02 (.315)	.13 (.000)	−.22 (.000)	−.06 (.019)	
GPA (17–20, W4)	.055 (.000)	.01 (.707)	.15 (.001)	−.15 (.000)	.01 (.728)	
DPGB (11–14, W1)	.059 (.000)	−.00 (.901)	−.13 (.000)	−.06 (.083)	.05 (.129)	−.18 (.000)
DPGB (14–17, W1)	.074 (.000)	−.03 (.379)	−.17 (.000)	−.06 (.115)	.04 (.312)	−.17 (.000)
DPGB (14–17, W4)	.100 (.000)	−.10 (.003)	−.10 (.002)	−.01 (.804)	.16 (.000)	−.23 (.000)
DPGB (17–20, W4)	.115 (.000)	−.06 (.101)	−.21 (.000)	.01 (.825)	.15 (.000)	−.21 (.000)

[a]p value based on F test for explained variance.
[b]p value based on t test for unstandardized regression coefficient.

plained in middle adolescence (when, presumably, whether one will go to college is most pertinent as an issue). Not surprisingly, higher grade point average, higher social class, and white ethnicity are all predictive of favorable perceptions of one's college chances. In early and middle adolescence, delinquent peer group bonding also appears to be predictive of one's college chances, but as noted earlier, there is some question about the causal direction of this relationship. Females in the older cohorts (14–17 in 1976, 17–20 in 1979) are less likely than males in the same cohorts to perceive their college chances as good. Except for an anomalous negative relationship between social disorganization and perceived college chances (probability in four trials p = 0.107), none of the other variables appears to have a significant impact on perceived college chances.

The most consistent influences on perceived job chances are perceived college chances (probably reflecting the perceived link between education and occupational success) and social disorganization, with individuals from more disorganized areas perceiving their job chances as poorer. There is also some suggestion that grade point average becomes increasingly important as a predictor of perceived job chances as respondents get older; the relationship is not statistically significant for early adolescence, but it is statistically significant and strongest in late adolescence. As with college chances, women in the older cohorts are less likely than men to view their job chances favorably. Also, nonwhite respondents are less likely than white respondents to view their job prospects as favorable in late adolescence (when they are likely to have had direct experience with the adult labor market), but the relationship between ethnicity and job chances is not statistically significant in early or middle adolescence.

Table 3 presents the ordinary least squares regression results for anomia. Explained variance ranges between 15 and 19 percent, and males, nonwhite respondents, and respondents with low grade point averages and high delinquent peer group bonding consistently have the highest levels of anomia. For nonwhites, the relationship with anomia increases with age, and the gender difference is more pronounced for the older than for the younger cohorts. For the younger cohorts, the relationship between delinquent peer group bonding and anomia is stronger than it is for the older cohorts. Social disorganization also appears to be positively related to anomia, but only for respondents in late adolescence and then only weakly. There is one anomalous statistically significant coefficient between social class and anomia (14–17-year-old respondents in 1979–80), but this may be attributable to sample variation (four-test p = 0.19).

Influences on Mode of Adaptation

In the analysis of Mertonian anomie theory (Menard, 1995), I found that the most informative results for analyzing mode of adaptation were produced by first analyzing the difference between conforming adaptations (conformity and ritualism) and nonconforming adaptations (innovation and retreatism). This strategy of analysis produces the results in Table 4. The first thing to note about Table 4 is the difference in levels of statistical significance and

TABLE 2. *College Chances (Educational Opportunity) and Job Chances (Employment Opportunity)*

Dependent variable (age, year)	Model X²/df (signif.)	Pseudo-R²	Logistic regression coefficients (significance)						
			Sex (F)	Ethnicity (nonwhite)	Lower class	Social disorganization	GPA	DPGB	College chances
College chances (11–14, W1)	167.378/6 (.000)	.149	–.041 (.799)	.734 (.001)	–.031 (.000)	.008 (.884)	.996 (.000)	–.006 (.007)	
College chances (14–17, W1)	201.653/6 (.000)	.202	–.598 (.001)	.376 (.153)	–.034 (.000)	–.046 (.517)	1.208 (.000)	–.004 (.072)	
College chances (14–17, W4)	238.051/6 (.000)	.201	–.251 (.123)	.607 (.004)	–.038 (.000)	–.113 (.028)	1.059 (.000)	–.007 (.000)	
College chances (17–20, W4)	154.488/6 (.000)	.156	–.372 (.035)	.586 (.015)	–.043 (.000)	.011 (.814)	.862 (.000)	–.001 (.517)	
Job chances (11–14, W1)	59.113/7 (.000)	.061	–.024 (.885)	.104 (.638)	–.006 (.299)	–.121 (.035)	.156 (.154)	.000 (.894)	1.041 (.000)
Job chances (14–17, W1)	39.090/7 (.000)	.045	–.536 (.003)	–.152 (.535)	–.005 (.384)	–.129 (.054)	.207 (.091)	–.002 (.217)	.558 (.005)
Job chances (14–17, W4)	107.571/7 (.000)	.112	–.129 (.450)	–.028 (.900)	–.003 (.573)	–.148 (.004)	.231 (.036)	–.002 (.343)	1.342 (.000)
Job chances (17–20, W4)	68.270/7 (.000)	.081	–.363 (.048)	–.563 (.015)	–.007 (.242)	–.120 (.014)	.313 (.008)	–.000 (.869)	.816 (.000)

TABLE 3. Anomia

Dependent variable (age)	R^2 (p)	Sex (F)	Ethnicity (nonwhite)	Lower class	Social disorg.	GPA	DPGB	College chances	Job chances
Anomia (11–14)	.148 (.000)	−.11 (.001)	.06 (.109)	−.04 (.298)	.02 (.595)	−.09 (.010)	.30 (.000)	−.03 (.390)	−.05 (.124)
Anomia (14–17)	.162 (.000)	−.16 (.000)	.08 (.040)	.01 (.789)	.02 (.627)	−.10 (.020)	.24 (.000)	−.08 (.048)	−.01 (.864)
Anomia (14–17)	.188 (.000)	−.12 (.000)	.07 (.028)	−.07 (.050)	.04 (.253)	−.12 (.001)	.31 (.000)	−.06 (.115)	−.04 (.241)
Anomia (17–20)	.178 (.000)	−.21 (.000)	.10 (.009)	−.05 (.161)	.08 (.030)	−.13 (.001)	.22 (.000)	−.03 (.477)	−.07 (.074)

Standardized regression coefficients (significance)

the pseudo-R^2 for the three comparisons. The model does fairly well (pseudo-R^2 = 0.14 to 0.17, p = 0.000) at explaining the differences between the conforming and nonconforming adaptations at every age. For the distinction between ritualists and conformists, the pseudo-R^2 statistic is less than 0.10 except for late adolescence (and in two cases, one in early and one in middle adolescence, the overall fit of the model shows no statistically significant improvement over chance in the explanation of the difference between ritualists and conformists). For the distinction between retreatists and innovators, the pseudo-R^2 is less than 0.10 and not statistically significant for early adolescence, but greater than 0.10 and statistically significant in middle and late adolescence.

The two consistent predictors of conforming versus nonconforming modes of adaptation are delinquent peer group bonding and anomia, both negatively related to conforming adaptations. The impact of ethnicity appears to increase gradually from early adolescence through middle adolescence to late adolescence. From early to late adolescence, the coefficient between being nonwhite and selecting a conforming mode (as opposed to a nonconforming mode) of adaptation more than doubles and goes from being not statistically significant (p = 0.232) to being statistically significant (p = 0.005). Grade point average, by contrast, appears to influence conforming/nonconforming mode of adaptation only in early adolescence. Social class shows a curious pattern, statistically significant in 1976–77 but not in 1979–80. This could reflect a period effect or the difference between the short-term and long-term impacts of parental social status. To the extent that there is an effect, lower-status individuals are more likely to adopt conforming modes of adaptation.

The findings with respect to ethnicity and social status are similar to my earlier results for Mertonian anomie theory, and may be explained in the same way. Recognizing that the model is controlling for delinquent peer group bonding and anomia, it appears that nonwhite and lower-class respondents with similar levels of illegal opportunities *who believe it is possible to succeed without breaking the rules* are even more likely to choose a conventional mode of adaptation than whites or middle-class individuals with the same beliefs.

From early to middle to late adolescence, gender becomes increasingly important as an explanation for the difference between ritualists and conformists, with females more likely than males (not statistically significantly in early adolescence but statistically significantly afterward) to adopt a ritualist rather than a conformist mode of adaptation, a mode of adaptation that accepts the normative constraints on legitimate means but abandons the cul-

TABLE 4. *Modes of Adaptation (Job Strain): Separate Logistic Regression Models*

Dependent variable (age)	Pseudo-R² (p)	Logistic regression coefficients (significance)								
		Sex (F)	Ethnicity (nonwhite)	Lower class	Social disorg.	GPA	DPGB	College chances	Job chances	Anomia
(Conformist + Ritualist vs. Innovator + Retreatist)										
Conformist (11–14)	.139 (.000)	-.03 (.888)	.32 (.232)	.02 (.000)	-.04 (.512)	.30 (.017)	-.02 (.000)	-.03 (.867)	.11 (.583)	-.12 (.000)
Conformist (14–17)	.174 (.000)	-.12 (.508)	.44 (.090)	.01 (.008)	.04 (.535)	.01 (.941)	-.02 (.000)	-.20 (.325)	-.02 (.906)	-.16 (.000)
Conformist (14–17)	.147 (.000)	-.30 (.066)	.49 (.026)	.01 (.133)	-.04 (.460)	.04 (.688)	-.02 (.000)	.05 (.796)	-.10 (.595)	-.12 (.000)
Conformist (17–20)	.144 (.000)	-.25 (.154)	.70 (.005)	.01 (.170)	-.01 (.856)	.09 (.419)	-.02 (.000)	-.29 (.143)	.06 (.750)	-.14 (.000)
(Ritualist vs. Conformist)										
Conformist (11–14)	.026 (.662)	-.37 (.333)	.78 (.190)	-.00 (.719)	-.14 (.266)	.23 (.336)	-.01 (.314)	-.00 (.998)	-.42 (.322)	.06 (.289)
Conformist (14–17)	.070 (.023)	-1.25 (.002)	.31 (.548)	-.01 (.407)	-.01 (.946)	-.34 (.170)	.01 (.388)	.16 (.681)	-.07 (.855)	-.08 (.114)
Conformist (14–17)	.061 (.136)	-1.13 (.014)	-.19 (.708)	.00 (.971)	.12 (.366)	.04 (.895)	.01 (.438)	.54 (.265)	.46 (.306)	.02 (.772)
Conformist (17–20)	.213 (.000)	-1.58 (.000)	1.00 (.134)	.03 (.022)	-.08 (.480)	-.14 (.586)	.00 (.736)	1.60 (.000)	1.23 (.002)	.08 (.215)
(Retreatist vs. Innovator)										
Innovator (11–14)	.075 (.482)	-.26 (.634)	.23 (.797)	.03 (.135)	-.02 (.899)	.74 (.049)	.00 (.893)	-.54 (.410)	.45 (.429)	.10 (.198)
Innovator (14–17)	.120 (.007)	-.139 (.004)	.54 (.502)	-.01 (.575)	.24 (.269)	.52 (.074)	.01 (.141)	.41 (.434)	.34 (.440)	.02 (.086)
Innovator (14–17)	.143 (.000)	.01 (.971)	2.58 (.015)	.01 (.495)	-.26 (.019)	-.37 (.149)	-.00 (.796)	1.03 (.049)	1.05 (.008)	.07 (.251)
Innovator (17–20)	.116 (.000)	-.64 (.067)	2.50 (.017)	.00 (.829)	-.11 (.226)	-.09 (.689)	.01 (.181)	.57 (.165)	.94 (.006)	-.07 (.189)

turally prescribed goal of occupational success. This is consistent with the literature on sex role socialization (for example, Renzetti and Curran, 1989) and may reflect differential sex role socialization with respect to economic goals. (Differential opportunity may also play a part, but this should be captured by the economic opportunity variable, job chances.) In late adolescence, social class, college chances, and economic opportunity also become salient predictors of ritualist as opposed to conformist modes of adaptation, with lower-class respondents, respondents with good perceived college chances, and respondents with good perceived job chances all the more likely to subscribe to the cultural goal of economic success and to adopt a conformist rather than a ritualist mode of adaptation. The influence of college and occupational opportunity is as expected, but again, it is *lower*-class individuals, all other things being equal, who are most likely to continue to subscribe to the goal of economic success.

Although the choice between retreatism and innovation is statistically significant when related to the variables in the model in middle and late adolescence, it is difficult to discern any systematic, consistent pattern in the relationships. In middle adolescence, gender appears to differentiate between innovators and retreatists in 1976–77 (with females again more likely to reject or abandon the goal of occupational success and thus to become retreatists rather than innovators) but not 1979–80. In the latter period, nonwhite ethnicity, low social disorganization, high college chances, and high job chances are statistically significant predictors of being an innovator as opposed to a retreatist. In late adolescence, respondents with nonwhite ethnicity and high job chances are statistically significantly more likely to be innovators as opposed to retreatists.

In summary, delinquent peer group bonding and anomia are useful for distinguishing between conforming and nonconforming adaptations but are not particularly useful for distinguishing within conforming adaptations (between conformists and ritualists) or within nonconforming adaptations (between innovators and retreatists). To the extent that statistically significant relationships are present, the most disadvantaged members of society (women, nonwhites, lower class) are more likely than their more advantaged counterparts to choose conforming modes of adaptation. If they do choose nonconforming modes of adaptation, however, females are more likely to reject the goal of occupational success and become retreatists, whereas nonwhites are more likely to retain the success goal and become innovators, particularly in later adolescence. Within the conforming modes of adaptation, women are again more likely to reject the goal of occupational success and become ritualists, but it is social class rather than ethnicity that affects the choice between ritualism and conformity, and lower-class respondents tend to adhere to the success goal and be conformists rather than ritualists. In late adolescence, perceived economic opportunity becomes significant as a predictor, not of conforming as opposed to nonconforming modes of adaptation but *within* conforming or nonconforming modes of adaptation, and individuals with little perceived opportunity are more likely to reject or abandon the goal of occupational success and become ritualists or retreatists as opposed to conformists or innovators.

Influences on Illegal Behavior

For minor offending, there is no clear developmental pattern in the explained variance for the model, which is lowest in early adolescence ($R^2 = 0.21$), then varies between 0.25 and 0.32 in middle and late adolescence. The most important influences on minor offending are delinquent peer group bonding and gender. Males and individuals with high DPGB have the highest rates of offending. Anomia is also a consistent influence, a little stronger for the younger cohorts than for the older cohorts, and not very strong overall. The influence of mode of adaptation declines with age; it is strongest in early adolescence (unstandardized regression coefficient $= 0.21$, $p = 0.000$) and weakest in late adolescence (unstandardized regression coefficient $= 0.07$, $p = 0.272$). This decline in the influence of mode of adaptation with age is *not* predicted by either Mertonian anomie theory or Cloward's differential-opportunity theory. In the test of Mertonian anomie theory, I found that mode of adaptation influenced minor offending throughout adolescence. Therefore, it is controlling only for the two opportunity structure variables, social disorganization and DPGB, that mode of adaptation shows this decline in influence with age.

The influence of social disorganization and DPGB both increase with age. The influence of social disorganization is not statistically significant in early adolescence but is statistically significant (albeit weak) in middle and late adolescence. The influence of DPGB increases from a standardized regression coefficient of .17 in early adolescence to .37 in late adolescence. It appears that as individuals get older, opportunity structure becomes more and more important in influencing minor offending. Two other variables, lower class (only in late adolescence) and GPA (for all except 14–17 year old respondents in 1976–77), also have weak influences on minor offending. Lower-class respondents were *less* likely than middle-class respondents to be involved in minor offending, as were individuals with higher GPAs. These results are presented in Table 5 and Figure 1 (presented earlier in this essay).

TABLE 5. Self-Reported Delinquency

Dependent variable (age)	R^2 (p)	Sex (F)	Ethnicity (nonwhite)	Lower class	Social disorg.	GPA	DPGB	College chances	Job chances	Anomia	Mode of adaptation
							Standardized regression coefficients (significance)				
Minor (11–14, W1)	.207 (.000)	-.13 (.000)	-.03 (.412)	-.03 (.462)	.04 (.182)	-.10 (.005)	.17 (.000)	.03 (.361)	-.06 (.069)	.10 (.005)	.21 (.000)
Minor (14–17, W1)	.247 (.000)	-.21 (.000)	-.01 (.731)	-.01 (.784)	.07 (.039)	-.05 (.212)	.23 (.000)	-.04 (.318)	.05 (.117)	.08 (.044)	.17 (.000)
Minor (14–17, W4)	.316 (.000)	-.13 (.000)	-.05 (.125)	-.06 (.086)	.09 (.002)	-.11 (.001)	.32 (.000)	.04 (.329)	.01 (.855)	.15 (.000)	.14 (.001)
Minor (17–20, W4)	.299 (.000)	-.17 (.000)	-.04 (.256)	-.09 (.012)	.09 (.005)	-.08 (.018)	.37 (.000)	.00 (.950)	.00 (.992)	.08 (.043)	.07 (.272)
Index (11–14, W1)	.112 (.000)	-.11 (.001)	-.02 (.587)	.04 (.234)	.06 (.063)	-.03 (.492)	.17 (.000)	-.04 (.292)	.01 (.715)	.11 (.005)	.07 (.276)
Index (14–17, W1)	.138 (.000)	-.13 (.000)	.07 (.071)	.10 (.015)	.05 (.126)	-.02 (.633)	.19 (.000)	-.03 (.455)	.02 (.512)	.08 (.060)	.06 (.471)
Index (14–17, W4)	.217 (.000)	-.13 (.228)	-.04 (.236)	-.02 (.667)	.12 (.000)	-.16 (.000)	.29 (.000)	.03 (.402)	.06 (.091)	.13 (.000)	.05 (.613)
Index (17–20, W4)	.213 (.000)	-.13 (.000)	-.02 (.542)	.02 (.664)	.11 (.001)	-.10 (.011)	.37 (.000)	-.05 (.191)	-.02 (.684)	-.03 (.406)	.03 (.899)

(continued)

TABLE 5. (Continued)

Dependent variable (age)	R² (p)	Sex (F)	Ethnicity (nonwhite)	Lower class	Social disorg.	GPA	DPGB	College chances	Job chances	Anomia	Mode of adaptation
					Standardized regression coefficients (significance)						
Marijuana (11–14, W1)	.171 (.000)	.03 (.342)	−.03 (.438)	−.06 (.092)	.01 (.826)	−.13 (.000)	.20 (.000)	.02 (.584)	.00 (1.000)	.07 (.064)	.22 (.000)
Marijuana (14–17, W1)	.321 (.000)	−.00 (.924)	−.01 (.810)	−.04 (.239)	−.00 (.920)	−.10 (.005)	.29 (.000)	−.01 (.689)	.06 (.061)	.05 (.209)	.33 (.000)
Marijuana (14–17, W4)	.379 (.000)	.04 (.183)	−.01 (.866)	−.01 (.667)	.04 (.116)	−.12 (.000)	.33 (.000)	.02 (.585)	.02 (.554)	.03 (.427)	.34 (.000)
Marijuana (17–20, W4)	.408 (.000)	−.06 (.062)	−.05 (.153)	−.01 (.726)	.04 (.223)	−.10 (.003)	.30 (.000)	−.02 (.522)	−.01 (.765)	.03 (.331)	.38 (.000)
Polydrug use (11–14, W1)	.050 (.000)	−.01 (.850)	−.02 (.602)	−.08 (.039)	.02 (.503)	−.06 (.105)	.17 (.000)	−.06 (.153)	.08 (.039)	−.01 (.732)	.05 (.649)
Polydrug use (14–17, W1)	.126 (.000)	.03 (.439)	−.07 (.059)	.00 (.963)	.09 (.017)	−.03 (.419)	.23 (.000)	−.07 (.119)	.10 (.006)	−.03 (.796)	.15 (.003)
Polydrug use (14–17, W4)	.263 (.000)	.10 (.002)	−.07 (.029)	−.04 (.227)	.04 (.247)	−.11 (.001)	.39 (.000)	.01 (.836)	.02 (.472)	.06 (.111)	.12 (.006)
Polydrug use (17–20, W4)	.297 (.000)	−.03 (.327)	−.07 (.036)	−.07 (.051)	.01 (.741)	−.11 (.002)	.40 (.000)	−.04 (.334)	.02 (.498)	.03 (.421)	.15 (.000)

Note: The single coefficient for the mode of adaptation, a nominal variable, is the beta coefficient adjusted for main effects and covariates from SPSS ANOVA. The formula may be found in SPSS, Inc. (1991).

Mode of adaptation is not a statistically significant influence on index offending at any age, a result that contrasts with my findings in testing Mertonian anomie theory. Again, the reason appears to be the controls for DPGB and social disorganization. DPGB is the strongest predictor of index offending, and the effect of DPGB increases with age, just as it did for minor offending. The effects of social disorganization and GPA are statistically significant for the 1979–80 period but not statistically significant at the 0.05 level for the earlier period. Anomia has a statistically significant influence on index offending in early and middle, but not late, adolescence. Besides DPGB, the strongest and most consistent influence on index offending was sex. As with minor offending, females had lower frequencies of index offending than males. Also similarly to minor offending, the explained variance is lowest in early adolescence ($R^2 = 0.11$) but shows no clear pattern thereafter, varying between 0.14 and 0.22 in middle and late adolescence.

Sex was not a statistically significant predictor of marijuana use. Instead,

FIGURE 2: *Minor and Index Offending, Marijuana and Polydrug Use*

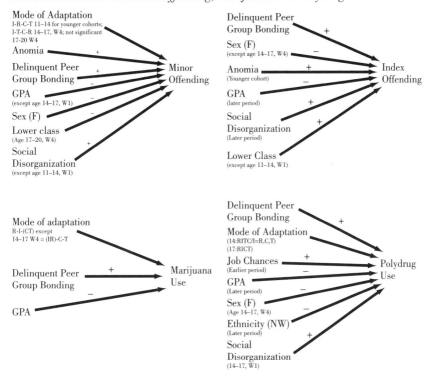

three variables, DPGB, GPA, and mode of adaptation, were consistent, statistically significant predictors of marijuana use. Of the three, mode of adaptation was consistently the strongest predictor of marijuana use, followed by DPGB and GPA in that order. Ritualists and conformists had similarly low rates of marijuana use, and with the exception of 14–17-year-old respondents in 1979–80, retreatists had the highest rates of marijuana use (and for 14–17-year-old respondents in 1979–80, the frequencies of marijuana use were almost identical). As we would expect, individuals with higher DPGB and lower GPA had higher frequencies of marijuana use. The explained variance for marijuana use increases with age, from 0.17 in early adolescence to 0.32–0.38 in middle adolescence, to over 40 percent, $R^2 = 0.41$, in late adolescence.

Polydrug use is poorly explained for 11–14-year-old respondents ($R^2 = 0.05$) and best explained for respondents in late adolescence ($R^2 = 0.30$). At all ages, DPGB is the best predictor of polydrug use, and except for early adolescence, when its influence is not statistically significant, mode of adaptation has the second strongest influence on polydrug use. The relationship between mode of adaptation and polydrug use is similar to the relationship between mode of adaptation and marijuana use. For 14–17-year-old respondents in 1979–80, innovators have higher rates of polydrug use than retreatists, but for 14–17-year-old respondents in 1976–77 and for 17–20-year-old respondents in 1979–80, retreatists have the highest rates of polydrug use. Ritualists consistently have the lowest rates of polydrug use, followed closely by conformists, for the years in which mode of adaptation is a statistically significant predictor of polydrug use.

Other statistically significant predictors of polydrug use are social class in early and late adolescence (lower social class is predictive of *lower* rates of polydrug use, possibly associated with financial availability of the drugs); GPA in 1979–80 (but not 1976–77, with higher GPA being predictive of lower frequency of polydrug use); and job chances in 1976–77 (but not in 1979–80, with better job chances being predictive of *higher* frequencies of illicit drug use, which may again reflect economic availability). There are two anomalously statistically significant coefficients, one for social disorganization for 14–17-year-old respondents in 1976–77 and one for sex for 14–17-year-old respondents in 1979–80.

Conditional Relationships

Table 6 summarizes the results of incorporating conditional relationships into the model. For minor offending, the explained variance is increased by less than 1 percent, and in three of the four tests, the increase in explained variance provided by the interaction terms is not statistically significant. In the fourth test, for 17–20-year-old respondents, the increase in the explained variance is 0.6 percent, the increase is barely statistically significant (p = 0.047), and placed in the context of four tests for an interaction effect, the observed effect could be attributed to sampling variation (four-test p = 0.175). Empirically, the simpler model without the interaction terms is preferable to the nonadditive model with the interaction terms. This also makes sense substantively, because as noted above, the offenses included in the minor offending scale are offenses for which a minimum of opportunity for learning or performance is necessary.

Although the influence of mode of adaptation on index offending is not statistically significant, the interaction between mode of adaptation and delinquent peer group bonding is statistically significant at the 0.05 level for all except 14–17-year-old respondents in 1979–80 (p = 0.071), and all of the standardized regression coefficients are greater than 0.10. This interaction term is strongest in early and late adolescence. The interaction term between mode of adaptation and social disorganization is also statistically significant but inconsistent for ages 14–17. The two interaction terms (DPGB with mode of adaptation and social disorganization with mode of adaptation) combined increase the explained variance only 1.3 to 2.5 percent. Whether this constitutes a sufficient impact on the model to justify their inclusion is questionable.

For marijuana use, there is a substantial and statistically significant increase in the explained variance (increase in R^2 = 3.4%, p = 0.000) as a result of adding the interaction terms in early adolescence. For middle adolescence, one increase is small and statistically significant, while the other is approximately zero and not statistically significant. In each instance in which the interaction terms produce a statistically significant increase in the explained variance, it is the interaction between DPGB and mode of adaptation, and not the interaction between social disorganization and mode of adaptation, that is statistically significant. For late adolescence, the increase is barely statistically significant (p = 0.049; four-test p = 0.182) and less than 1 percent. Substantively, this could reflect the more problematic nature of obtaining marijuana for younger respondents, compared with middle- and late-adolescent respondents. Inclusion of the interaction term is probably justifiable for young adolescents but questionable for middle or late adolescents.

For polydrug use, addition of the interaction terms consistently increases

TABLE 6. Conditional Relationships

Offense	Age	Year	Increase in explained variance (p)	Standardized regression coefficients (p) for interactions between . . .	
				DPGB and mode of adaptation	Social disorganization and mode of adaptation
Minor	11–14	1976–77	.0056 (.062)	.100 (.035)	.042 (.378)
	14–17	1976–77	.0023 (.343)	.077 (.186)	.033 (.516)
	14–17	1979–80	.0003 (.821)	−.001 (.992)	.028 (.532)
	17–20	1979–80	.0062 (.047)	.193 (.015)	.007 (.903)
Index	11–14	1976–77	.025 (.000)	.233 (.000)	−.059 (.235)
	14–17	1976–77	.013 (.005)	.140 (.024)	−.121 (.022)
	14–17	1979–80	.024 (.000)	.116 (.071)	.214 (.000)
	17–20	1979–80	.024 (.000)	.359 (.000)	.068 (.253)
Marijuana	11–14	1976–77	.034 (.000)	.277 (.000)	−.040 (.405)
	14–17	1976–77	.016 (.000)	.216 (.000)	−.056 (.230)
	14–17	1979–80	.0002 (.985)	−.005 (.926)	.007 (.874)
	17–20	1979–80	.0052 (.049)	.144 (.047)	−.087 (.097)
Polydrug	11–14	1976–77	.018 (.001)	.196 (.000)	.036 (.483)
	14–17	1976–77	.022 (.000)	.259 (.000)	.052 (.328)
	14–17	1979–80	.015 (.000)	.241 (.000)	.049 (.292)
	17–20	1979–80	.025 (.000)	.395 (.000)	−.045 (.419)

the explained variance by about 2 percent, and the increase in R^2 is consistently statistically significant. In every instance, it is the interaction between DPGB and mode of adaptation, not the interaction between social disorganization and mode of adaptation, that is statistically significant. Once again, the increase in the explained variance is small, and the justifiability of complicating the model (moving from an additive to a nonadditive model) is open to question.

In every case when the interaction between DPGB and mode of adaptation is statistically significant, the nature of the interaction is to increase the impact of DPGB for individuals with nonconforming modes of adaptation (retreatist, innovator) as opposed to conforming modes of adaptation (conformists, ritualists). In other words, illegitimate opportunity matters most to individuals who are predisposed to take advantage of it. Still, the small impact of the interaction terms on the model suggests that the predisposition to take advantage of illegitimate opportunity is largely rooted in a rational assessment of the extent to which one has illegitimate opportunities to take advantage of (note the impact of DPGB on the choice between conforming and nonconforming modes of adaptation). The discrepancy between the will and the ability to use illegitimate means exists but is perhaps less than we might be led to expect from Cloward (1959) and the social-disorganization tradition.

Separate Models for Conditional Relationships

Given the initial results of the analysis of the interaction terms, further exploration of the conditional relationships of illegitimate opportunity and mode of adaptation to illegal behavior was undertaken by calculating separate models for conforming and nonconforming modes of adaptation. In the separate models, modes of adaptation are dichotomized into conforming versus ritualist for the conforming modes and innovator versus retreatist for the nonconforming modes, so the full impact of mode of adaptation on illegal behavior is not observed in these models. The results are presented in Table 7. For all the dependent variables and for all age groups, both the explained variance and the effects of delinquent peer group bonding are higher for innovators and retreatists than for conformists and ritualists. For all practical purposes, the variance in marijuana use at ages 11–14, and in polydrug use for all ages except 14–17 in 1979–80, is unexplained for conformists and ritualists. Explained variance is less than 10 percent for conformists and ritualists for minor offending at ages 11–14 and 17–20, for marijuana use at all ages except ages 14–17 in 1979–80, and for index offending and polydrug use at all ages. Explained variance for innovators and retreatists is greater than 10 percent for all offenses at all ages, and greater than 20 percent with three exceptions (marijuana use at ages 14–17, 1979–80, and polydrug use at ages 11–14 and 14–17, 1976–77). In addition, the pattern of relationships in Figure 1 and Table 5 clearly reflects the pattern for innovators and retreatists, not for conformists and ritualists. The power of the differential-opportunity model is greatest for the respondents who are most heavily involved in illegal behavior.

All the explained variances for conformists and ritualists are less than the explained variances for the full sample in Table 5. For innovators and retreatists, however, six of the sixteen models (one for minor offending, three for marijuana use, and two for polydrug use) have explained variances smaller than the explained variances for the full sample. What is missing from the separate models, again, is the full influence of mode of adaptation (all four categories instead of just the two being used in each of the separate models). The principal point of Table 7 is not to suggest an alternative model but to clarify the nature of the interaction effects. Even for minor offending and marijuana use, it is evident that the explanatory power of the model and the effect of illegitimate opportunity are both conditional on the mode of adaptation.

Differential Opportunity, Anomie, and Social Control

On the whole, the differential-opportunity model fares well, but how does it compare with alternative theoretical explanations of illegal behavior? Table 8 compares the variance explained by the model of differential-opportunity theory with the variance explained by Merton's anomie theory (Menard, 1995) and control theory (Menard et al., 1993). The explained variance for differential-opportunity theory does not include interaction terms for marijuana use (except at ages 11–14) or for minor offending, but it does include the interaction terms for marijuana use at ages 11–14 and for index offending and polydrug use at all ages. Control theory and differential-opportunity theory do equally well at explaining the variance in polydrug use for ages 11–14 and 14–17 in 1976–77 if we exclude the interaction terms. Otherwise, differential-opportunity theory does better at explaining the variance in illegal behavior than control theory and Mertonian anomie theory in every comparison. The improvement over Mertonian anomie theory is consistent and sometimes substantial, with increases in explained variance of over 10 percent

TABLE 7. *Self-Reported Delinquency: Conditional Effects with Separate Models*

Dependent variable (age)	R² (p)	Sex (F)	Ethnicity (nonwhite)	Lower class	Social disorg.	GPA	DPGB	College chances	Job chances	Anomia	Mode of adaptation
						Standardized regression coefficients (significance)					
Conformists and Ritualists											
Minor (11–14, W1)	.065 (.000)	−.15 (.000)	.02 (.656)	.01 (.859)	.02 (.676)	−.05 (.296)	.09 (.035)	−.03 (.467)	−.06 (.124)	.07 (.095)	.01 (.762)
Minor (14–17, W1)	.129 (.000)	−.23 (.000)	−.07 (.175)	−.02 (.637)	.08 (.108)	−.02 (.769)	.16 (.001)	−.10 (.056)	.01 (.785)	.06 (.235)	−.03 (.572)
Minor (14–17, W4)	.153 (.000)	−.14 (.000)	−.02 (.665)	−.03 (.455)	.09 (.029)	−.08 (.078)	.25 (.000)	.03 (.540)	.06 (.159)	.11 (.011)	.01 (.892)
Minor (17–20, W4)	.097 (.000)	−.13 (.019)	−.02 (.720)	−.07 (.241)	.09 (.088)	−.05 (.411)	.18 (.001)	.11 (.067)	−.03 (.589)	.07 (.270)	.02 (.770)
Innovators and Retreatists											
Minor (11–14, W1)	.292 (.000)	−.12 (.069)	−.10 (.123)	−.13 (.062)	.08 (.213)	−.28 (.000)	.27 (.000)	−.21 (.004)	−.03 (.710)	.14 (.043)	−.00 (.967)
Minor (14–17, W1)	.249 (.000)	−.21 (.000)	.08 (.164)	.01 (.901)	.08 (.140)	−.10 (.101)	.27 (.000)	.04 (.512)	.09 (.094)	.12 (.033)	.10 (.053)
Minor (14–17, W4)	.305 (.000)	−.16 (.002)	−.09 (.112)	−.09 (.104)	.09 (.109)	−.15 (.015)	.31 (.000)	.03 (.674)	−.06 (.297)	.18 (.002)	.05 (.371)
Minor (17–20, W4)	.328 (.000)	−.23 (.000)	−.05 (.276)	−.12 (.018)	.10 (.036)	−.10 (.043)	.38 (.000)	−.07 (.168)	.01 (.915)	.10 (.051)	−.01 (.749)

Conformists and Ritualists

Index (11–14, W1)	.039 (.008)	−.10 (.015)	.03 (.528)	.05 (.258)	.08 (.061)	−.02 (.624)	.02 (.585)	−.03 (.505)	.02 (.683)	.08 (.065)	.04 (.371)
Index (14–17, W1)	.097 (.000)	−.09 (.077)	−.01 (.801)	.13 (.016)	.16 (.001)	.03 (.635)	.08 (.110)	−.05 (.355)	−.01 (.850)	.12 (.021)	.01 (.813)
Index (14–17, W4)	.065 (.000)	−.09 (.034)	−.02 (.721)	.02 (.652)	.02 (.614)	−.04 (.394)	.17 (.000)	.04 (.445)	.03 (.507)	.09 (.050)	−.04 (.391)
Index (17–20, W4)	.061 (.020)	−.16 (.003)	−.08 (.163)	.05 (.437)	.14 (.012)	−.08 (.159)	.07 (.230)	.01 (.819)	−.03 (.567)	−.03 (.575)	−.00 (.954)

Innovators and Retreatists

Index (11–14, W1)	.221 (.000)	−.16 (.021)	−.09 (.212)	.05 (.493)	−.01 (.840)	−.03 (.659)	.29 (.000)	−.08 (.302)	.04 (.598)	.16 (.030)	−.01 (.911)
Index (14–17, W1)	.209 (.000)	−.21 (.000)	.18 (.002)	.05 (.358)	−.05 (.342)	−.08 (.250)	.22 (.000)	−.03 (.713)	.06 (.320)	.05 (.407)	.05 (.332)
Index (14–17, W4)	.305 (.000)	−.03 (.592)	−.06 (.308)	−.03 (.546)	.22 (.000)	−.26 (.000)	.25 (.000)	.02 (.777)	.10 (.062)	.16 (.005)	−.04 (.482)
Index (17–20, W4)	.252 (.000)	−.15 (.004)	.00 (.939)	.01 (.869)	.13 (.009)	−.10 (.069)	.36 (.000)	−.09 (.131)	−.02 (.709)	−.00 (.930)	−.02 (.627)

Conformists and Ritualists

Marijuana (11–14, W1)	.024 (.155)	−.03 (.418)	.03 (.540)	.00 (.941)	.01 (.889)	−.08 (.093)	.01 (.839)	−.07 (.139)	.06 (.356)	.05 (.278)	.06 (.149)
Marijuana (14–17, W1)	.061 (.003)	−.04 (.412)	−.00 (.991)	.03 (.613)	−.06 (.343)	.05 (.258)	.12 (.019)	−.08 (.131)	.11 (.038)	.07 (.204)	−.04 (.427)
Marijuana (14–17, W4)	.129 (.000)	.07 (.101)	.00 (.976)	.01 (.760)	.06 (.168)	−.15 (.001)	.31 (.000)	−.00 (.936)	−.03 (.455)	−.03 (.505)	.04 (.342)
Marijuana (17–20, W4)	.085 (.001)	.00 (.961)	−.08 (.196)	−.02 (.791)	.14 (.011)	−.04 (.503)	.19 (.001)	−.04 (.473)	.19 (.130)	.03 (.566)	.03 (.541)

(continued)

TABLE 7. (Continued)

Dependent variable (age)	R² (p)	Sex (F)	Ethnicity (nonwhite)	Lower class	Social disorg.	GPA	DPGB	College chances	Job chances	Anomia	Mode of adaptation
					Standardized regression coefficients (significance)						
Innovators and Retreatists											
Marijuana (11–14, W1)	.250 (.000)	.11 (.094)	−.07 (.303)	−.17 (.016)	−.04 (.554)	−.23 (.002)	.36 (.000)	.16 (.028)	−.02 (.769)	.08 (.245)	−.10 (.130)
Marijuana (14–17, W1)	.215 (.000)	.02 (.714)	−.00 (.970)	−.10 (.084)	−.04 (.426)	−.16 (.012)	.40 (.000)	.07 (.276)	.02 (.731)	.04 (.470)	−.01 (.920)
Marijuana (14–17, W4)	.183 (.000)	.02 (.743)	−.01 (.835)	−.04 (.483)	.06 (.307)	−.13 (.044)	.36 (.000)	.06 (.359)	.07 (.224)	.07 (.239)	.00 (.957)
Marijuana (17–20, W4)	.216 (.000)	−.11 (.029)	−.04 (.431)	−.03 (.614)	−.00 (.953)	−.16 (.003)	.33 (.000)	−.02 (.686)	.00 (.969)	.05 (.337)	−.08 (.119)
Conformists and Ritualists											
Polydrug use (11–14, W1)	.018 (.386)	.02 (.593)	.03 (.437)	−.06 (.194)	−.02 (.696)	−.09 (.049)	.04 (.407)	−.04 (.420)	.05 (.272)	−.07 (.115)	.02 (.603)
Polydrug use (14–17, W1)	.024 (.421)	.02 (.697)	−.05 (.360)	.05 (.406)	.09 (.082)	−.01 (.821)	.03 (.510)	−.07 (.187)	.08 (.108)	−.06 (.263)	−.04 (.453)
Polydrug use (14–17, W4)	.066 (.000)	.12 (.005)	−.09 (.043)	.03 (.552)	.02 (.677)	−.04 (.390)	.19 (.000)	−.05 (.374)	−.05 (.308)	.02 (.639)	.07 (.114)
Polydrug use (17–20, W4)	.046 (.099)	.07 (.219)	−.11 (.075)	.01 (.825)	.07 (.202)	−.03 (.565)	.07 (.217)	−.12 (.053)	−.05 (.441)	.02 (.749)	.06 (.299)
Innovators and Retreatists											
Polydrug use (11–14, W1)	.178 (.000)	−.07 (.320)	−.11 (.124)	−.10 (.177)	.05 (.503)	−.04 (.648)	.27 (.000)	−.10 (.188)	.17 (.022)	.09 (.209)	.02 (.733)
Polydrug use (14–17, W1)	.131 (.000)	.02 (.716)	−.07 (.232)	−.01 (.857)	.10 (.076)	−.04 (.519)	.28 (.000)	−.06 (.434)	.11 (.069)	.07 (.241)	.00 (.952)
Polydrug use (14–17, W4)	.247 (.000)	.07 (.187)	−.09 (.116)	−.09 (.118)	.07 (.188)	−.16 (.008)	.42 (.000)	.04 (.514)	.08 (.148)	.07 (.240)	−.00 (.974)
Polydrug use (17–20, W4)	.272 (.000)	−.08 (.109)	−.10 (.050)	−.12 (.020)	.01 (.904)	−.16 (.002)	.43 (.000)	−.02 (.765)	.03 (.571)	.04 (.414)	−.04 (.381)

for minor offending, index offending, and polydrug use for 17–20-year-old respondents. As with Mertonian anomie theory, explanatory power tends to be lowest in early adolescence and highest in late adolescence, a pattern more clearly in evidence for illicit drug use than for other forms of illegal behavior.

Explained variance is not the only criterion by which the different theories should be judged, however. Equally important is the extent to which the results of the theory testing are consistent with the specific predictions of the theory. In this respect, anomie theory fares best. None of my earlier findings (Menard, 1995) was contradictory to the predictions from Merton's anomie theory. Social-control theory represents the opposite situation. Much of the variance explained by control theory (Menard et al., 1993) was attributable to the positive effect of involvement with friends on illegal behavior, an effect whose sign was the opposite of what control theory predicted. Differential-opportunity theory represents an intermediate case, closer to anomie than to control theory. Most of the results are consistent with the predictions derived from differential-opportunity theory. The principal exception is the absence of any impact of mode of adaptation on index offending, and even this exception is largely eliminated if we rely on the model for index offending that includes the interaction terms (particularly DPGB with mode of adaptation) as influences on illegal behavior.

TABLE 8. *Comparison of Control, Anomie, and Differential-Opportunity Theories (R²)*

Explained variance	R^2	Age			
		11–14, W1	*14–17, W1*	*14–17, W4*	*17–20, W4*
Control	Minor	.17	.18	.24	.19
	Index	.10	.08	.13	.11
	Marijuana	.16	.30	.34	.34
	Polydrug	.05	.13	.25	.25
Cloward— opportunity theory	Minor	.21	.25	.32	.30
	Index	.14	.15	.24	.24
	Marijuana	.21	.32	.38	.41
	Polydrug	.07	.15	.28	.32
Merton—Anomie	Minor	.17	.19	.23	.19
	Index	.08	.10	.14	.10
	Marijuana	.14	.25	.30	.34
	Polydrug	.02	.08	.15	.18
Difference	Minor	.04	.06	.09	.11
	Index	.03	.04	.08	.11
	Marijuana	.03	.07	.08	.07
	Polydrug	.03	.05	.11	.12

Conclusion

It is evident from the foregoing analysis that differential-opportunity theory does quite well as an explanation for illegal behavior and that the explanatory power of the model increases with age. The relationships are consistent with expectations from the theory, especially when full consideration is given to the nature of conditional relationships suggested by the theory. In every case, the mode of adaptation affects the explanatory power of the model and the strength of the influence of illegitimate opportunity, specifically delinquent peer group bonding, on illegal behavior. This conditional relationship is especially important for more serious forms of illegal behavior (index offending and polydrug use) and for early adolescent (age 11–14) marijuana use.

It remains to be seen whether the power of the theory holds as well for adult respondents. It would also be interesting to see whether the model does as well for males as for females, for majority and minority ethnic group members, and for individuals from different social strata. These concerns are beyond the scope of this essay but deserve careful attention in future research. Another issue that deserves more attention in future research is the causal ordering of delinquent peer group bonding relative to several other variables in the model, as discussed earlier. The competing ordering suggested by the integrated theory of Elliott et al. (1985, 1989), in particular, deserves consideration. It is worth noting that many of the same variables used in testing the integrated theory were used in testing differential-opportunity theory, but they were used in different ways. Differences include the treatment of beliefs as a component of mode of adaptation and the extraction of elements of the normlessness scales to construct the anomia scale. This serves to highlight the integrated nature of differential opportunity, often overlooked prior to Cullen's (1988) discussion of Cloward and Ohlin's differential-opportunity theory as an integrated theory. A conceptual and empirical comparison of differential opportunity and the integrated theory of Elliott et al. is another promising possibility for future research.

In the past decade, the anomie/strain theory tradition in criminology has been invigorated by new theoretical statements (Agnew 1985, 1992), by careful reconsideration of the content of anomie and strain theories, and by reexamination of earlier tests of those theories (Bernard, 1987; Cullen, 1988). In addition, better methods of analysis and better data have made it possible to model the complex theories developed in the anomie/strain tradition more fully and to do so with full attention to the possibility that the explanatory power and the relationships described by those theories may vary over the life course. As more appropriate models and data are brought to bear, the result has been new and powerful support for anomie and strain theory as an explanation for illegal behavior. Whether these results can be consistently replicated, and whether anomie and differential-opportunity theories can do as well as other integrated theoretical perspectives for explaining illegal behavior, still remains to be resolved by future research.

Notes

1. With the data used in the present study, it is not possible to distinguish between retreatists and rebels. For a more detailed discussion of these modes of adaptation, see Merton (1968). For details on their operationalization in the present study, see Menard (1995). Note that Cloward and Ohlin (1960) paralleled Merton's individual modes of adaptation with a typology of three subcultures: conflict (not corresponding precisely to any of Merton's modes of adaptation), criminal (corresponding to Merton's innovators), and retreatist (corresponding to Merton's retreatists).

2. Limited empirical testing of the plausibility of this ordering was also undertaken with an analysis of Granger causality (Granger, 1969; see also Menard, 1991, pp. 56–58). This involves regressing each variable on past values of that same variable and on a proposed cause to see whether the proposed cause has an effect above and beyond the past values of the proposed effect. The Granger causality analysis for delinquent peer group bonding suggested placement of delinquent peer group bonding causally subsequent to grade point average, college chances, job chances, and anomia. This ordering was not selected because it was not considered as consistent with differential-opportunity theory as an ordering in which DPGB precedes college chances, job chances, and anomia, but it further reinforces the point that the causal ordering of DPGB relative to these other variables deserves further consideration.

References

Agnew, Robert S. 1985. A revised strain theory of delinquency. *Social Forces* 64:151–66.
———. 1992. Foundation for a general strain theory of crime and delinquency. *Criminology* 30:47–87.
Agresti, Alan, and Barbara Finlay. 1986. *Statistical methods for the social sciences*. 2d ed. San Francisco: Dellen/Macmillan.
Bernard, Thomas J. 1984. Control criticisms of strain theory: An assessment of theoretical and empirical adequacy. *Journal of Research in Crime and Delinquency* 21:353–72.
———. 1987. Testing structural strain theories. *Journal of Research in Crime and Delinquency* 21:353–72.
Blumstein, Alfred, Jacqueline Cohen, Jeffrey A. Roth, and Christy A. Visher, eds. 1986. *Criminal careers and career criminals*. Vol. I. Washington, D.C.: National Academy Press.

Boocock, Sarane S. 1980. *Sociology of education: An introduction.* Boston: Houghton Mifflin.

Cloward, Richard A. 1959. Illegitimate means, anomie, and deviant behavior. *American Sociological Review* 24:164–76.

Cloward, Richard A., and Lloyd E. Ohlin. 1960. *Delinquency and opportunity: A theory of delinquent gangs.* New York: Free Press.

Cohen, Albert K. 1955. *Delinquent boys.* Glencoe, Ill.: Free Press.

Cohen, Lawrence E., and Marcus Felson. 1979. Social change and crime rate trends: A routine activities approach. *American Sociological Review* 44:588–608.

Cohen, Lawrence E., James Kluegel, and Kenneth Land. 1981. Social inequality and predatory criminal victimization: An exposition and test of a formal theory. *American Sociological Review* 46:505–24.

Covey, Herbert C., Scott Menard, and Robert J. Franzese. 1992. *Juvenile gangs.* Springfield, Ill.: Charles C. Thomas.

Cullen, Francis T. 1988. Were Cloward and Ohlin strain theorists? *Journal of Research in Crime and Delinquency* 25:214–41.

Durkheim, Emile. (1951). *Suicide.* Edited by George Simpson. Translated by John A. Spaulding and George Simpson. New York: Free Press.

Elliott, Delbert S., and Suzanne S. Ageton. 1980. Reconciling race and class differences in self-reported and official estimates of delinquency. *American Sociological Review* 40:95–110.

Elliott, Delbert S., Suzanne S. Ageton, David H. Huizinga, Brian A. Knowles, and Rachelle J. Canter. 1983. *The prevalence and incidence of delinquent behavior: 1976–1980.* National Youth Survey Report No. 26. Boulder, Colo.: Behavioral Research Institute.

Elliott, Delbert S., David Huizinga, and Suzanne S. Ageton. 1985. *Explaining delinquency and drug use.* Beverly Hills, Calif.: Sage.

Elliott, Delbert S., David Huizinga, and Scott Menard. 1989. *Multiple problem youth: Delinquency, substance use, and mental health problems.* New York: Springer-Verlag.

Felson, Marcus, and Lawrence E. Cohen. 1980. Human ecology and crime: A routine activity approach. *Human Ecology* 8:289–406.

Granger, C. W. J. 1969. Investigating causal relations by econometric models and cross-spectral methods. *Econometrica* 37:424–38.

Hindelang, Michael, Michael Gottfredson, and James Garofalo. 1978. *Victims of personal crime: An empirical foundation for a theory of personal victimization.* Cambridge, Mass.: Ballinger.

Kobrin, Solomon. 1951. The conflict of values in delinquency areas. *American Sociological Review* 16:653–61.

Menard, Scott. 1991. *Longitudinal research.* Newbury Park, Calif.: Sage.

———. 1995. A developmental test of Mertonian anomie theory. *Journal of Research in Crime and Delinquency* 32:136–74.

Menard, Scott, and Delbert S. Elliott. 1994. Delinquent bonding, moral beliefs, and illegal behavior: A three-wave panel model. *Justice Quarterly* 11:173–88.

Menard, Scott, Delbert S. Elliott, and Sharon Wofford. 1993. Social control theories in developmental perspective. *Studies in Crime and Crime Prevention* 2:69–87.

Merton, Robert K. (1938). Social structure and anomie. *American Sociological Review* 3:672–82.

———. 1957. *Social theory and social structure*. Rev. ed. New York: Free Press.

———. 1959. Social conformity, deviation, and opportunity structures: A comment on the contributions of Dubin and Cloward. *American Sociological Review* 24:177–89.

———. 1964. Anomie, anomia, and social interaction: Contexts of deviant behavior. In *Anomie and Deviant Behavior: A Discussion and Critique*, edited by M. B. Clinard, 213–42. New York: Free Press.

———. 1968. *Social Theory and social structure*. Enlarged ed. New York: Free Press.

Renzetti, Claire M., and Daniel J. Curran. 1989. *Women, men, and society: The sociology of gender*. Boston: Allyn and Bacon.

Roitberg, Thalia, and Scott Menard. 1995. Adolescent violence: A test of integrated theory. *Studies on Crime and Crime Prevention* 4:177–96.

Shaw, Clifford R. 1930. *The Jack-roller*. Chicago: University of Chicago Press.

———. 1931. *The natural history of a delinquent career*. Chicago: University of Chicago Press.

Shaw, Clifford R., and Henry D. McKay. 1942. *Juvenile delinquency and urban areas*. Chicago: University of Chicago Press.

SPSS, Inc. 1991. *SPSS statistical algorithms*. 2d ed. Chicago: SPSS, Inc.

Sutherland, Edwin H., ed. 1937. *The professional thief*. Chicago: University of Chicago Press.

———. 1947. *Principles of criminology*. 4th ed. Philadelphia: J. B. Lippincott.

———. 1949. *White collar crime*. New York: Dryden.

Weber, Max. 1920 (1947). *The theory of social and economic organization*. Edited by Talcott Parsons. Translated by A. M. Henderson and Talcott Parsons. New York: Free Press.

FRANCIS T. CULLEN & JOHN PAUL WRIGHT

Liberating the Anomie-Strain Paradigm: Implications from Social-Support Theory

For much of its history, American criminological theory has developed within neatly defined paradigms sporting names familiar even to students in introductory courses (e.g., strain, control, cultural deviance, labeling, critical). Of course, attempts at theoretical integration have not been unknown or without value (Messner, Krohn, and Liska, 1989). Nonetheless, the lines demarcating prevailing paradigms have been brightly drawn, and criminologists have tended to convey standard accounts of these theories in their classes and, within their scholarship, to test repeatedly traditional statements of the theories against one another (see Burton, 1990).

This developmental pathway has produced a wealth of useful empirical information but also has had a dysfunctional side: theoretical paradigms have been stunted in their growth. Once packaged into neat paradigms, the theories tend to be reduced to their central propositions, reified, and then transmitted and tested in this bare-bones form. The richness of the initial statements is not fully appreciated, and thus the lines for advancing the theory are closed off.

Until recently, Robert K. Merton's paradigm of social structure and anomie had suffered this fate (Burton and Cullen, 1992). In *Causes of Delinquency*, Hirschi (1969) conceptualized Merton's work as being a "strain theory" and as being in competition with cultural-deviance theory and his own social-bond theory (see also Kornhauser, 1978). Hirschi's approach was innovative and allowed him to undertake a pathbreaking empirical analysis. But Hirschi's success had a downside: Too many criminologists uncritically embraced his portrayal of criminological theory and, in particular, his truncated version of "strain theory" became reified as the standard statement of the paradigm.

Few scholars asked whether Hirschi's rendering of strain theory captured the full complexity of what Merton and his followers, such as Cohen and

Cloward and Ohlin, had written. For example, there was little examination of factors in addition to strain that these theorists highlighted as being important (Cullen, 1984, 1988), and there was little consideration of whether Hirschi's operationalization of strain was adequate (Burton and Cullen, 1992; Farnworth and Leiber, 1989). And there was little thought given to the fact that Merton conceived his work as a macrolevel theory oriented toward the explanation of rates of deviance—and not as an individual-level theory which linked crime ineluctably to personal feelings of strain. In fact, this anomie portion of his theory was, as Messner (1988, p. 33) points out, "the road not taken" (see also Messner and Rosenfeld, 1994).

In the past half decade or so, however, there has been not only a revival of interest in Merton's paradigm but also concerted efforts to expand anomie-strain theory in new directions (Adler and Laufer, 1995; Agnew, 1992; Agnew, Cullen, Burton, Evans, and Dunaway, 1996; Bernard, 1987; Burton and Dunaway, 1994; Burton and Cullen, 1992; Burton, Cullen, Evans, and Dunaway, 1994; Cullen, 1988; Menard, 1995; Messner, 1988; Messner and Rosenfeld, 1994; Passas, 1990; Paternoster and Mazerole, 1994; Rosenfeld, 1989; Rosenfeld and Messner, 1995). Taken together, these writings have succeeded in *liberating* anomie-strain theory from the prepackaged versions most criminologists learned in graduate school and by reading theory textbooks.

Although these writings might be mined for a variety of profitable lines of inquiry, two perspectives already have captured criminologists' imagination. First, on the individual level, Agnew's (1992) "general strain theory" offers the commonsensical, but nonetheless overlooked, observation that strains other than blocked success goals—the causal factor central to traditional strain theory—can result in wayward conduct (see also Agnew, 1985, 1989, 1995; Agnew and White, 1992). Second, on the macrolevel, Messner and Rosenfeld's (1994; Rosenfeld and Messner, 1995) "institutional-anomie theory" expands Merton's anomie theory by showing how crime rates are shaped not only by anomie within economic institutions but also by anomie and the attenuation of controls within a variety of other social institutions (e.g., the family).

The purpose of this essay is to contribute to the recent movement to liberate anomie-strain theory from the strictures imposed by its traditional conceptualization in the discipline. In particular, we attempt to show how these two prominent developments in the anomie-strain paradigm—general strain theory and institutional-anomie theory—might be extended further by considering the role of "social support" in crime causation (Cullen, 1994;

Wright, Cullen, and Wooldredge, 1995). Social-support theory has been used widely to explain dysfunctional human development (Thoits, 1995; Vaux, 1988), but it has been largely neglected by criminologists. We argue that this oversight potentially impoverishes our understanding of crime causation and, in particular, that social-support theory is complementary and consistent with both individual-level and macrolevel strain theories.

Before beginning this analysis, we will note that Merton never intended his theory to be static—a theoretical shrine to be visited for purposes of paying homage. Instead, Merton (1959, 1964, 1995) sees his theory as dynamic, as evolving to incorporate fresh ideas that explain larger chunks of social reality. He has frequently observed, of course, that knowledge grows not by standing in the obscuring shadow of intellectual giants but by standing on their shoulders and seeing horizons not visible from a lower vantage point (Merton, 1965). Criminologists, therefore, do not do justice to Merton's tradition by clinging to a static, truncated version of his theory but rather by standing on his broad shoulders and exploring new theoretical vistas (see also Passas, 1995).

Advancing General Strain Theory

As alluded to above, Agnew advanced Merton's paradigm of social structure and anomie by arguing that people can be exposed to an array of strains that might result in crime and delinquency. This insight is not fully new, because various forms of strain previously had been linked to criminality and an array of wayward activities (Cullen, 1984, pp. 55–75; see also Vaux and Ruggerio, 1983; Peirce, Frone, Russell, and Cooper, 1994). Agnew's unique contribution, however, was to make the explicit observation that Merton had identified only one category of strain: the blockage of positively valued goals—in concrete terms, the denial of the goal of success. He observed that in their empirical tests, criminologists relied almost exclusively on the strain models developed by Merton and his followers, while simultaneously concluding that empirical support for strain theory was shaky (but see Burton and Cullen, 1992). This tendency to "cling to the early strain models," continued Agnew, only obfuscated the possibility that other strains existed and should be explored to "fully exploit the potential of strain theory" (1992, p. 75). Agnew then moved to liberate strain theory by delineating two sources of strain that criminologists had previously ignored: "the actual or anticipated removal of valued stimuli" and "the actual or anticipated presentation of negatively valued stimuli" (1992, p. 47).

It seems likely that this portion of Agnew's theory will receive much empirical test in the time ahead, for the research task appears clear: test to see how various measures of strain are related to crime and delinquency. However, Agnew understood that strain does not lead ineluctably to criminal conduct. "Virtually all strain theories," he noted, "acknowledge that only *some* strained individuals turn to delinquency" (1992, p. 66; emphasis in original). Accordingly, he argued for the necessity of exploring "those factors that influence whether one adapts to strain using delinquent or nondelinquent means" (1992, p. 66).

In essence, Agnew conveyed that a complete strain model needs to delineate not only sources of strain but also the *intervening variables* that determine when strain does, or does not, result in criminal behavior. In the past, however, criminologists testing strain theory have only rarely assessed the effects of intervening variables in specifying when strain eventuates in crime or delinquency (Cullen, 1984). (This neglect will be explored below in more detail.) Given this narrow perspective, it remains problematic whether the criminologists who assess general strain theory will examine *systematically* not only diverse strains but also the intervening variables that shape when these strains prove criminogenic.

Again, Agnew has furnished leads as to the social-psychological and macrolevel "constraints to nondelinquent and delinquent coping" (1992, pp. 71–73). For our purposes, it is instructive that Agnew explicitly recognized the compatibility between general strain theory and social-support theory. He contended that the presence of social support "facilitates . . . coping. . . . Adolescents with conventional social supports, then, should be better able to respond to objective strains in a nondelinquent manner" (1992, pp. 71–72). We will argue that social support is a major intervening variable that insulates strained individuals from coping through criminal means.

THE NEGLECT OF INTERVENING VARIABLES

With few exceptions, criminological tests of strain theory proceed in a uniform fashion: Individuals are measured for how much strain they have, and then the researcher determines if the strain index is related to the (self-report) crime measure. This approach is similar to how other theories are assessed; researchers typically explore whether having a greater dose of a causal variable defined by the theory increases crime. But such a research design makes it impossible to assess a proposition integral to strain theory: Having high levels of strain—the theory's causal variable—does *not* necessarily mean that individuals will break the law. As noted, crime is held to occur only when strain interacts with certain theoretically relevant intervening variables. Unless this issue is addressed, tests of strain theory will be misspecified and conclusions regarding the adequacy of the perspective will be misleading.

Revisiting Merton's writings reveals the origins of this matter. His "typology of adaptations" suggests that anomic strain can be coped with in one of five ways, including four deviant modes of adaptation and conformity. The presence of strain might make deviance more likely (Merton, 1995), but this conclusion is qualified in two ways. First, most people in society do not respond to strain by deviant conduct; "conformity . . . is the most common and widely diffused" adaptation (Merton, 1968, p. 141). Second, Merton recognized that uncovering the source of deviance—his chief theoretical concern—did not complete the explanatory task, for it was still necessary to account for the factors that made certain adaptations more likely than others. He cautioned that his essay "Social Structure and Anomie" has "not included a detailed treatment of the structural elements which predispose toward one rather than another of the alternative responses open to individuals; it has neglected, but not denied the relevance of, the social-psychological processes determining the specific incidence of these responses" (1968, p. 160).

Merton's observations that strain can produce different responses and that factors *other than strain* determine which adaptation is chosen have, at most, been given passing attention by all but a few criminologists (Cullen, 1984). As noted, scholars have reduced Merton's paradigm to a theory of a single adaptation: the more strain there is, the more crime (or delinquency) will occur. The problem with this reductionism is that it obscures the need to consider whether factors might intervene to suppress criminal responses to strain, making conformity or other deviant behaviors more likely.

Consider one example of how the neglect of intervening variables can potentially result in theoretical confusion. A criminologist operating in the strain tradition would argue that men have higher rates of crime because they are under more strain than women. But scholars looking at mental illness, where the evidence suggests that women have higher rates of psychiatric symptomatology, would draw the opposite conclusion: women are under more strain (Gove and Tudor, 1973). An alternative perspective, however, would be that men and women may have similar levels of strain, but because of distinctive gender roles, they respond to that strain in different ways (Cloward and Piven, 1979; Cullen, 1984). This possibility cannot be explored—

theoretically or empirically—unless the causal role of intervening variables is contemplated.

This is not to say, of course, that responses to strain are fully indeterminate—that strain can give rise to a virtually unlimited range of responses. It may well be that certain types of strain are more strongly related to crime than to other forms of deviance. Further, it may well be that the effects of strain are, to a greater or lesser degree, "general," in the sense that they may make all, or most, forms of deviance more probable. Even so, these are issues to be sorted out empirically, and they do not obviate the need to include intervening variables in assessments of strain theory.

Although not often fully understood (Cullen, 1984, 1988), the case for a theory of intervening variables was the goal underlying Richard Cloward's (1959) work on "illegitimate opportunity structures" (see also Cloward and Ohlin, 1960; Cloward and Piven, 1979; Cloward and Piven, with Cullen and Tichen, 1977). Most criminologists view Cloward as offering a strain model of delinquency or, at best, as offering a "mixed model" that merges strain and cultural deviance theories to explain subcultural delinquency (Cullen, 1984, 1988; Kornhauser, 1978). But this is a narrow reading of Cloward's writings.

By revisiting Cloward's (1959) initial statement on illegitimate means, it is clear that his major contribution was to draw from the writings of the Chicago school the insight that people could not simply deviate in any way of their choosing. Rather, learning (values, skills) and performance (opportunity) structures—the components of illegitimate means—limit criminal and other deviant options available to them. By focusing on how access to the values, skills, and opportunities needed for criminal or deviant roles is socially patterned, it would be possible to discern when specific adaptations would transpire. "Once processes generating differentials in pressures are identified," Cloward (1959, p. 167) contended, "there is then the question of how these pressures are resolved, or how men respond to them."

This perspective informed his investigation with Lloyd Ohlin (1960) of types of delinquent subcultures. Scholars have questioned the substantive accuracy of this work—in particular, whether pure forms of conflict, criminal, and retreatist subcultures exist (Short and Strodtbeck, 1965)—but the empirical defensibility of this one application of the theory does not undermine the central points Cloward makes regarding intervening variables. The core principle is expressed in *Delinquency and Opportunity*. According to Cloward and Ohlin (1960, p. 43), "some variables help us to explain why predispositions to deviate from accepted norms arise; other variables tell us why delin-quent rather than other types of deviance are selected."

It is instructive that in assessing Cloward's 1959 article, Merton recog-nized the value of the illegitimate means idea. "Pressures for deviant behav-ior are one thing," observed Merton (1959, p. 188), "actual rates of deviant behavior quite another." Cloward's work on illegitimate means is valuable because it illuminates the need "to identify other sociological variables that intervene between structurally induced pressure for deviant behavior and actual rates of such behavior" (1959, p. 188).

In summary, a complete strain theory is not merely a theory of sources of strain but of how people respond to strains. Although this point has not shaped understandings or empirical tests of Merton's work, Agnew (1992) fully understood the importance of intervening variables when he set forth his general strain theory. Hopefully, Agnew will not suffer the fate of Cloward (and Ohlin) and have his work reduced to nothing more than a theory of the sources of strain. In this regard, we would suggest that social support is one category of intervening variables that should be considered in the continuing effort to build a more systematic general strain theory of crime and delin-quency.

SOCIAL SUPPORT AS AN INTERVENING VARIABLE

Although examined only infrequently by criminologists (for exceptions, see Cullen, 1994; Currie, 1985; Drennon-Gala, 1995; Hepburn, 1977; Wright, 1996; Wright, Cullen, and Wooldredge, 1995), the concept of social support has exerted a major influence among scholars investigating the psychosocial origins of health (Cohen and Wills, 1985; House, Landis, and Umberson, 1988; Lin and Ensel, 1986; Thoits, 1995; Vaux, 1988). Noteworthy for our purposes, the social-support paradigm was formulated as a way of extending existing research on the relationship between "stress"—or "strain" in our terms—and health outcomes, ranging from psychiatric problems to alcohol-ism to physical ailments. These researchers understood that stress (or strain) did not lead ineluctably to deviance or ill health, for its effects might be diminished if a person were to be enmeshed in social relationships that pro-vided support. As noted above, we are proposing a similar intellectual mar-riage within criminology: coupling general strain theory with social-support theory.

Detailed analyses of the concept of social support are available and do not need to be repeated here (see, in particular, Vaux, 1988). For the uninitiated reader, however, we will briefly share a typical definition of support. Lin

(1986, p. 18) defines social support as "the perceived or actual instrumental and/or expressive provisions supplied by the community, social networks, and confiding partners." The distinguishing feature of social support is that it involves the transfer of resources—such as money, information, emotional understanding, the expression of positive regard—from one person to another. In this respect, the social-support paradigm intersects with the current interest in how "social capital" resides in the quality of relationships and may work to reduce criminal involvement (Hagan, 1994).

In the health literature, social support is viewed as reducing unhealthy outcomes in two ways. First, support has a direct or main effect on well-being; those who have supportive relationships generally are healthier physically and psychologically. Second and more closely related to our concerns here, support can have a "buffering effect" on stress (usually measured by the interaction term of stress X support). When individuals experience a stressful life event or are under chronic life stresses, social support is mobilized to mitigate the potentially pathological consequences of the stress (Cohen and Wills, 1985; Thoits, 1995; Vaux, 1988). For example, in times of financial crisis, support might involve providing a loan or a place to live; in times of emotional crisis, support might involve serving as a confidante or facilitating entry into psychotherapy. Thoits (1995, p. 64) captures this process by likening social support to a "social 'fund' from which people may draw when handling stressors."

Criminologists interested in the causal effects of support on crime might profitably explore both these effects—direct and buffering (Cullen, 1994; Wright, 1996). With regard to general strain theory, however, social support would be explored more as an intervening variable that buffers against strain. This effect could occur in either of two ways. On one hand, social support could function to provide the resources that allow individuals to cope effectively when they experience strains generated by blocked goals and noxious stimuli. On the other hand, supportive relations could help to inoculate individuals against the strains that normally would impinge on those similarly situated in society. We will return to these issues below when we link research on "resiliency" to the general strain/social-support paradigm.

Although the research is limited and must be gathered from diverse sources, the existing evidence suggests that social support has direct and buffering effects on delinquency (Alexander, 1973; Farrell, Barnes, and Banerjee, 1995; Drennon-Gala, 1995; Hepburn, 1977; Johnson, Su, Gerstein, Shin, and Hoffman, 1995; Rothbaum and Weisz, 1994; Yoshikawa, 1994; see also Cullen, 1994). Recent research by Wright (1996) lends credence to this conclusion (see also Wright, Cullen, and Wooldredge, 1995). Based on a representative subsample of 1,775 adolescents and their parents interviewed for the National Survey of Families and Households, he examined the impact on juvenile delinquency of three sets of variables: parental supports; family risk factors, most of which would fall into Agnew's (1992) categories of strain (e.g., family conflict); and direct parental controls. Parental supports reduced delinquent involvement both directly and indirectly by buffering the risk (strain) factors and by increasing the effectiveness of direct controls. The analysis also revealed that the effects of family structural variables, such as poverty and "broken homes," influence delinquency mainly by diminishing the amount of support parents are able to supply their children.

IMPLICATIONS FOR THEORETICAL CRIMINOLOGY

The utility of integrating general strain and social-support theories will hinge not only on the confirmation the model can secure in narrow empirical tests of the buffering hypothesis but also on whether this integrated approach can illuminate issues central to contemporary criminological theory. In a beginning way, we are able to suggest three areas to which this integrated approach might contribute to our understanding: the generality of deviance and stability and change in offending; the selection of adaptations; and the resiliency of at-risk children.

Generality of Deviance—Stability and Change in Offending. Gottfredson and Hirschi's (1990) *A General Theory of Crime* has been much debated and studied (mostly with favorable results). Regardless of whether one is a fan of their theory, Gottfredson and Hirschi must be credited with forcing criminologists to face two empirical "facts" that demand theoretical explanation: the tendency for deviance to be general, and the tendency for the roots of crime to extend to childhood and remain stable over time (see also Wilson and Herrnstein, 1985). Sampson and Laub (1993) have revised the stability thesis, noting that criminal careers, although often characterized by continuity in offending, are not uniformly stable but can be marked by "turning points" that prompt change and a move into conformity.

Gottfredson and Hirschi (1990) correctly point out that most prevailing criminological theories operate poorly when asked to explain the generality of deviance and stability. This theoretical inadequacy largely stems from two factors. First, scholars simply fail to consider the issue of generality and thus do not investigate whether their causal variables can explain why criminals also tend to engage in a variety of other deviant activities. Second, because the scholars' theories give causal primacy to experiences during adolescence (e.g., association with gangs, frustration in school), they cannot shed light on why the roots of juvenile delinquency can be traced to stable problem behaviors that emerge in childhood and develop into criminality during the life course.

An integrated general strain/social-support approach, however, is not plagued by these limitations. From the stress-support literature, it is clear that stress increases and support decreases participation in a range of deviant behaviors (Cohen and Wills, 1985; Thoits, 1995; Vaux, 1988). In short, the effects of these factors are *general*.

Similarly, unlike other dominant sociological models of crime, strain and support are not tied exclusively to the adolescent years. Rather, research reveals that family processes can function both as powerful strains or as salient supports during the *first years of childhood* (Rothbaum and Weisz, 1994). Accordingly, strain and support become prime candidates for explaining dysfunctional and nurturant developmental sequences that can help account for the early emergence and stability of problem behaviors.

Finally, because strain and support can occur across the life course, they can help to explain not only continuity but also change in offending. Thoits (1995, p. 57), for example, highlights "how events and strains in one stage of life can influence psychological well-being both in contiguous and much later life stages." And Vaux (1988, p. 226) explicitly recognizes that "social-support constructs have applicability throughout the life cycle. Related to development," he continues, "there are changes in the individual's capacity to engage supportive others, changes in opportunities to do so, and changes in the need for support" (1988, p. 226). In this regard, it seems profitable to explore how changes in support and in strains might serve as a turning point out of crime. In fact, Sampson and Laub (1993) have demonstrated that quality marriages make desistance from crime more likely. They interpret this result largely within the framework of social-bond theory, arguing that marriages increase informal social controls. But this finding is equally interpretable from a social-support perspective (Cullen, 1994). As Thoits (1995, p. 65) notes, "married individuals report higher perceived support than the unmarried."

In short, the life-course perspective is becoming increasing central to criminological theory. Many existing crime theories are not well equipped to address the puzzles at the core of this perspective. In contrast, although hard evidence of their utility is in short supply, general strain theory and social-support theory—alone or in combination—ostensibly are compatible with a life-course perspective and thus are worthy of further investigation.

Adapting to Strain. As noted above, a problem virtually ignored by criminologists is why people under strain commit a particular type of crime as opposed to some other adaptation—whether deviant or conformist. As Agnew (1992, p. 75) cautions, it is essential to "describe those factors affecting the choice of delinquent versus nondelinquent adaptations. The failure to consider such factors is a fundamental reason for the weak empirical support for strain theory." Although a number of intervening variables are likely to shape this choice—cultural, structural, and individual (Cloward and Piven, 1979; Cullen, 1984; Hoffmann and Ireland, 1995, pp. 257–59)—social support may potentially influence whether a criminal response is taken (Agnew, 1992, pp. 71–72). Admittedly, it remains to be seen whether social support's effects are general, reducing the probability of all forms of deviance, or whether they are specific to crime, reducing all or particular forms of criminality. Even so, we can envision three ways in which social support would reduce the likelihood that individuals would respond to strain through crime.

First, Agnew (1992, p. 49; see also Bernard, 1990) contends that "adolescents are pressured into delinquency by the negative affective states—most notably anger and related emotions—that often result from negative relationships." The anger-crime link, however, is not ironclad. To the extent that individuals have personality traits that allow them to repress or control feelings of anger, strain is not likely to generate the emotions that make a criminal response probable. In this light, we propose that quality parental support increases healthy human development and the likelihood that an individual will develop the personal traits or "temperaments" to resist acting on feelings of anger (Rothbaum and Weisz, 1994).

Second, Agnew (1992; Agnew and White, 1992) proposes that a variable that channels youths into crime—and presumably not other adaptations—is having delinquent friends and the delinquent values these associations impart (Cloward 1959). Youths enmeshed in supportive networks, however, are less likely to hold such values. Instead, the provision of support—by parents and significant others—provides individuals with conventional modeling and inculcates prosocial values. In short, supportive relationships increase the odds that definitions unfavorable to the violation of the law will exceed those favoring normative departures.

Third and relatedly, we propose that social support diminishes the availability of criminal opportunities. Situationally, supportive relationships can be drawn on to diffuse potentially volatile interpersonal conflicts. Structurally, supportive relationships strengthen community-level "social capital." Neighborhoods that are "communitarian" and "reintegrative" arguably create a web of relationships in which individuals are tied more closely to one another (Braithwaite, 1989). Social support creates opportunities for intimacy and for reciprocity—in short for the creation of social capital (Hagan, 1994; Sullivan, 1989). In these contexts, strained individuals have more constraints to delinquent coping: others know and can identify them and are willing to exercise social control (Sampson and Groves, 1989). They also have more opportunities to escape aversive locations. In contrast, residents of under-class areas suffering a depletion of social capital, argues Agnew (1992, p. 73), "often lack the resources to escape legally from adverse environments—by, for example, quitting their job (if they have a job) or moving to another neighborhood."

Resiliency in Strain-Inducing Environments. High-risk, strain-inducing neighborhoods and families seemingly promote numerous individual patholo-gies, such as mental illness, hard drug use, and chronic delinquency. However, a remarkable number of adolescents—perhaps as many as half—emerge from these conditions relatively unscathed, experiencing little psy-chosocial maladjustment (Werner and Smith, 1982). This finding raises the question as to why some youths are "resilient" even when faced with the strains pervasive in these difficult circumstances. Social support appears to play an integral role in inoculating youths from these strain-inducing envi-ronments and in buffering the strains that cannot be escaped.

Research indicates that resilient youths are more likely to be enmeshed in supportive, nurturant relationships. For example, attachments to parents or significant others, having received consistent and reliable caregiving early in life, and the presence of an external support system inoculate and buffer against the effects of "noxious environments" (Garmezy, 1985; Rutter, 1985). Moreover, parental supports have been associated with higher levels of adolescent self-worth, academic achievement, and associations with proso-cial peers—factors also associated with resiliency (Smith, Lizotte, Thorn-berry, and Krohn, 1995).

It is instructive that the positive effects of supportive relationships have been replicated in research involving early interventions with high-risk fami-lies—research that furnishes insight into the potential programs that might be consistent with an integrated support-strain theory. Yoshikawa (1994), for example, reviewed successful early intervention programs designed for high-risk populations. The evidence to date, argues Yoshikawa (1994, p. 44), shows that successful programs have several key features: "(a) an interven-tion of at least two years in length, (b) provision of a high quality educational infant day-care or preschool program for children, (c) provision of informa-

tional and emotional support focused on development and child-rearing issues for parents, and (d) provision of prenatal-postnatal care and educational
and vocational counseling or training when otherwise unavailable." Successful delinquency prevention programs also target multiple early family risk
factors and supply the family with support in multiple settings. In short,
points out Yoshikawa, long-term prevention aimed at creating resiliency in
children at risk for chronic delinquency is accomplished most effectively
through a multifaceted supportive intervention that elevates the cognitive and
school competencies of youths and that stabilizes the nurturant strands of the
parent-child relationship.

Advancing Anomie Theory

It is ironic that Merton's paradigm of social structure and *anomie* is most
often described and tested without reference to his concept of anomie. Following Hirschi (1969), most criminologists treat Merton's paradigm as an
analysis of the social sources of strain that individuals feel and then respond
to in deviant ways. Although Merton's work can be read in this way—
particularly his typology of "individual adaptations"—his paradigm was
chiefly formulated as a macrolevel theory that explored the social sources of
anomie, which in turn explained differential rates of deviance across and
within societies (Cullen, 1984; Messner, 1988). In brief, Merton examined
how anomie was fostered by the excessive cultural emphasis on success goals
and by the disjuncture between America's cultural prescriptions of universal
economic mobility—the "American Dream"—and structural inequality that
limits opportunities for such mobility.

As noted earlier, Messner and Rosenfeld (1994) have taken a major step
in reviving interest in the anomie portion of Merton's paradigm (see Chamlin
and Cochran, 1995). Standing on Merton's shoulders, they embrace the essentials of his approach but then make a major contribution by showing how
his model can be expanded into an "institutional-anomie theory."

Similar to Merton, Messner and Rosenfeld argue for the criminogenic effects of the American Dream, which they define as "a commitment to the goal
of material success, to be pursued by everyone in society, under conditions of
open, individual competition" (1994, p. 69). The resulting "intense pressures for monetary success" weaken the power of normative standards to
regulate behavior (p. 69). In short, "anomie" sets in, and individuals are free
to achieve economic goals through the "technically most efficient means,"
which frequently are illegal.

Messner and Rosenfeld's truly innovative elaboration of Merton's paradigm, however, is their insight that the cultural hegemony of the American Dream causes economic concerns to dominate other institutional spheres, such as the family, school, and political arena. Merton had all but ignored noneconomic institutions, but Messner and Rosenfeld believe that the power of these institutions relative to the economy is integral to why the United States has a high rate of serious crime.

Unlike advanced industrial societies in which the economy is balanced by other institutional interests, they contend, U.S. social institutions are so penetrated by the American Dream that they are arranged to serve the pursuit of material success. For example, families are expected to uproot and move to a new community if a breadwinner's employer so demands; schools are seen as advancing career prospects and not as a means of learning for learning's sake; and politicians are expected to facilitate capital accumulation. The result is that institutional controls in the United States are weak. As Messner and Rosenfeld (1994, p. 86) propose, "to the degree that noneconomic institutions are relatively devalued, the attractiveness of the roles that they offer for members of society is diminished. There is, accordingly, widespread detachment from these institutions and weak institutional control." In societies in which the institutional balance of power is more equal, controls are less attenuated. In the end, this differential in control helps to explain America's high rate of serious crime compared with advanced industrial nations.

It certainly is plausible that the salience of the American Dream heightens crime by weakening both normative controls (anomie) and institutional (informal) controls. Or, as Rosenfeld and Messner (1995, p. 175) put it, "The American dream . . . has a direct effect on crime through the creation of an anomic normative order, that is an environment in which social norms are unable to exert a strong regulatory force on the members of society. It has an indirect effect on crime by contributing to an institutional balance of power that inhibits the development of strong mechanisms of external social control." It is not clear, however, that the criminogenic effects of the American Dream occur only, or perhaps even primarily, through its impact on *control*. We propose that a more complete "institutional-anomie" theory would explore how the American Dream fosters crime by weakening the provision of *support*.

First, as Messner and Rosenfeld note, the American Dream emphasizes *individual* material success. The by-product of this excessive cultural embrace of individual success—what Bellah, Madsen, Sullivan, Swidler, and

Tipton (1985) call "utilitarian individualism"—is not only the attenuation of normative controls but also the corrosion of communal ties. Because Americans tend to place their own good above the "common good," concern for community and mutuality of support are devalued; their status will not be raised without a fundamental "transformation of American culture" (Bellah et al., 1985, pp. 275–96). In turn, as the culture prescribes individual success at the expense of caring for others, the society becomes less "communitarian," and its members are less "densely enmeshed in interdependencies which have the special qualities of mutual help and trust" (Braithwaite, 1989, p. 100). The result, according to Braithwaite, is higher levels of crime. In short, the American Dream undermines social support and thus contributes to the nation's lawlessness.

Second, the institutional imbalance of power enjoyed by the economy undermines the capacity of other institutions to deliver support that might insulate against criminogenic forces. Families, for example, are expected to accommodate to work schedules, even if time spent with children is forfeited. When faced with choices between social welfare and fostering capital accumulation, the government leans in the direction of capital. These choices have consequences. "The industrial societies that have escaped our extremes of criminal violence," observes Currie (1985, pp. 171–72), "tend either to have highly developed sectors with fairly generous systems of income support, relatively well-developed employment policies, and other cushions against the 'forces of the market,' or (like Japan) to accomplish much the same ends through private institutions backed by an ethos of social obligation and mutual responsibility." In short, to the extent that social institutions are unable to deliver support because they are subservient, as Messner and Rosenfeld (1994) argue, to economic imperatives, the United States will suffer the cost of crime.

THE FUTURE OF ANOMIE-STRAIN THEORY

The genius of Robert K. Merton's anomie-strain theory is that it is a dynamic paradigm, which offers opportunities for further evolution and a broader understanding of crime and deviance. In its early days, this paradigm dominated the discipline by furnishing important puzzles for criminologists to solve (Cole, 1975). As the paradigm aged and the puzzles became more familiar, however, criminologists' interest in Merton's work waned. Even worse, scholars frequently made the mistake of reifying the theory, reducing it to a form that borders on the vacuous (e.g., the disjunction between aspirations and expectations causes delinquency), and relegating it to the dustbin of the discipline (Burton and Cullen, 1992). As a result, anomie-strain theory largely lost its capacity to direct criminological inquiry. Instead, it became mostly a site for theoretical archaeology, digging up the past out of historical curiosity.

But the best archaeology, of course, tells us something new about the present. Merton's writings should be explored mostly because they can prompt new insights. Fortunately, a revisionist group of scholars has taken up this challenge. They have stood on Merton's shoulders and in so doing have broadened the horizons of his work (Passas, 1995). General strain theory and institutional-anomie theory are prima facie evidence of the theoretical advances still to be unearthed in the anomie-strain paradigm.

For the immediate future, it seems likely that these perspectives will offer fresh puzzles and thus will prompt empirical research (see, for example, Chamlin and Cochran, 1995; Paternoster and Mazerole, 1994). As time proceeds, however, the risk is that these two branches on the anomie-strain paradigm will, like Merton's work before them, be conceptualized narrowly and treated as static perspectives. If so, their full value is unlikely to be realized; they, too, will await "liberation."

In this context, we have set forth one avenue for the elaboration of anomie-strain theory: the integration of the paradigm with social-support theory. We have tried to demonstrate that social-support theory is compatible with both Agnew's general strain theory and Messner and Rosenfeld's institutional-anomie theory. In the former case, we have proposed that social support is an intervening variable that mitigates strain, reduces the likelihood of criminal adaptations, and is integral to the resiliency of youths in at-risk environments. We also have suggested that general strain and social-support theories can help to illuminate psychosocial factors that shape continuity and change in criminal careers across the life course—a central concern of today's theoretical criminology. With regard to Messner and Rosenfeld's contribution, we have proposed that social support can be an important intervening variable between the American Dream and crime. In this scenario, the emphasis on individual material success weakens communitarianism and the ability of noneconomic institutions to furnish supports—processes that ultimately are criminogenic.

The utility of integrating social-support and anomie-strain theories, of course, remains to be determined. Moreover, each perspective stands on its own, and each perspective might find opportunities for integration with other theories of crime. Nonetheless, we hope that we have, in a small way, created a new avenue of inquiry and thus have contributed to the continuing liberation of the anomie-strain paradigm.

References

Adler, Freda, and William S. Laufer, eds. 1995. *The legacy of anomie theory.* New Brunswick, N.J.: Transaction.

Agnew, Robert. 1985. A revised strain theory. *Social Forces* 64:151–67.

———. 1989. A longitudinal test of the revised strain theory. *Criminology* 5:373–87.

———. 1992. Foundation for a general strain theory of crime and delinquency. *Criminology* 30:47–86.

———. 1995. The contributions of social-psychological strain theory to the explanation of crime and delinquency. In *The Legacy of Anomie Theory*, edited by Freda Adler and William S. Laufer, 113–37. New Brunswick, N.J.: Transaction.

Agnew, Robert, Francis T. Cullen, Velmer S. Burton Jr., T. David Evans, and R. Gregory Dunaway. 1996. A new test of classic strain theory. *Justice Quarterly* 13:681–704.

Agnew, Robert, and Helene Raskin White. 1992. An empirical test of general strain theory. *Criminology* 30:475–99.

Alexander, James F. 1973. Defensive and supportive communications in normal and deviant families. *Journal of Consulting and Clinical Psychology* 40:223–31.

Bellah, Robert N., Richard Madsen, William M. Sullivan, Ann Swidler, and Steven M. Tipton. 1985. *Habits of the heart: Individualism and commitment in American life.* New York: Harper and Row.

Bernard, Thomas J. 1987. Testing structural strain theories. *Journal of Research on Crime and Delinquency* 24:262–80.

———. 1990. Angry aggression among the "truly disadvantaged." *Criminology* 28:73–96.

Braithwaite, John. 1989. *Crime, shame and reintegration.* Cambridge: Cambridge University Press.

Burton, Velmer S., Jr. 1990. Explaining adult criminality: Testing strain, differential association, and control theories. Unpublished Ph.D. dissertation, University of Cincinnati.

Burton, Velmer S., Jr., and Francis T. Cullen, 1992. The empirical status of strain theory. *Journal of Crime and Justice* 15:1–30.

Burton, Velmer S., Jr., Francis T. Cullen, T. David Evans, and R. Gregory Dunaway. 1994. Reconsidering strain theory: Operationalization, rival theories, and adult criminality. *Journal of Quantitative Criminology* 10:213–39.

Burton, Velmer S., Jr., and R. Gregory Dunaway. 1994. Strain, relative deprivation, and middle-class delinquency. In *Varieties of Criminology: Readings from a Dynamic Discipline*, edited by Gregg Barak, 79–96. Westport, Conn.: Praeger.

Chamlin, Mitchell B., and John K. Cochran. 1995. Assessing Messner and Rosenfeld's institutional anomie theory: A partial test. *Criminology* 33:411–29.

Cloward, Richard A. 1959. Illegitimate means, anomie, and deviant behavior. *American Sociological Review* 24:164–76.

Cloward, Richard A., and Lloyd Ohlin. 1960. *Delinquency and opportunity: A theory of delinquent gangs.* New York: Free Press.

Cloward, Richard A., and Frances Fox Piven. 1979. Hidden protest: The channeling of female innovation and resistance. *Signs* 4:651–69.

Cloward, Richard A., and Frances Fox Piven, with the assistance of Francis T. Cullen and Roslyn Tichen. 1977. *The structuring of deviant behavior: A preliminary perspective.* First Year Report to the Law Enforcement Assistance Administration.

Cohen, Sheldon, and Thomas Ashby Wills. 1985. Stress social support, and the buffering hypothesis. *Psychological Bulletin* 98:310–57.

Cole, Stephen. 1975. The growth of scientific knowledge: Theories of deviance as a case study. In *The Idea of Social Structure: Papers in Honor of Robert K. Merton,* edited by Lewis A. Coser, 175–220. New York: Harcourt Brace Jovanovich.

Cullen, Francis T. 1984. *Rethinking crime and deviance theory: The emergence of a structuring tradition.* Totowa, N.J.: Rowman & Allenheld.

———. 1988. Were Cloward and Ohlin strain theorists? Delinquency and opportunity revisited. *Journal of Research in Crime and Delinquency* 25:214–41.

———. 1994. Social support as an organizing concept for criminology: Presidential address to the Academy of Criminal Justice Sciences. *Justice Quarterly* 11:527–59.

Currie, Elliott. 1985. *Confronting crime: An American challenge.* New York: Pantheon.

Drennon-Gala, Don. 1995. *Delinquency and high school dropouts: Reconsidering social correlates.* Lanham, Md.: University Press of America.

Farnworth, Margaret, and Michael J. Leiber. 1989. Strain theory revisited: Economic goals, educational means, and delinquency. *American Sociological Review* 54:263–74.

Farrell, Michael P., Grace M. Barnes, and Sarbani Banerjee. 1995. Family cohesion as a buffer against the effects of problem-drinking fathers on psychological distress, deviant behavior, and heavy drinking adolescents. *Journal of Health and Social Behavior* 36:377–85.

Garmezy, Norman. 1985. Stress resistant children: The search for protective factors. In *Recent Research in Developmental Psychopathology,* edited by John Stevenson, 213–33. Oxford: Pergamon Press.

Gottfredson, Michael R., and Travis Hirschi. 1990. *A general theory of crime.* Stanford, Calif.: Stanford University Press.

Gove, Walter R., and Jeannette F. Tudor. 1973. Adult sex roles and mental illness. *American Journal of Sociology* 78:812–35.

Hagan, John. 1994. *Crime and disrepute.* Thousand Oaks, Calif.: Pine Forge.

Hepburn, John R. 1977. Testing alternative models of delinquency causation. *Journal of Criminal Law and Criminology* 67:450–60.

Hirschi, Travis. 1969. *Causes of delinquency.* Berkeley: University of California Press.

Hoffman, John P., and Timothy Ireland. 1995. Cloward and Ohlin's strain theory reexamined: An elaborated model. In *The Legacy of Anomie Theory,* edited by Freda Adler and William S. Laufer, 247–70. New Brunswick, N.J.: Transaction.

House, James S., Karl R. Landis, and Debra Umberson. 1988. Social relationships and health. *Science* 241:540–45.

Johnson, Robert A., S. Susan Su, Dean R. Gerstein, Hee-Chon Shin, and John P. Hoffman. 1995. Parental influences on deviant behavior in early adolescence: A logistic response analysis of age- and gender-differential effects. *Journal of Quantitative Criminology* 11:167–93.

Kornhauser, Ruth Rosner. 1978. *Social sources of delinquency: An appraisal of analytic models.* Chicago: University of Chicago Press.

Lin, Nan. 1986. Conceptualizing social support. In *Social Support, Life, Events, and Depression*, edited by Nan Lin, Alfred Dean, and William Ensel, 17–30. Orlando: Academic Press.

Lin, Nan, Alfred Dean, and Walter Ensel, eds. 1986. *Social support, life events, and depression.* Orlando: Academic Press.

Menard, Scott. 1995. A developmental test of Mertonian anomie theory. *Journal of Research in Crime and Delinquency* 32:136–74.

Merton, Robert K. 1959. Social conformity, deviation, and opportunity structures: A comment on the contributions of Dubin and Cloward. *American Sociological Review* 24:177–89.

———. 1964. Anomie, anomia, and social interaction: Contexts of deviant behavior. In *Anomie and Deviant Behavior*, edited by Marshall B. Clinard, 213–42. New York: Free Press.

———. 1965. *On the shoulders of giants: A Shandean postscript.* New York: Free Press.

———. 1968. *Social theory and social structure*, enlarged ed. New York: Free Press.

———. 1995. Opportunity structure: The emergence, diffusion, and differentiation of a sociological concept, 1930s–1950s. In *The Legacy of Anomie Theory*, edited by Freda Adler and William S. Laufer, 3–78. New Brunswick, N.J.: Transaction.

Messner, Steven F. 1988. Merton's "social structure and anomie": The road not taken. *Deviant Behavior* 9:33–53.

Messner, Steven F., Marvin D. Krohn, and Allen E. Liska, eds. 1989. *Theoretical integration in the study of deviance and crime: Problems and prospects.* Albany: State University of New York Press.

Messner, Steven F., and Richard Rosenfeld. 1994. *Crime and the American dream.* Belmont, Calif.: Wadsworth.

Passas, Nikos. 1990. Anomie and corporate deviance. *Contemporary Crises* 14:157–78.

———. 1995. "Continuities in the anomie tradition. In *The Legacy of Anomie Theory*, edited by Freda Adler and William S. Laufer, 91–112. New Brunswick, N.J.: Transaction.

Paternoster, Raymond, and Paul Mazerole. 1994. General strain theory and delinquency: A replication and extension. *Journal of Research in Crime and Delinquency* 31:235–63.

Peirce, Robert S., Michael R. Frone, Marcia Russell, and M. Lynne Cooper. 1994. Relationship of financial strain and psychological resources to alcohol use and abuse: The mediating role of negative affect and drinking motives. *Journal of Health and Social Behavior* 35:291–308.

Rosenfeld, Richard. 1989. Robert Merton's contributions to the sociology of deviance. *Sociological Inquiry* 59:453–66.

Rosenfeld, Richard, and Steven F. Messner. 1995. Crime and the American dream: An institutional analysis. In *The Legacy of Anomie Theory*, edited by Freda Adler and William S. Laufer, 159–81. New Brunswick, N.J.: Transaction.

Rothbaum, Fred, and John R. Weisz. 1994. Parental caregiving and child externalized behavior in nonclinical samples: A meta-analysis. *Psychological Bulletin* 116:55–74.

Rutter, Michael. 1985. Resilience in the face of adversity: Protective factors and resistance to psychiatric disorders. *British Journal of Psychiatry* 147:598–611.

Sampson, Robert J., and W. Byron Groves. 1989. Community structure and crime: Testing social-disorganization theory. *American Journal of Sociology* 94:774–802.

Sampson, Robert J., and John H. Laub. 1993. *Crime in the making: Pathways and turning points through life*. Cambridge: Harvard University Press.

Short, James F., Jr., and Fred L. Strodtbeck. 1965. *Group process and gang delinquency*. Chicago: University of Chicago Press.

Smith, Carolyn, Alan J. Lizotte, Terence P. Thornberry, and Marvin D. Krohn. 1995. Resilient youth: Identifying factors that prevent high risk youth from engaging in delinquency and drug use. *Current Perspectives on Aging and the Life Cycle* 4:217–47.

Sullivan, Mercer L. 1989. *"Getting Paid": Youth crime and work in the inner city*. Ithaca: Cornell University Press.

Thoits, Peggy A. 1995. Stress, coping, and social support processes: Where are we? What next? *Journal of Health and Social Behavior* (Extra Issue):53–79.

Vaux, Alan. 1988. *Social support: Theory, research, and intervention*. New York: Praeger.

Vaux, Alan, and Mary Ruggerio. 1983. Stressful life change and delinquent behavior. *American Journal of Community Psychology* 11:169–83.

Werner, Emmy E., and Ruth S. Smith. 1982. *Overcoming the odds: High risk children from birth to adulthood*. Ithaca: Cornell University Press.

Wilson, James Q., and Richard J. Herrnstein. 1985. *Crime and human nature*. New York: Simon and Schuster.

Wright, John P. 1966. Parental support and juvenile delinquency: A test of social support theory. Unpublished Ph.D. dissertation, University of Cincinnati.

Wright, John Paul, Francis T. Cullen, and John D. Wooldredge. 1995. Parental support and juvenile delinquency: A social capital approach. Paper presented at the annual meeting of the American Society of Criminology, Boston.

Yoshikawa, Hirokazu. 1994. Prevention as cumulative protection: Effects of early family support and education on chronic delinquency and its risks. *Psychological Bulletin* 115:28–54.

RICHARD ROSENFELD & STEVEN F. MESSNER

Markets, Morality, and an Institutional-Anomie Theory of Crime

But after so may failed prophesies, is it not in the interest of
social science to embrace complexity, be it at some sacrifice
of its claim to predictive power? —Albert O. Hirschman

Do markets enhance or erode the moral order of a capitalist society? This question has been at the center of a longstanding debate in social theory—a debate that gave rise to sociology as a distinctive orientation to the study of human behavior. Although the markets-and-morality debate is a defining feature of much of modern social theory, it has had relatively little impact on the sociological study of crime.[1] This is quite curious because the "moral order," understood in a broad sense to encompass the shared sentiments and values that provide the foundation for social life, is intimately related to the phenomenon of crime. Crime involves the violation of those collective sentiments that are so central to the social order that they have been formally codified in the criminal law. Identification of the basic sources of order and disorder in a society, therefore, would seem to be indispensable for explaining the overall level of crime.

The purpose of this essay is to bring the markets-and-morality debate closer to the center of contemporary theory and research on crime. To this end, we review the core arguments of the debate in classical social thought and highlight the more important sociological insights to emerge from it. Several of these insights are elaborated in the "institutional-anomie theory" of crime. This perspective offers a useful framework for understanding the broad social and cultural sources of crime, and for identifying the conditions under which market forces strengthen or weaken the moral foundations of capitalist societies in particular. We present the main arguments of the theory, show their relevance to the markets-and-morality debate, and discuss some of the more important similarities and differences between this approach and other criminological perspectives. We conclude with a brief assessment of the research implications of our arguments and their relevance to contemporary societies in the midst of the uneasy transition to market economies.

The Debate over Markets and Morality

Albert O. Hirschman (1992) provides a cogent exegesis of the classical debate beginning in the eighteenth century and continuing to the present on the question of whether markets bolster or erode the moral order in capitalist societies.[2] Hirschman organizes this debate in terms of two opposing views. The first, which he labels the *doux-commerce thesis*, argues that the marketplace replaces the barbarism of feudal society with a new form of morality based on trust and mutual obligation (1992, pp. 105–41). In sharp contrast, what Hirschman terms the *self-destruction thesis* holds that markets erode institutional controls and ultimately destroy their own social and moral foundations.[3]

The doux-commerce thesis grows out of the liberal political philosophy and economic theory of the Enlightenment. It envisions a social order in market societies that is characterized by mutually satisfying relationships centered around voluntary exchange. Moreover, involvement in the commercial transactions of the marketplace is seen as having a "civilizing" influence on social conduct. Market involvement promotes personal attributes such as thrift, industriousness, honesty, and reliability, behaviors that are required to sustain the central organizing principle of markets: reciprocity (Hirschman, 1992, pp. 106–9).

Discussions of the civilizing functions of markets can be found in the writings of prominent philosophers such as Montesquieu and Condorcet, as well as David Hume, Adam Smith, and other early contributors to the intellectual edifice of modern capitalism (Hirschman, 1992, pp. 106–9). A particularly glowing account is provided by Thomas Paine in *The Rights of Man*:

> Commerce is a pacific system, operating to cordialise mankind, by rendering Nations, as well as individuals, useful to each other. . . . The invention of commerce is the greatest approach towards universal civilization that has yet been made by any means not immediately flowing from moral principles. (quoted in Hirschman, 1992, p. 108)

The doux-commerce thesis thus envisions a happy marriage between individual and collective welfare in market societies. Collectivities are best served, the argument goes, when persons are free to pursue their self-interests through market exchanges. The image is one of sovereign and rational individualists with a strong self-interest in preserving mutually beneficial, cooperative, and trusting exchange relations with others. By promoting such relations, markets pacify the irrational brutalities of precapitalist social relations and enhance the moral order of society.

The opposite position, the self-destruction thesis, maintains that capitalist markets have a corrosive impact on institutional controls, which leads ultimately to social disorder and moral decline. Markets, in this view, function at peak efficiency precisely to the extent that they free persons from the restraints on self-interested behavior imposed by political, social, or moral obligations and ties. The development of market capitalism is thus accompanied by the destruction of traditional social relations and by the weakening of social regulation. The classic characterization of this process comes from Marx:

> Constant revolutionizing of production, uninterrupted disturbance of all social conditions, everlasting uncertainty and agitation distinguish the bourgeois epoch from all earlier ones. All fixed, fast-frozen relations, with their train of ancient and venerable prejudices and opinions are swept away, all new-formed ones become antiquated before they can ossify. (Marx and Engels, [1848], 1964, p. 63)

Furthermore, for Marx and other radical critics, capitalism is intrinsically incapable of offering any effective substitute for the traditional ties that have been "torn asunder" in the process of capitalist development. What remains in a capitalist order is "no other nexus between man and man than naked self-interest, than callous 'cash payment' " (Marx and Engels, [1848], 1966, p. 61).

The image of modern capitalist relations as inherently weak and unstable is not restricted to Marxist accounts of capitalism. It also figures centrally in the conservative reaction to industrialism and to the French Revolution (Nisbet, 1953, pp. 23–25). Indeed, as Nisbet observes, "the indictment of capitalism that comes from the conservatives in the nineteenth century is often more severe than that of the socialists" (Nisbet, 1966, p. 26). For example, the French conservative Balzac offers an appraisal of the "cash nexus" of capitalism that is as damning as any leveled by Marx. Balzac writes that in this new social order "there is no kin but the thousand-franc note" (quoted in Nisbet, 1966, p. 26). In short, both conservative and radical critics of capitalism arrive at the same gloomy prognosis for this new form of social organization. As market principles and practices spread throughout a society, they undermine nonmarket relations and their concomitant behavioral controls, ultimately destroying even the minimal level of social order required for the effective functioning of markets themselves.

In sum, two very different images of the relationship between capitalist markets and moral order can be found in classical social thought. According to one, markets civilize behavior and create harmonious and peaceful societies by bringing people into relations of mutual dependency, trust, and profit. According to the other, markets demoralize economic activities in particular and social relations in general by unleashing actors from institutional restraints.

Neither of these classical views by itself offers a satisfactory analysis of the social and moral impact of markets, and both have been criticized in the sociological literature. A major deficiency of the doux-commerce thesis is the implicit assumption that the operation of markets requires only free, rational actors pursuing their self-interest. The problem with this assumption is that it ignores the social conditions that enable persons to engage in market transactions in the first place. As Durkheim ([1893], 1964, pp. 200–229) explains, the contractual agreements arrived at in the marketplace are ultimately dependent on a variety of "non-contractual solidarities." Markets alone cannot produce morality or solidarity, according to Durkheim, because the distinctive motivating force behind market transactions—self-interest—does not provide a sufficient foundation for lasting social relationships:

> . . . where interest is the only ruling force each individual finds himself in a state of war with every other. . . . There is nothing less constant than interest. Today it unites me to you; tomorrow, it will make me your enemy. (Durkheim, [1893], 1964, pp. 203–4).

More recently, Smelser has echoed Durkheim's remarks in his critique of rational-choice theories of social behavior:

> What is forgotten [in these theories] is that the free economic agent and the free citizen are themselves in, and products of, a specific complex of cultural values and institutions. They are certainly not "natural persons." They behave according to norms that endorse and reward such behavior. (Smelser, 1990, p. 781)

The doux-commerce thesis is flawed, then, because it is predicated on an untenable conception of human social behavior, accompanied by a naive functionalism that stipulates that markets necessarily produce the morality necessary for markets to function. Yet, the self-destruction thesis contains an equally serious and in some ways quite similar deficiency. The collapse of capitalism is regarded as predetermined and inevitable. In Hirschman's (1992, p. 138) account, capitalism is depicted as "a wild, unbridled force which, having swept away everything in its path, finally does itself in by successfully attacking its own foundations." Such a view rests on an untenable determinism and a crude materialism: markets necessarily dominate other social formations, because material interests always supersede norms. The self-destruction thesis is unable to account for either the persistence of capitalist economies, long after they should have succumbed to their own contradictions, or for the variety of social arrangements observed across different capitalist societies.

Despite these analytic deficiencies, however, each of the classic positions in the markets-and-morality debate identifies an important facet of social relations in capitalist societies. The doux-commerce thesis calls attention to the reciprocity inherent in exchange relations and to the tendencies for market transactions to develop into ongoing social relationships. To the extent that they do so, markets enhance social integration and strengthen the moral order. The self-destruction thesis, on the other hand, highlights the tension between markets and other social institutions. The logic of the marketplace cultivates an orientation toward action that is calculating, instrumental, and guided by self-interest. Insofar as this market-driven orientation permeates noneconomic aspects of social life, integration is jeopardized, and the moral order is weakened (Hirschman, 1992, p. 139; see also Schwartz, 1994).

The important insight to be drawn from the classical debate is that capitalist markets have dialectical consequences. The answer to the question posed at the onset of this essay—"Do markets enhance or erode the moral order of a capitalist society?"—is, then, "it depends." Markets simultaneously enhance and threaten the moral order. The moral foundations of capitalist societies are being "constantly depleted and replenished at the same time" (Hirschman, 1992, p. 139). There is no reason to assume that capitalist societies are either doomed to self-destruction or immune from serious disorder. Rather, the level of order or disorder in a capitalist society will reflect the balance between the integrative and destructive forces associated with the principal feature of its economic system—markets—and therefore will vary depending on the historical circumstances in which these forces are played out.

This resolution of the opposing images of market society in the classical debate is important but hardly sufficient if it is to be used as an analytical tool in the sociological study of crime. An adequate appraisal of the role of markets in capitalist societies, and of the relationship between market arrangements and crime, requires more than merely recognizing that markets have variable "net" moral consequences under different conditions. It is also necessary to ask: What are the distinctive conditions under which markets exhibit variable consequences, and what are the social processes through which these conditions lead specifically to crime? The institutional-anomie theory of crime directly engages these questions.

The Institutional-Anomie Theory of Crime

Institutional-anomie theory applies basic sociological concepts and ideas to formulate a macrosocial explanation of crime (Messner and Rosenfeld, 1994a; Rosenfeld and Messner, 1995). Its main epistemological premise is that a comprehensive sociological analysis of any phenomenon must be cast in terms of the fundamental features of social organization: *culture* and *social structure*. In standard usage, culture refers to commonly held values, goals, symbols, cognitions, and beliefs that motivate, regulate, and give meaning to social action. Social structure refers to the social positions and roles through which behavior is enacted. The mechanisms linking these core elements of social organization are *social institutions*.[4]

A basic principle of institutional-anomie theory is that major social institutions are simultaneously interdependent and in conflict with one another. Institutions are interdependent in the sense that the functioning of any one depends to some extent on the functioning of others. Recognition of such interdependence is implicit in Durkheim's classic insight about the role of "non-contractual solidarities" in market transactions, referred to earlier. Durkheim observes that economic activity always occurs within a context of preexisting understandings and expectations, that is, within a larger noneconomic institutional context. More recently, Polanyi has used the concept of embeddedness to make a similar point about the interconnections between economic institutions and noneconomic institutions:

> The human economy is embedded and enmeshed in institutions, economic and noneconomic. The inclusion of the noneconomic is vital. For religion or government may be as important to the structure and functioning of the economy as monetary institutions or the availability of tools and machines themselves that lighten the toil of labor. (quoted in Smelser and Swedberg, 1994, p. 15)

Despite the necessary interdependence of major social institutions, however, their integration is inherently problematic. There is always a certain degree of conflict or tension between them, because in any complex society the claims of some institutional roles will inevitably differ from and often contradict those of others. For example, the value orientations and associated demands of economic roles are, especially in market societies, not easily reconciled with those of familial roles. Being a "good parent" at times must come at the expense of being a "valued employee," and vice versa. The resolution of these conflicting claims in the course of ongoing social interaction yields a distinctive pattern of institutional relationships for the society at large. We have referred to the outcome of this balancing of competing institutional demands and claims as the "institutional balance of power" in a society (Messner and Rosenfeld, 1994a, pp. 75–88).

The type of institutional arrangement that is the focus of institutional-anomie theory is one in which the economy dominates the institutional balance of power. Our notion of economic dominance in the institutional balance of power is similar to Currie's concept of a "market society" as distinct from a "market economy." According to Currie (1991, p. 255), in a market society "the pursuit of private gain becomes the organizing principle of all areas of social life—not simply a mechanism that we may use to accomplish certain circumscribed economic ends." Economic dominance in the institutional balance of power is manifested in at least three important ways. First, noneconomic functions and roles tend to be devalued in comparison with economic ones. Social success is defined and measured primarily in terms of market achievements. Second, noneconomic roles typically must be accommodated to the requirements of economic roles when conflicts emerge. For example, the schedules, routines, and demands of the workplace take precedence over those of the home, school, church, and the larger community. Finally, economic standards and norms penetrate into noneconomic realms. The economy reproduces itself within other institutions in the sense that its calculating, utilitarian logic informs discourse and thinking about noneconomic aspects of social life.[5]

How does this type of domination of other institutions by the economy contribute specifically to crime? The answer provided by institutional-anomie theory involves two interrelated processes. Economic dominance stimulates the emergence of anomie at the cultural level, and it erodes the structural restraints against crime associated with the performance of institutional roles.

CRIME AND ANOMIC CULTURE

To understand the linkage between economic dominance and anomie, it is useful to consider the distinctive value complex that characterizes market societies in general. This complex stresses individual competition as the primary basis for allocating social rewards. It also defines success in economic terms, thereby encouraging individuals to orient their behavior toward the pursuit of monetary rewards. These market values and their accompanying behavioral guidelines socialize people in appropriate market behaviors and legitimate markets as essential and desirable mechanisms for producing and distributing goods and services. Accordingly, a strong cultural emphasis on competition for monetary rewards is a functional requisite for the long-run viability of any market society.

There is nothing inherently criminogenic about the market values of competition and materialism. As proponents of the doux-commerce thesis correctly point out, the pursuit of individual interest in competition with others can promote relationships of mutual obligation and trust, which are likely to inhibit "malfeasance" (Granovetter, 1985). Market values of competition and materialism lead to crime, we suggest, only when they occur in combination with what can be termed an "anomic ethic." Following Merton, the anomic ethic refers to the excessive emphasis on the goals of social action regardless of the moral status of the means used to achieve social goals. Under this cultural condition, persons are encouraged to use whatever means are technically most expedient to attain goals of all types (see Merton, 1968, p. 189).

Anomie in this sense refers to more than the absence or weakening of social rules, as in the common definition of anomie as "normlessness." It is itself a social rule or standard, albeit a highly permissive one, that motivates the pursuit of goals, in common idiom, "by any means necessary." As used in institutional-anomie theory, then, anomie does not result from the absence of culture but instead reflects a strong cultural emphasis on ends over means (cf. Orrù, 1987).

Unlike the value placed on the competitive pursuit of monetary success through the market, which is not intrinsically criminogenic, the ethic of anomie has a very direct relationship with criminal behavior. Persons who pursue goals by any means necessary have no *moral* qualms about using criminal means. The selection of means turns entirely on utilitarian, cost-benefit considerations, which include the perceived probability and severity of the penalties for criminal behavior. Hence, persons in an anomic environment may prefer to use legal rather than illegal means to achieve a goal, but this preference is not rooted in the cultural prohibition of illegal means. In other words, the selection of the legal means has little expressive significance, and results instead from an instrumental calculation that, in this particular situation, "crime does not pay."

Perhaps the most important point to make about the anomic ethic is that, unlike the values of competition and materialism, which receive strong emphasis in all market societies, the anomic ethic does not. Although it may be a distinguishing characteristic of some developed capitalist societies, the United States being perhaps the most prominently cited example (Merton, 1968; Messner and Rosenfeld, 1994a), anomie is not a functional requisite of market society itself. Accordingly, the level of anomie can, and does, vary considerably across market societies.

An illustration of the analytic independence of anomie and market arrangements is provided by Weber's ([1904–5], 1976) classic discussion of the functions of the Protestant Ethic in the early stages of capitalist development. Weber's early capitalists were strongly motivated to compete for monetary rewards, but they were also very sensitive to the legitimacy of the means by which these rewards were acquired and used. Indeed, the Protestant Ethic is often used interchangeably with the "work ethic," a term that explicitly emphasizes the legitimate means and attendant personal qualities for acquiring wealth: dedication to task, deferred gratification, industriousness, in short, hard work. According to this ethic, wealth is the reward for hard work in a calling; it is not the only or even the primary reason for work. The economic rewards of work are to be reinvested in productive activity for the greater good of the community, as well as for the benefit of the individual producer.

The Protestant Ethic accompanying early capitalism contrasts starkly with the anomic ethic as we have described it. The anomic ethic by definition is indifferent to the moral status of the means used to secure economic ends, and it encourages people to think only of themselves as they acquire money to secure and display personal worth and social status.

Does the work ethic inevitably become emptied of broader cultural significance and in the course of capitalist development degenerate into the ethic of anomie? Weber's position on this issue is characteristically ambivalent. More recent critics, such as Daniel Bell, have tended to adopt a soft version of the self-destruction thesis. While rejecting the thesis of social collapse, Bell (1976, pp. 21–22) has described how the "transcendental ethic" of the early stages of economic development associated with Protestantism has been undermined by inherent features of the capitalist system. We prefer a more contingent view and maintain that an important factor associated with the declining significance of the Protestant Ethic, and its replacement by the ethic of anomie, is the degree to which the economy dominates the institutional balance of power. In any event, the great variety of "capitalisms" in the world belies the thesis that a single institutional form is more "inevitable" than others.

In summary, whatever the ultimate fate of noneconomic institutions in market societies, their common function is to confer moral legitimacy on the means of social action. From a purely economic standpoint, technical efficiency is the sole criterion for the evaluation of the suitability of means. The presence of meaningful moral prohibitions against illegal behavior, therefore, presupposes reasonably vital noneconomic institutions. To the extent that the economy dominates other institutions, cultural messages that imbue the means of social action with moral significance lack institutional backing. Under such institutional conditions, the ethic of anomie will tend to emerge, leading in turn to high levels of crime.

CRIME AND SOCIAL CONTROL

Economic dominance is conducive not only to an anomic cultural ethic—it also weakens social control. An important function of all social institutions is to align the behavior of actors with the main cultural patterns of the society. This is the essence of social control. A strong institution by definition is one that imposes effective controls over persons involved in its specific functional tasks. Economic dominance signals the evisceration of noneconomic institutions. As noneconomic institutions are relatively devalued, are forced to accommodate to economic imperatives, and are ever more penetrated by economic standards and criteria, they are less able to fulfill their distinctive functions effectively, including that of social control. Feeble institutions do not offer attractive roles to which individuals are likely to become strongly attached. As a consequence, the bonds to such conventional institutions will be tenuous, and the constraints against crime associated with these bonds will be weak (Hirschi, 1969).

Economic dominance has important implications not only for the functioning of noneconomic institutions but also for the nature of economic activity itself. As noted in our review of the markets-and-morality debate, economic activity occurs within a broader cultural and structural context. Markets operate in, and are to some degree shaped by, nonmarket social relations. As Granovetter (1985, p. 490) observes, economic action is always "overlaid" with social content and is embedded in networks of ongoing social relations.

This embedding of economic activity places restraints on economic actors, thereby promoting social control.

The degree of embeddedness of economic activity in social relations varies considerably across different capitalist societies and reflects the level of economic dominance. The notion of "embeddedness" as used by economic sociologists is essentially the obverse of institutional domination. A market economy that is strongly embedded in nonmarket institutions is less able to degrade, penetrate, or force accommodations from those institutions. Under such institutional arrangements, anomic cultural pressures are curbed, and economic activity serves to enmesh actors in more general social ties and obligations. In contrast, when the economy dominates other institutions, economic transactions occur to a greater extent without interference from the countervailing claims of other institutions. As a result, these economic transactions are less likely, in Granovetter's terms, to be "overlaid" with social content. Ironically, then, an institutional balance of power characterized by economic dominance undermines the social control functions of all institutions—economic and noneconomic alike.

We are now in a position to answer the question posed earlier concerning the variable consequences of markets for the moral order in capitalist societies. To the extent that economic and noneconomic institutions are reasonably balanced, the "harmonizing" processes emphasized by proponents of the doux-commerce thesis are likely to predominate. Markets will serve to "replenish" the moral foundations of capitalist societies by enmeshing economic actors in noneconomic social relations. In contrast, when the economy dominates the institutional balance of power, the more corrosive, "depleting" effects of markets on the moral foundations of society, cited by advocates of the self-destruction thesis, are likely to prevail. Such an "excess of depletion over replenishment" (Hirschman, 1992, p. 139) promotes social disorder and, we contend, leads to high levels of crime in market societies.

Theoretical Convergence and Divergence

Institutional-anomie theory directs attention to the complex interplay of cultural conditions, institutional arrangements, and features of social control in its explanation of crime. The theory draws liberally on traditional criminological perspectives, but it also differs from these perspectives in important respects. The most obvious point of convergence is with traditional anomie theory. Institutional-anomie theory incorporates the Durkheimian notion that high levels of deviant behavior, including crime, result from a permissive normative order that places few restraints on individual actions. We deviate, however, from the most popular interpretations of anomie theory, which are commonly associated with Robert Merton's writings.

Correctly or not, Merton is often depicted as a "relative deprivation" theorist (see Box, 1981, pp. 99–100; Davis, 1980, p. 135; Messner, 1988, p. 39). According to this view, individuals who are unable to achieve what they have been socialized to expect, particularly with regard to economic goals, experience feelings of frustration and strain. As a consequence, they are driven to "do things that they normally would not do" (Bernard, 1984, p. 353), such as engage in crime. Although not denying the criminogenic potential of relative deprivation and goal frustration, institutional-anomie theory directs attention to a fundamentally different causal dynamic: an anomic cultural orientation, which flourishes under conditions of institutional imbalance and encourages the use of whatever means are technically expedient in the pursuit of goals. Some persons may commit crimes because they feel deprived, frustrated, or strained, but these psychological states are not prerequisites for criminal involvement. The theoretically strategic determinant of crime is exposure to anomic cultural pressures in the absence of effective, counterbalancing institutional restraints.

Institutional-anomie theory also differs from traditional anomie theory by virtue of its expanded structural focus. For Merton, the critical feature of social structure is the stratification system. In his view, inequality of opportunity in conjunction with universal success goals is the structural source of anomie. Once again, although not dismissing the role of criminogenic consequences of economic inequality, we regard the stratification system as but one of many institutions that collectively comprise the social structure of a society and give rise to its more or less distinctive level and pattern of crime.

In this respect, we are sympathetic to those critics who have charged that Merton drifted away from Durkheim in his formulation of anomie theory by neglecting the larger institutional context. Nanette Davis writes, for example, that "if Merton had remained faithful to the original Durkheimian rendition of anomie, he would have considered the more general issue of breakdown in the controlling and regulatory functions of institutional life" (Davis, 1980, p. 135; see also Besnard, 1990, pp. 252–53; Box, 1981, p. 99). Institutional-anomie theory seeks to overcome this limitation of Merton's work by explicitly incorporating the multiple dimensions of institutional dynamics in its analytic framework.

Finally, our arguments are heavily indebted to insights associated with traditional bonding and social-disorganization theories. From Durkheim

([1897], 1966) to Parsons (1951, 1990) to Hirschi (1969), scholars have appreciated the critical role played by social institutions in the regulation of human behavior. Institutional-anomie theory begins with the basic premise that bonds to institutions regulate human conduct and proceeds to address a question that has been left largely unanswered in traditional bonding theory: Under what specific macrosocial conditions do institutions fulfill this regulatory function more or less successfully? Institutional-anomie theory, in other words, attempts to move beyond bonding theory by identifying the social-organizational preconditions for weak or strong social control. We stress the macrosocial character of these preconditions. They reside in the fundamental structure of whole societies and therefore are not fully captured by social-disorganization perspectives that locate the sources of crime in the weakened social controls of local communities (e.g., Bursik, 1988; Sampson and Groves, 1989; Shaw and McKay, 1969).[6]

We also argue that culture must be considered to understand fully the motivations underlying criminal behavior. Control theorists try to dispense with the need for cultural factors in the explanation of crime by adopting a view of human nature that regards the motivation for crime as unproblematic. In their recent statement of self-control theory, Gottfredson and Hirschi (1990, p. 117) express the basic control position as follows: "A theory can assume, as ours does, that people naturally pursue their own interests and unless socialized to the contrary will use whatever means are available to them for such purposes."

Our examination of the classical markets-and-morality debate raises serious questions about the plausibility of the notion of "natural persons" implicit in Gottfredson and Hirschi's conception of criminal motivations. We prefer to leave to philosophers the task of deciding just what kinds of behavior are "natural" to the human species. We also remain skeptical, as stated earlier, of conceptions of anomie that very explicitly throw out culture by equating anomie with normlessness (e.g., Kornhauser, 1978, pp. 165–66). In any event, the important sociological point is that societies can and do vary in the extent to which they provide cultural support for the individualistic pursuit of self-interest by the technically most expedient means. In our view, a full understanding of the restraining role of institutions requires explicit attention to those features of the cultural environment that encourage, perhaps ironically, the very behaviors that are at the same time subject to normative restraint.

In sum, the institutional-anomie theory of crime represents an effort to build upon the contributions of both control and anomie theory but to overcome their more important limitations. It combines Merton's incisive analysis of the anomic cultural ethic characterized by a disproportionate emphasis on goals over means with the Durkheimian emphasis on the regulatory role of social institutions. By joining the cultural component of traditional anomie theory with the structural component of control theory, institutional-anomie theory offers an explanation of crime that, whatever its other limitations, is sociologically complete.

Criminological Research in a Global Market Economy

It is hardly an exaggeration to say that the present era is one of extraordinary social transformations, perhaps on a par with those accompanying the initial emergence of capitalism on a significant scale in the late eighteenth and nineteenth centuries. The fall of communist regimes in Eastern Europe and the former Soviet Union and the drive for economic reforms in the People's Republic of China have greatly expanded the relative size of the world's population exposed to the vicissitudes of the market. Expansions in global markets, in turn, have increased the competitive pressures on the economies of the developed nations, heightening concerns about the costs of the modern welfare state (Olsen, 1996; Teeples, 1995).

With respect to the issue of crime, there are good reasons to be wary of the rapid charge toward market systems in developing nations and of proposals to curtail radically the social-welfare policies of the advanced societies, thereby exposing their populations more directly to global market forces. Markets can be compatible with strong social control, as we have argued at length in this essay, but only to the extent that they are integrated with other social institutions. Efforts to impose or unleash market arrangements without careful consideration of the consequences for other features of social organization and without systematic planning to adjust noneconomic institutions to market conditions are likely to lead to precisely the kinds of institutional imbalances and social dislocations that engender anomie and high rates of crime.

Levels of crime increased dramatically after the collapse of communist regimes in the former Soviet Union and many parts of Eastern Europe. Journalistic accounts have linked rising crime rates in the former Soviet world and China to the weakened controls and heightened individualism that have accompanied market reforms (Mufson, 1996; *New York Times*, 1994). For example, a *New York Times* article on conditions in Russia attributes rising crime rates after *Glasnost* to a "breakdown in . . . trust and discipline" and the popular perception that "people are out for themselves and anything goes" (Bohlen, 1992, p. 1). In the same article, a political advisor to President Boris Yeltsin describes the emergence of rough-and-tumble markets in which "everything has been divided between groups which have taken definite shape and are engaged in tough competition, resorting to whatever means are available" (p. 6). Although the social landscape depicted in such accounts is consistent with our arguments connecting unfettered markets with heightened anomie and reduced social control, these connections remain only suggestive. The social and cultural sources of instability and crime in the postcommunist world is an important and still very much open empirical issue.

The relationship between crime and social-welfare policy in the advanced capitalist nations also warrants close attention from researchers. From the perspective of institutional-anomie theory, by reducing political controls on pure market forces, cutbacks in the welfare state can be viewed as tipping the institutional balance of power toward the economy and away from the polity. Rates of crime should increase as a result, assuming no change in other conditions. Consistent with this expectation, we found in a study of more than forty nations that those with broader and more generous social-welfare policies had lower rates of homicide than those with restrictive policies, even when measures of economic development, inequality, and other factors associated with crime were controlled (Messner and Rosenfeld, 1994b; cf. Fiala and LaFree, 1988; Gartner, 1990).

These results are promising, but they represent only the initial steps in marshaling evidence for the arguments we have advanced in this paper. Future research should examine other aspects of the political systems of market societies (e.g., levels of voting and other forms of political participation). In addition, other social institutions—the family, education, religion—have to be considered in any comprehensive empirical assessment of the institutional-anomie theory of crime.[7] Perhaps the most difficult empirical challenge facing researchers who would test this perspective is the development of valid indicators of *anomie* at the macrolevel of analysis (see Chamlin and Cochran, 1995, pp. 413–15, 425–26). This problem is not unique to institutional-anomie theory but confronts any theory of crime that assigns an important role to values, goals, beliefs, and other elements of culture.

If we are correct in our view that sociological explanation necessarily requires attention to cultural as well as structural dimensions of social organization, then the development of an empirically grounded understanding of the culture of market societies is essential if sociology is to contribute to knowledge and policy on crime and the market system at the close of the twentieth century. The nineteenth-century debate surrounding the emergence of the capitalist system and its impact on moral and social order remains remarkably pertinent to this project. Now, as a century ago, a distinctive challenge for researchers is to incorporate sociological insights from the debate over markets and morality within empirically valid and policy-relevant explanations of crime and social control in a changing global economy. The institutional-anomie theory of crime, we propose, provides a productive point of departure for this urgent intellectual and practical task.

Notes

1. Marxist and "critical" criminology are important exceptions to this generalization (see, especially, Bonger, 1969; Greenberg, 1981; Quinney, 1977; Taylor, Walton, and Young, 1973). However, scholars working in the marxist intellectual tradition have tended to focus their attention more on the legal system as an instrument of class rule than on the social sources of criminal offending.

2. Not all markets are capitalist markets. As Lindblom observes, a "market" is simply an arrangement for signaling producers about what and how much to produce on the basis of prices (see Swedberg, 1987, p. 107). Because our present concern is with the operation of markets in capitalist societies, for linguistic convenience we use "markets" and "capitalist markets" interchangeably.

3. Hirschman identifies two additional views concerning the moral and social functions of markets, the feudal-shackles thesis and the feudal-blessings thesis. These are not so much separate conceptions of market functioning as they are opposing evaluations of precapitalist social forms that logically accompany the two major rival views (see Hirschman, 1992, pp. 124–39).

4. For an excellent introduction to sociological approaches to the study of culture, see Griswold (1994). Parsons (1964, 1990) provides classic statements of the role of institutions in society (see also Bellah et al., 1991).

5. John Gagnon notes that the tendency for the logic of a market economy to permeate discourse over an ever increasing range of social phenomena can be observed both inside and outside academic social science: "Within the social sciences there has been a 100-year struggle to extend the reach of economic metaphors and analyses to include all aspects of mental and social life. Outside the social sciences, in practical society, a parallel attempt to subject all forms of conduct to the discipline of commodification and pricing has become part of the normal order" (Gagnon, 1994, p. 1078). See Schwartz (1994, pp. 359–66) for an extended discussion of how "our language is suffused with market terminology" (pp. 359–60).

6. Bursik and Grasmick's (1993) recent discussion of "public controls" is a suggestive departure from the more local orientation of conventional social-disorganization theories.

7. A recent study that reveals empirical support for institutional-anomie theory at the subnational level incorporates indicators of several different institutions. In a cross-sectional study of U.S. states, Chamlin and Cochran (1995) found that the effect of economic deprivation on crime is conditioned by family, religious, and political involvement,

a result consistent with the proposition that the influence of market forces on crime rates will vary according to the strength of noneconomic institutions.

References

Bell, Daniel. 1976. *The cultural contradictions of capitalism*. New York: Basic Books.

Bellah, Robert N., Richard Madsen, William M. Sullivan, Ann Swidler, and Steven M. Tipton. 1991. *The good society*. New York: Alfred A. Knopf.

Bernard, Thomas J. 1984. Control criticisms of strain theory. *Journal of Research in Crime and Delinquency* 21:353–72.

Besnard, Philippe. 1990. "Merton in Search of Anomie." In *Robert K. Merton: Consensus and Controversy*, edited by Jon Clark, Celia Modgil, and Sohan Modgil, 243–54. London: Falmer Press.

Bohlen, Celestine. 1992. The Russians' new code: If it pays, anything goes. *New York Times* (30 August), pp. 1, 6.

Bonger, William A. 1969. *Criminality and economic conditions*. Abridged and with an introduction by A. T. Turk. Bloomington: Indiana University Press.

Box, Steven. 1981. *Deviance, reality, and society*, 2d ed. London: Holt, Rinehart and Winston.

Bursik, Robert J., Jr. 1988. Social disorganization and theories of crime and delinquency: Problems and prospects. *Criminology* 26:519–51.

Bursik, Robert J., Jr., and Harold G. Grasmick. 1993. *Neighborhoods and crime: The dimensions of effective community control*. New York: Lexington.

Chamblin, Mitchell B., and John K. Cochran. 1995. Assessing Messner and Rosenfeld's institutional anomie theory: A partial test. *Criminology* 33:411–29

Currie, Elliott. 1991. Crime in the market society. *Dissent* (Spring):251–59.

Davis, Nanette J. 1980. *Sociological constructions of deviance: Perspectives and issues in the field*. 2d ed. Dubuque, Iowa: Wm. C. Brown.

Durkheim, Emile. [1893], 1964. *The division of labor in society*. New York: Free Press.

———. [1897], 1966. *Suicide: A study in sociology*. New York: Free Press.

Fiala, Robert, and Gary LaFree. 1988. Cross-national determinants of child homicide. *American Sociological Review* 53:432–45.

Gagnon, John H. 1994. Review essay: The dismal science and sex. *American Journal of Sociology* 99:1078–82.

Gartner, Rosemary. 1990. The victims of homicide: A temporal and cross-national comparison. *American Sociological Review* 55:92–106.

Gottfredson, Michael R., and Travis Hirschi. 1990. *A general theory of crime*. Stanford, Calif.: Stanford University Press.

Granovetter, Mark. 1985. Economic action and social structure: The problem of embeddedness. *American Journal of Sociology* 91:481–510.

Greenberg, David F. 1981. *Crime and Capitalism*. Palo Alto, Calif.: Mayfield.

Griswold, Wendy. 1994. *Cultures and societies in a changing world*. Thousand Oaks, Calif.: Pine Forge Press.

Hirschi, Travis. 1969. *Causes of delinquency*. Berkeley: University of California Press.

Hirschman, Albert O. 1992. *Rival views of market society and other recent essays*. Cambridge: Harvard University Press.

Kornhauser, Ruth. 1978. *Social sources of delinquency: An appraisal of analytic models*. Chicago: University of Chicago Press.

Marx, Karl, and Friedrich Engels. [1848], 1964. *The communist manifesto*. New York: Washington Square Press.

Merton, Robert K. 1968. *Social theory and social structure*. New York: Free Press.

Messner, Steven F. 1988. Merton's "social structure and anomie": The road not taken. *Deviant Behavior* 9:33–53.

Messner, Steven F., and Richard Rosenfeld. 1994. *Crime and the American dream*. Belmont, Calif.: Wadsworth.

———. 1994. Political restraint of the market and levels of criminal homicide: A cross-national application of the institutional-anomie theory of crime. Presented at the meeting of the American Society of Criminology, Miami, Florida.

Mufson, Steven. 1996. As rigid controls ease, violent crime mounts in china. *Washington Post* (13 February), p. A14.

New York Times. 1994. Warsaw shops close to protest crime (7 August), p. 4

Nisbet, Robert A. 1953. *The quest for community*. New York: Oxford University Press.

———. 1966. *The sociological tradition*. New York: Basic Books.

Olsen, Gregg M. 1996. Re-modeling Sweden: The rise and demise of the Swedish compromise in a global economy. *Social Problems* 43:1–20.

Orrù, Marco. 1987. *Anomie: History and meanings*. Boston: Allen & Unwin.

Parsons, Talcott. 1951. *The social system*. New York: Free Press.

———. 1964. *Essays in sociological theory*. Rev. ed. New York: Free Press.

———. 1990. Prolegomena to a theory of social institutions. *American Sociological Review* 55:319–33.

Quinney, Richard. 1977. *Class, state, and crime*. New York: Longman.

Rosenfeld, Richard, and Steven F. Messner. 1994. Crime and the American dream: An institutional analysis. *Advances in Criminological Theory* 6:159–81.

Sampson, Robert J., and W. Byron Groves. 1989. Community structure and crime: Testing social disorganization theory. *American Journal of Sociology* 94:774–802.

Schwartz, Barry. 1994. *The costs of living*. New York: W. W. Norton.

Shaw, Clifford R., and Henry D. McKay. 1969. *Juvenile delinquency in urban areas*. Rev. ed. Chicago: University of Chicago Press.

Smelser, Neil J. 1990. Can individualism yield a sociology? *Contemporary Sociology* 19:778–83.

Smelser, Neil J., and Richard Swedberg. 1994. The sociological perspective on the economy. In *The Handbook of Economic Sociology*, edited by N. J. Smelser and R. Swedberg, 3–26. Princeton, N.J.: Princeton University Press.

Swedberg, Richard. 1987. Economic sociology: Past and present. *Current Sociology* 35:1–215.

Taylor, Ian, Paul Walton, and Jock Young. 1973. *The new criminology: For a social theory of deviance*. London: Routledge & Kegan Paul.

Teeples, Gary. 1995. *Globalization and the decline of social reform*. Atlantic Highlands, N.J.: Humanities Press.

Weber, Max. [1904–5], 1976. *The Protestant ethic and the spirit of capitalism*. With an Introduction by Anthony Giddens. New York: Charles Scribner's.

About the Contributors

ROBERT AGNEW is Professor of Sociology at Emory University in Atlanta. His research and publications focus on the causes of delinquency and especially on his general strain theory.

ALBERT K. COHEN earned his Ph.D. in sociology from Harvard University and taught at the University of Connecticut for twenty-three years before becoming Professor Emeritus. He has been a visiting scholar at universities in the United States, England, Ireland, Israel, and Japan. He has served as president of the Society for the Study of Social Problems (SSSP) and is the author of numerous articles. His books include *Delinquent Boys: The Culture of the Gang* (1955) and *Deviance and Control* (1965).

FRANCIS T. CULLEN is Distinguished Research Professor of Criminal Justice and Sociology at the University of Cincinnati. His works include *Reaffirming Rehabilitation* (1982), *Rethinking Crime and Deviance Theory* (1984), *Corporate Crime under Attack* (1987), *Criminology* (1992), and *Criminological Theory* (1995). He has served as president of the Academy of Criminal Justice Sciences and as editor of *Justice Quarterly*.

JOHN HAGAN is a German Marshall Fund Fellow and Professor of Sociology and Law at the University of Toronto. He is co-author, with Bill McCarthy, of *Mean Streets: Youth Crime and Homelessness* (forthcoming) and, with Fiona Kay, of *Gender in Practice: A Study of Lawyers' Lives* (1995). He is editor of the *Annual Review of Sociology* and continues his research on lawyers and crime in North America and on the transition to adulthood in Berlin.

BILL MCCARTHY is Associate Professor in Sociology at the University of Victoria in British Columbia. He is co-auther, with John Hagan, of *Mean Streets: Youth Crime and Homelessness* (forthcoming) and in addition to his research on adolescent homelessness, he currently is studying with Rosemary Gartner the change in homicide victimization and patterns of offending.

SCOTT MENARD is a Research Associate in the Institute of Behavioral Sciences at the University of Colorado, Boulder. He received his baccalaureate from Cornell University and his doctorate from the University of Colorado. His publications include *Longitudinal Research* (1991), *Applied Logistic Regression Analysis* (1995), and, with Herbert C. Covey and Robert J. Franzese, *Juvenile Gangs* (2d edition, 1997), as well as other books and papers on crime, delinquency, drug use, population, and quantitative methods.

ROBERT K. MERTON is University Professor Emeritus at Columbia University, Foundation Scholar of the Russell Sage Foundation, and a member of the adjunct faculty of The Rockefeller University. He is the author of various works in theoretical sociology and the sociology of science and has had an abiding interest in the paradigm of anomie and opportunity structure for some sixty years. His dual interests in science and the humanities have been recognized by his being the only sociologist to receive the nation's highest scientific honor, the National Medal of Science, awarded by the president, and also the only sociologist to receive the Prize for Distinguished Scholarship in the Humanities, awarded by the American Council of Learned Societies.

STEVEN F. MESSNER is Professor of Sociology at the University at Albany, State University of New York. In collaboration with Richard Rosenfeld, with whom he co-authored *Crime and the American Dream* (1994), he is currently studying the relationships among institutional structure, the moral order, and patterns of crime in postindustrial society. He is also engaged in research on crime and delinquency in China.

NIKOS PASSAS is Associate Professor at Temple University. His work focuses on social theories of deviance, and international, white-collar, and organized crime. His publications include *Organized Crime* (1995) and *Transnational Crime* (1998). He is series editor on transnational crime at Northeastern University Press.

RICHARD ROSENFELD is Professor of Criminology at the University of Missouri–St. Louis. He is a member of the National Consortium on Violence Research and is co-author, with Steven F. Messner, of *Crime and the American Dream* (1994). He and Professor Messner are currently studying crime and the institutional structure of postindustrial society. He is also engaged in research on patterns of urban homicide.

DIANE VAUGHAN is Professor of Sociology at Boston College. She received her Ph.D. from Ohio State University. Her perennial research focus is on how macrolevel factors affect interpretation, meaning, and action at the micro-level. She has pursued this agenda in *Controlling Unlawful Organizational Behavior* (1983), *Uncoupling* (1986), and *The Challenger Launch Decision* (1996). The last received the 1996 Robert K. Merton Book Award, Science, Knowledge, and Technology section, American Sociological Association, and was nominated for the National Book Award and Pulitzer Prize for that year. She currently is writing *Theorizing: The Heuristics of Case Analysis.*

JOHN PAUL WRIGHT is Assistant Professor of Criminal Justice at East Tennessee State University. His interests include quantitative tests of criminological theories, particularly in the area of social support. His recent work examines the effects of adolescent employment on juvenile delinquency.

Index

Mental illness
  factors affecting, 85, 86, 191, 193, 198
  see also Suicide
Mentoring and tutoring networks for street
    youth, 133–34
  see also Learning structure; Reference
    groups
Merton's theory
  analysis of, 27–46, 142–45, 187–89
  SSAT
    development, 96–97
    and organizations, 99–101
    typology of adaptations, 191
Morality, relation to markets and crime, 9,
    16, 207–23
Motivation
  effect on individuals, 58–59, 73–74
  social regulation affecting, 3
  see also Desire; Goals

NASA, organizational deviance in, 13–14,
    95–120
National Survey of Families and House-
    holds, 195
National Youth Survey (NYS), 149–51,
    153, 156, 161
Natural persons, in markets-and-morality
    debate, 29
Neighborhood. *see* Community
Nonconformity
  as adaptive response, 160, 167, 177
  compared to conformity, 84, 169
  innovative, 83
  social structure affecting choice for, 3
  see also Adaptation
Normlessness
  effect on individual, 85, 217–18
  effect on society, 37
  relation to anomie, 219
  social structure affecting, 38, 214
  see also Social norms
Norms
  adaptive selection of, 69
  economic, 10
  reference group standards affecting, 54,
    64–66, 152

relation to deviance, 62–63, 83, 102,
    106
  in work-group culture, 109–10, 113,
    118–19
  see also Social norms

Occupation
  effect on status set, 40, 133–34
  as escape from strain, 135–36, 151, 198
  opportunities for within lower classes,
    164
  relation to drug use, 174
  role of in current economy, 79–80, 200
  see also Social class; Workplace
Opportunity structure
  aspirations affecting, 33–34, 58–59
  factors affecting access to, 72, 80–81,
    85, 99–100
  illegitimate, 159–64, 167, 177, 192–93
  as method for deviance, 102, 156, 158
  relation to goals, 58, 68, 125, 129, 143,
    145–46
  relation to reference groups, 42, 70, 73
  relation to status set, 40
  relation to strain, 124
  see also Goal blockage; Legitimate chan-
    nels
Organizations
  accountability in, 114–16
  criminogenic, 95
  institutional deviance in, 13–14, 20,
    95–120
  SSAT as explanatory tool for, 99–100
  see also Corporate society

Parents. *See* Family; Marriage
Patterning, social structure affecting, 65,
    67–68, 71
Performance structure
  relation to deviance, 154, 192
  relation to opportunity structure, 146
Pharmacists, prescription violations by, 95
Physical capital, 130
  see also Human capital; Social capital
Politics
  conservative, 5